Jihad in
Islamic History

Jihad in Islamic History

Doctrines and Practice

MICHAEL BONNER

PRINCETON UNIVERSITY PRESS

PRINCETON AND OXFORD

First published in France by Téraèdre under the title
Le jihad, origines, interprétations, combats © Téraèdre
48 rue Sainte-Croix-de-la-Bretonnerie 75004 Paris

English edition copyright © 2006 by Princeton University Press
Published by Princeton University Press, 41 William Street,
Princeton, New Jersey 08540
In the United Kingdom: Princeton University Press, 6 Oxford Street,
Woodstock, Oxfordshire OX20 1TW

All Rights Reserved

Fourth printing, and first paperback printing, 2008
Paperback ISBN: 978-0-691-13838-1

The Library of Congress has cataloged the cloth edition of this book as follows

Bonner, Michael David.
[Jihad. English]
Jihad in Islamic history : doctrines and practice / Michael Bonner.
p. cm.
Includes bibliographical reference and index.
ISBN-13: 978-0-691-12574-9 (hardcover : alk. paper)
ISBN-10: 0-691-12574-0 (hardcover : alk. paper)
1. Jihad—History. 2. War—Religious aspects—Islam. I. Title.
BP182.B6513   2006
297.7′209—dc22   2005034086

British Library Cataloging-in-Publication Data is available

This book has been composed in Janson

Printed on acid-free paper. ∞

press.princeton.edu

Printed in the United States of America

5 7 9 10 8 6 4

To the memory of my sister

Alisa Bonner

Contents

Maps

Symbols and Accent Marks

This book uses a limited system of transliteration for non-Latin alphabets, namely Arabic, Greek, Hebrew, and Persian. For these alphabets it does not indicate long and short vowels, and it does not use special signs to indicate consonants that do not occur in the English alphabet. The only exceptions are the Arabic glottal stop *hamza* indicated as ʾ and the deep guttural stop *ʿayn*, indicated as ʿ.

Preface

My intention in this short book is to offer an introduction to the jihad and, more specifically, to the origins of the jihad within the broader history of Islam. I have not provided a systematic overview of the doctrine of jihad, which would have required a longer book of an entirely different character. Nor have I given a comprehensive summary of the history of Islam, or even of its early history, as seen from the perspective of the jihad. Instead I have worked with two goals in mind.

My first goal is to provide the reader with an introduction to some of the most important debates, both premodern and modern, over the jihad. I think of this reader as someone who may or may not have basic knowledge of the political and religious history of the Islamic world, but who wishes to find a way through this particular terrain. I have tried to give this reader a sense of what happened—the structure and the most important particulars of historical events—without, however, simply rehashing the history of Islam, which is available now in a number of good books in English. I have tried to keep my analytic focus on the jihad, even as I touched on other broad historical topics, and even as I outlined some of the debates regarding methods and approaches that have gone on among modern specialists in the study of Islamic society, religion, and culture. In this way, I have sought to acquaint the reader with the most important ways in which the jihad has been identified and approached, both in the past and in the present. I have tried to identify the most important and challenging problematics regarding this theme which, as everyone now knows, has far more than academic importance.

My second goal is to present a connected series of theses of my own regarding the jihad and its origins. Some of these have been presented in earlier work of mine, some not; they boil down to the following.

One thesis has to do with the Quranic message and its lasting heritage in Islamic societies. In chapter 2, I identify two different thematic areas within the Quran. One of these has to do with the notions of gift and reciprocity, and with generosity, charity, and the care of the poor and unfortunate. The other has to do with recompense, requital, and reward, relating especially to jihad and the conduct of war. These two thematic areas do not conflict with each other; in fact, it is impossible to have either of them without the other. It is precisely the combination of the two that provided much of the transforming power of the Quran and the early message of Islam. This has implications for our contemporary world, which I allude to at the end of the book.

Another thesis has to do with the extended origins of the jihad. The basic elements of the jihad as we know it came into existence during the first rise of Islam and the lifetime of Muhammad (around 570–632 CE). Other elements of the jihad came into the world soon afterward. However, I argue that the doctrine of jihad, as we recognize it today, and the distinctive set of social practices that are associated with it, did not come into existence until considerably later, toward the end of the eighth century of the Common Era, when the ʿAbbasid Caliphate was consolidating its power. It is only then that the jihad becomes fully recognizable as a doctrine, as a source of inspiration and guidance in the building of a series of new Islamic states, and as what we may call, in Linda Darling's phrase, a piece of "contested territory" among a variety of groups within Islamic society.[1] This view of extended origins has a number of consequences for our view of the jihad in history, which I will spell out as I go along.

Another thesis grows directly from the one just mentioned. This has to do with the long series of dynastic states that arose and succeeded one another in the various parts of the Islamic world, over the centuries. I propose to view many of these as frontier societies and thus, to a large extent, as an outcome of the doctrine and practice of the jihad. A key to this thesis—and what made

---

[1] Linda Darling, "Contested Territory."

me notice the phenomenon in the first place—is the participation in warfare along the frontiers of many religious scholars who were specialists in the holy law, mystics, preachers, and sometimes simply fighters (chapter 7).

These three themes—reciprocity/gift and recompense/reward in the original Quranic message, the prolonged gestation period of the jihad, and the rise and growth of many Islamic states as frontier societies—correspond broadly to three stages in the development of the jihad within Islamic societies and states.

An earlier version of this book has appeared in France, in a new series called Islam in Debates.[2] In the spirit of that series, it provides nonspecialist readers with a concise introduction to a complex and controversial area of study. It points out what the main areas of contention are within this field and where its main arguments seem to be headed. It also provides suggestions for further reading. This English-language version is somewhat longer than the French one, in large part because I have taken into account the highly useful suggestions made by three anonymous readers for Princeton University Press.

Any study of the jihad runs the risk of including an unmanageably large amount of Islamic history and doctrine. I have sought to avoid this by limiting myself to a fairly precise set of questions, set out in the introduction. I concentrate mainly on the early period of Islam, and it is there that my own contributions and ideas stand the best chance of being considered original, and perhaps even right. However, I also sketch out certain aspects of the jihad over the many centuries of Islamic history. At the end I include a quick look at aspects of the jihad in the modern and contemporary periods, not to provide a survey but to consider the question of whether and, if so, to what extent there is continuity of the jihad, from the beginnings of Islam until the present.

Much of this book, especially in its earlier chapters, consists of presentation and analysis of various kinds of historical narrative. Here I try to give the reader an idea of some of the most important debates that have gone on in regard to both the narratives and the doctrines of early Islam where these have related most directly to

---

[2] L'Islam en débats, published by Éditions du Téraèdre, Paris, under the general editorship of Jocelyne Dakhlia and Françoise Micheau. The book's title is Le Jihad: Origines, interprétations, combats.

the jihad. Though I have not tried to hide my own preferences among the various arguments that have been made, I did try to treat them all fairly and dispassionately. At the same time, with so much territory to cover in so few pages, I had to leave out many arguments and ideas that some readers may no doubt consider to be the most important ones.

Translations from the Quran are my own wherever there is no indication otherwise. In some places, as indicated in the notes, I have used the translation of Arthur J. Arberry, *The Koran Interpreted.* The verses of the Quran are cited according to the modern Egyptian system.

I wish to thank my editor at Princeton University Press, Fred Appel, for his discerning judgment and encouragement. I also wish to thank the academic editors of the French series in which it first appeared, Jocelyne Dakhlia and Françoise Micheau, and Jean Ferreux, editor of Les Editions du Téraèdre, for having first proposed that I write on this theme and for all their expert advice. Over the years, I have learned about jihad from several teachers and friends. Here I can mention especially Michael Cook, David Eisenberg, Andras Hamori, Rudi Lindner, Roy Mottahedeh, and Houari Touati. Two scholars, recently deceased and much regretted, Albrecht Noth and John Wansbrough, are cited throughout the book. Three anonymous readers for Princeton University Press have offered advice that has proved uncommonly precise and useful. I have also profited from discussions on several of these topics with Michigan graduate students including (but not limited to) Rob Haug, David Hughes, Mohammad Khalil, Derek Mancini-Lander, and Kristina Richardson. Rob Haug has also provided expert help with maps, here and elsewhere. Layla Hourani has provided technical help in several areas. Finally, I wish especially to thank my wife Daniela for her intellectual precision and discerning literary judgment.

Jihad in
Islamic History

CHAPTER ONE

Introduction

What Is Jihad?

In the debates over Islam taking place today, no principle is invoked more often than jihad. Jihad is often understood as the very heart of contemporary radical Islamist ideology.[1] By a sort of metonymy, it can refer to the radical Islamist groups themselves.[2] Some observers associate jihad with attachment to local values and resistance against the homogenizing trends of globalization.[3] For others, jihad represents a universalist, globalizing force of its own: among these there is a wide spectrum of views. At one end of this spectrum, anti-Islamic polemicists use jihad as proof of Islam's innate violence and its incompatibility with civilized norms.[4] At the other end of the spectrum, some writers insist that jihad has little or nothing to do with externally directed violence. Instead, they declare jihad to be a defensive principle,[5] or else to be utterly pacific, inward-directed, and the basis of the true meaning of Islam which, they say, is peace.

[1] Kepel, *Jihad: The Trail of Political Islam*.
[2] Rashid, *Jihad: The Rise of Militant Islam in Central Asia*.
[3] Barber, *Jihad versus McWorld*.
[4] Pipes, "What Is Jihad?"
[5] For a nuanced argument along these lines, see Sachedina, "The Development of Jihad in Islamic Revelation and History," and "Justifications for Just War in Islam."

Thus Islam, through jihad, equals violence and war; or else, through jihad, it equals peace. Now surely it is not desirable, or even possible, to reduce so many complex societies and polities, covering such broad extents of time and space, to any single governing principle. And in fact, not all contemporary writers view the matter in such stark terms. Many do share, however, an assumption of nearly total continuity, in Islam, between practice and norm and between history and doctrine. And it is still not uncommon to see Islam described as an unchanging essence or a historical cause. The jihad then conveniently provides a key to understanding that essence or cause, and so we are told that Islam is fundamentally "about" war, that it "accounts for" the otherwise inexplicable suicidal activity of certain individuals, that it "explains" the occurrence of wars in history, and so on.

None of this so far has told us what jihad actually is, beyond its tremendous resonance in present and past. Is it an ideology that favors violence? A political means of mass mobilization? A spiritual principle of motivation for individuals?

While we do not wish for this to be an argument over words alone, we cannot understand the doctrines or the historical phenomena without understanding the words as precisely as possible. The Arabic word *jihad* does not mean "holy war" or "just war." It literally means "striving." When followed by the modifying phrase *fi sabil Allah*, "in the path of God," or when—as often—this phrase is absent but assumed to be in force, *jihad* has the specific sense of fighting for the sake of God (whatever we understand that to mean). In addition, several other Arabic words are closely related to *jihad* in meaning and usage. These include *ribat*, which denotes pious activity, often related to warfare, and in many contexts seems to constitute a defensive counterpart to a more activist, offensive *jihad*. *Ribat* also refers to a type of building where this sort of defensive warfare can take place: a fortified place where garrisons of volunteers reside for extended periods of time while holding Islamic territory against the enemy. *Ghazw, ghazwa*, and *ghaza'* have to do with raiding (from which comes the French word *razzia*). *Qital*, or "fighting," at times conveys something similar to jihad/ribat, at times not. *Harb* means "war" or "fighting," usually in a more neutral sense, carrying less ideological weight than the other terms. All these words, however, have wide semantic ranges and frequently overlap with one other. They also change with distance and time.

Jihad refers, first of all, to a body of legal doctrine. The comprehensive manuals of classical Islamic law usually include a section called *Book of Jihad*. Sometimes these sections have different names, such as *Book of Siyar* (law of war) or *Book of Jizya* (poll tax), but their contents are broadly similar. Likewise, most of the great compendia of Tradition (*hadith*; see chapter 3) contain a *Book of Jihad*, or something like it. Some Islamic jurists also wrote monographic works on jihad and the law of war. Not surprisingly, these jurists sometimes disagreed with each other. Some, but not all, of these disagreements correlated to the division of the Sunni Muslim legal universe into four classical schools (*madhhabs*), and of Islam as a whole into the sectarian groupings of Sunnis, Shi'is, Kharijis, and others. Like Islamic law in general, this doctrine of jihad was neither the product nor the expression of the Islamic State: it developed apart from that State, or else in uneasy coexistence with it. (This point will receive nuance in chapter 8.)

These treatments of jihad in manuals and other works of Islamic law usually combine various elements. A typical *Book of Jihad* includes the law governing the conduct of war, which covers treatment of nonbelligerents, division of spoils among the victors, and such matters. Declaration and cessation of hostilities are discussed, raising the question of what constitutes proper authority. A *Book of Jihad* will also include discussion of how the jihad derives from Scripture (the Quran) and the Example of the Prophet (the Sunna), or in other words, how the jihad has been commanded by God. There are often—especially in the hadith collections—rhetorical passages urging the believers to participate in the wars against the enemies of God. There is usually an exposition of the doctrine of martyrdom (see chapter 5), which is thus part of jihad. The list of topics is much longer, but this much can begin to give an idea of what the jihad of the jurists includes.

Jihad is also more than a set of legal doctrines. Historians of Islam often encounter it and try to understand its meaning and especially when they think about such things as motivation, mobilization, and political authority. For instance, regarding the earliest period of Islam, why did the Muslims of the first generations fight so effectively? What was the basis of their solidarity? How did they form their armies? Why did they assume the attitudes that they did toward their own commanders and rulers? For historians interested in such questions, it is impossible to study the historical manifestations of jihad apart from the legal doctrine, for several reasons. First, some—though far from all—of the historical narratives that are available to us regarding early Islam seem to have been formed by juridical perspectives, no doubt in part because many of the early Muslim historians were jurists themselves.[6] Second, the doctrine of jihad had a role of its own in events, a role that increased over time (see chapter 8). And not only the doctrine, but also its exponents and champions: the jurists and scholars known collectively as the "learned," the *ulama*: many of these were protagonists in the ongoing drama of the jihad in several ways including, at critical junctures, their participation (both symbolic and physical) in the conduct of warfare (see chapter 7). Jihad, for the historian, is thus not only about clashes between religions, civilizations, and states but also about clashes among groups within Islamic societies. Equally important, jihad has never ceased changing, right down to our own day. If it ever had an original core, this has been experienced anew many times over.

Just War and Holy War

The concept of just war, *bellum iustum*, has a long history in the West.[7] The medieval part of this history is particularly Christian, in part because of the emphasis on love (*agapē, caritas*) in Christian doctrine and the difficulties this created for Christian thinkers and political authorities in their conduct of war. Then, with the introduction of natural law theory into the law of war in the sixteenth and seventeenth centuries, and with Europe's increasing domination of the seas, Western doctrines of just war came to prevail over both Christian and non-Christian states—whether they liked it or not—and their interactions in war and peace.

[6] Brunschvig, "Ibn ʿAbdalhakam et la conquête de l'Afrique du Nord par les Arabes."

[7] A starting point is provided by the essays collected in Kelsay and Johnson, eds., *Just War and Jihad*. See especially Johnson's "Historical Roots and Sources of the Just War Tradition in Western Culture," 3–30; also his *The Holy War Idea in Western and Islamic Traditions*; and Russell, *The Just War in the Middle Ages*.

Now, it is possible to draw meaningful parallels between these Western doctrines of just war and the classical doctrine of jihad expressed by the Muslim jurists. However, there are also differences. For the most part, the Muslim jurists do not make the "justice" of any instance of jihad the term of their discussion. Likewise, the concept of holy war, at least as we use it now, derives from Christian doctrine and experience, especially relating to the Crusades. Scholars of the ancient Near East and the Hebrew scriptures have broadened the concept, and so too have anthropologists. This anthropological literature on holy war may help us to ask about the links between the jihad, as it first emerged, with warfare in Arabia before Islam. It may also help us to see the role of jihad in the conversion to Islam of other nomadic and tribal peoples, such as the Berbers in North Africa and the Turks in Central Asia. At the same time, we must remember that the Muslim jurists did not usually discuss these matters in these terms; for them any authentic instance of jihad was necessarily both holy and just.

In the medieval Islamic world, there were philosophers who, unlike the jurists, were willing to foreground questions of justice and injustice in their discussions of warfare. They did this by adapting Islamic concepts into a Greek, mainly Platonic field of reference.[8] The most important of these philosophers was the great al-Farabi (d. 950). Al-Farabi considers a range of situations in which wars may be considerered just or unjust. They are unjust if they serve a ruler's narrow, selfish purposes or if they are devoted solely to conquest and bloodshed. Just wars may, of course, be defensive, but they may also, under some circumstances, be offensive: what makes them just is their role in achieving the wellbeing of the "virtuous city," that association which we all need in order to attain happiness.[9] Here al-Farabi uses not only the Arabic word *harb* (war) but also, on occasion, the word *jihad*, though not quite in the technical sense assigned to it by Islamic legal doctrine. It seems likely, all the same, that al-Farabi was trying to find a philosophical place for the juridical doctrine of jihad within his teachings regarding the virtuous city and its ruler, the Islamic philosopher-king.

[8] Kraemer, "The Jihād of the Falāsifa"; Heck, "*Jihad* Revisited," esp. 103–106.
[9] Butterworth, "Al-Fârâbî's Statecraft," 79–100.

6   CHAPTER ONE

We find a synthesis of juridical and philosophical views in the famous *Muqaddima*, or introduction to the study of history, of Ibn Khaldun (d. 1406).[10] Ibn Khaldun begins his discussion of wars by saying that these "have always occurred in the world since God created it," naturally and unavoidably, because of men's desire for revenge and their need for self-defense. Ibn Khaldun then identifies four types of war. The first of these "usually occurs between neighboring tribes and competing families." The second is "war caused by hostility," whereby "savage nations living in the desert" attack their neighbors, solely with a view to seizing their property. These two types are "wars of outrage and sedition" (*hurub baghy wa-fitna*). The third type is "what the divine law calls *jihad*." The fourth consists of "dynastic wars against seceders and those who refuse obedience." Of these four types, "the first two are unjust and lawless," while the last two are "wars of jihad and justice" (*hurub jihad wa-ʿadl*). In this way, as Charles Butterworth remarked, Ibn Khaldun "distinguishes just war from jihad and allows neither to encompass the other."[11]

The juridical discourse on jihad had incomparably more influence on intellectual life within premodern Muslim societies than did these philosophical discussions. The same applies to its influence over preaching, the popular imagination in general, and the running of the affairs of armies and states. Modern and contemporary Muslim thinkers, on the other hand, have had a great deal to say about justice and injustice in relation to the doctrine of jihad and war in general,[12] but this takes us farther than we can go here.

Warfare and Jihad

We have seen that certain philosophical writers distinguished between, on the one hand, jihad, which they understood to be a part of the divine law of Islam, and, on the other hand, the phenomenon of warfare, which has occurred throughout history in all places inhabited by humans. In addition to this philosophical discourse, the premodern Islamic world was familiar with several other ways

[10] Ibn Khaldun, *The Muqaddimah*, trans. Franz Rosenthal, 2:73–74; Kraemer, "The Jihād of the Falāsifa," 288–289.
  [11] Butterworth, "Al-Fârâbî's Statecraft," 96–97, n. 17.
  [12] See, for example, Sachedina, "Justifications for Just War in Islam."

of speaking and writing about warfare, distinct from—though often related to—the practice and doctrine of jihad. Here we may briefly mention a few of these.[13]

Islam arose in an environment where warfare—or at any rate, armed violence with some degree of organization and planning—was a characteristic of everyday life. Even if it often amounted to little more than livestock-rustling, its threat was never far away, especially in those regions of the Arabian peninsula that lay beyond the control of rulers and states. We see this in the great corpus of pre-Islamic poetry, our most vivid and extensive source of information about Arabia on the eve of Islam. Some of this poetry was devoted entirely to the joys and travails of fighting, especially in the poems collected afterward under the rubric of *hamasa* (valor). War also loomed large in the countless dirges composed in honor of its victims. And in the songs of praise that the poets recited in honor of their patrons, their kin, and themselves, martial valor usually topped the list of virtues, followed closely by generosity. In all these poems, war typically appears as something ordained by fate, unwelcome but necessary, often imposed by the obligation to seek revenge for wrongs done to one's kin. Sometimes we find a willingness to be the first aggressor, together with a grim enthusiasm for the activity of fighting itself: "Yea a son of war am I—continually do I heighten her blaze, and stir her up to burn whenever she is not yet kindled."[14] Most often, however, this enthusiasm is tempered by patient endurance (*sabr*) in the face of the constant, lurking possibility of violent death, as well as the inevitability of death itself, which here is the extinguishing of the individual, the end of everything. Thus the old Arabic poems, together with the prose narratives that accompany them, express a heroic ideal, where the courage and endurance of a few individuals illuminate a dark, violent world.

Long after the arrival of Islam, this ancient heroic ethos continued to hold considerable power and attraction. So for instance, when our sources report the death of a commander in the Islamic armies, they sometimes give the text of a dirge that was recited

---

[13] For the following, see also Donner, "The Sources of Islamic Conceptions of War."

[14] Charles Lyall, *The Diwans of ʿAbid ibn al-Abras, of Asad, ʿAmir ibn al-Tufail, and of ʿAmir ibn Saʿsaʿa*, 29, verse 10; cited by Donner, "The Sources of Islamic Conceptions of War," 36.

on the occasion. Here we still find the thematics of the pre-Islamic poetry, praising the deceased for his courage and generosity, and for his steadfast defense of his kin and all those who sought his protection. More often, however, and in a great variety of contexts, we find the old Arab heroism blended together with Islamic piety. We do not have to consider this a contradiction, for it is precisely this combination of self-denying monotheistic piety and swashbuckling derring-do that we find in many genres of Islamic literature relating to the jihad—for instance, in popular poems and romances and even in (apparently) sober biographical literature (see chapter 7). Nonetheless, the old heroic ethos was not, in the end, an Islamic virtue, and it constituted, for many people, a point of controversy.

Rulers in the Islamic world sometimes supported the activity of religious and legal scholars who produced, among other things, learned treatises on the jihad. However, within the royal courts, and in the concentric circles of influence and prestige that emanated outward from them, there was also a keen interest in viewing warfare from a broader perspective. We find an early example of this attitude in the lengthy chapter on war (*kitab al-harb*) written, in the mid-to-late ninth century, by the polymath man of letters Ibn Qutayba.[15] This chapter opens with citations from the sayings of the Prophet (the hadith) and the Quran, and some narratives from the early, heroic period of Islam. Soon, however, Ibn Qutayba begins to quote from the literature of "the Indians" and especially "the Persians" of the Sasanian dynasty, which had been defeated and destroyed during the early Islamic conquests some two centuries previously. Here we find counsel on many matters, including strategy, tactics, and the correct demeanor to observe in battles and on campaigns. The sources of this advice are utterly non-Islamic, which implies that any civilized belligerent, of any religion, may take advantage of it if he wishes. And at times the advice is indeed quite worldly, as when the "stratagems of war" ascribed to an anonymous Persian king include "distracting people's attention away from the war they are involved in by keeping them busy with other things."[16] This material is mainly in the mode—highly fashionable in Ibn Qutayba's day and

---

[15] Ibn Qutayba, *'Uyun al-akhbar*, 1:107–222.
[16] Ibid., 1:112.

long afterward—of advice for princes. At the same time, however, Ibn Qutayba returns repeatedly to narratives from the early Islamic campaigns and to religious norms regarding the conduct of warfare. He thus tries to integrate two different conceptions of war (Sasanian/imperial and Islamic/jihad), which nonetheless remain distinct.

Throughout the centuries there was a steady, if not enormous, production of manuals and treatises on technical matters such as tactics, siegecraft, armor, weapons, and horsemanship.[17] The audience for this literature must have consisted of military professionals—a group which, as we shall see, stood apart from the military amateurs who made up the units of "volunteers." This technical literature tended to show less interest in the precedents of centuries past and more interest in the practices and activities of the enemy in the present time. For these and other reasons, it stands apart from the literature of jihad.

Finally, war is a central theme of the apocalyptic literature that flourished intermittently among medieval Muslims, as well as among their Christian and Jewish neighbors. Here war fills out the catastrophic scenarios that culminate in the end of this world as we know it—even though in these scenarios we do find, after a cataclysmic evil war, a just war led by the redeeming figure of the Mahdi. These apocalyptic wars are, of course, related to the Islamic notions of jihad and martyrdom,[18] but to a surprising extent, the relationship does not appear very close. It is noteworthy that at least from the second century of the Hijra/eighth century CE onward, Islamic tradition considered these matters under two different rubrics, *fitan* (wars of the Last Days) and *jihad*.[19]

Thus there were several ways available of thinking and arguing about warfare, its conduct, and its justifications. All the same, for most times and places in the premodern Islamic world, we must consider the religious discourse of jihad as the dominant one in this area, not only because of its prestige and its place in the central

---

[17] See Elgood, ed., *Islamic Arms and Armour*; and Kennedy, *The Armies of the Caliphs*, with bibliography.

[18] Heck, "*Jihad* Revisited," 102. Perhaps it is true, as Heck says, that "religious martyrdom . . . requires the addition of an eschatological climate." However, the mature Islamic doctrine of martyrdom (see chapter 5, below) seems to have washed out this "eschatological climate" rather thoroughly.

[19] See Cook, "Muslim Apocalyptic and Jihad," and below, p. 131–132.

system of values but also because it comprehended so much. Jihad, at least as it emerged in its full articulation toward the end of the eighth century of the Common Era, included exhortations to the believers to attain religious merit through striving and warfare. It also gave an account of the will of God, as this had become known to mankind through God's Word and through the Example of His Prophet, and as it had then become realized, over and over again, through the martial activities of the community of believers. At the same time, the jihad included a large body of precise instructions regarding the conduct of warfare, very much in the here and now, answering to the technical requirements of recruitment, tactics, and strategy. This does not mean, however, that the jihad—as expressed in the first instance by jurists—was preeminently practical in nature: in fact it often tended to be backward-looking, seeking models of conduct in an idealized past. Now we may consider how these Islamic jurists, and others, have construed the jihad and how they have argued about it.

Fields of Debate

Over the centuries, as Muslim jurists reiterated and refined the criteria for jihad, they referred constantly to several underlying questions. We may begin by singling out two of these.

Who Is the Enemy?

If we think of jihad first of all as a kind of organized warfare against external opponents, then who precisely are those opponents? How and under what conditions must war be waged against them? What is to be done with them once they have been defeated? Questions of this kind predominated in many of the juridical debates about the jihad, especially during the early, formative centuries of Islam.

Once some sort of consensus has been achieved regarding these enemies from outside, then what about internal adversaries? All agree that war may be waged, at least as a last resort, against Muslims who rebel against a constituted Muslim authority. Is such war then a kind of jihad? And must these internal Muslim rebels be treated in the same way as the external non-Muslim opponents just mentioned? Here we find that in actual historical experience, the contending parties in intra-Muslim conflicts did often have recourse to the doctrine and above all, the rhetoric of jihad. In juridical discourse, however, the matter is somewhat complicated.

Organized armed action against the Muslim political rebel (*baghi*), as well as against two other types of malfeasor, the apostate (*murtadd*) who renounces his own religion of Islam, and the brigand (*muharib*) who threatens the established order while seeking only his own personal gain, is indeed often described as a form of jihad. Loyal Muslims who die in combat against these rebels, apostates, and brigands achieve the status of martyr (see chapter 5). On the other hand, the status of the adversaries in these conflicts is considered to be different from that of the non-Muslim adversaries in the "external" jihad. Here we see differences in approach between Sunni and Shiʿi jurists.[20] For the most part, however, we find that these matters are actually dealt with under headings of Islamic law other than jihad. In fact, it is possible to provide a nuanced, theoretical discussion of political rebels and rebellion in Islam while referring to jihad only intermittently or even minimally.[21] Thus, while the discussion of rebels is part of the juridical discourse on jihad, it is not, at least in a consistent way, at the heart of that discourse. Here, as elsewhere, we encounter the temptation of allowing the notion of jihad to apply to almost everything—a temptation that is best for us to avoid.[22]

The Quran and Tradition often speak of oppressors. What happens if oppressors arise within the Muslim community itself? Must we carry out jihad against them? Here, of course, we are looking at the problem of rebellion from the point of view of the ruled, instead of the rulers: is there a right to resistance against an unjust ruler? From very early on in the history of Islam, some Muslims have deployed the ideology and vocabulary of jihad against what

[20] Kraemer, "Apostates, Rebels and Brigands," esp. 58–59: "Whereas Sunnīs seldom characterized warfare against rebels as *ǧihād*, although one killed fighting them was considered a martyr, the Šīʿīs regarded suppression of rebellion as *ǧihād* and the *buǧāt* [rebels] as infidels."

[21] As in Abou El Fadl, "Ahkâm al-Bughât"; idem, *Rebellion and Violence in Islamic Law*.

[22] We see this in Alfred Morabia's masterful *Le Ǧihâd dans l'Islam médiéval* (hereafter *Le Ǧihâd*), which tends to make jihad into an all-embracing principle governing almost everything: so the discussion of "internal, coercive" jihad (against rebels, etc.), 298–309.

they have seen as oppressive and tyrannous (though Muslim) rulers. From a later perspective, these oppressors might be described as political rebels or religious heretics—though here we run the risk of using the terminology and conceptual patterns of Christianity. The point for now is simply that jihad has a long history as an ideology of internal resistance (discussed in chapter 8 below).

Finally, many have claimed that the authentic jihad, the "greater jihad," is not warfare waged in the world against external adversaries but is rather an internal spiritualized war waged against the self and its base impulses. What does it mean to have such an adversary and to make war against it? This question will be taken up again very shortly.

Who Is in Charge?

Early Muslim jurisprudence provided an answer to this question: the imam, which then meant much the same thing as the caliph, the supreme ruler and head (after God Himself) over the entire Muslim community and polity. The imam has ultimate responsibility for military operations, both offensive and defensive; in particular, offensive campaigns outside the Islamic lands, against external foes, require his permission and supervision. However, since the imam or caliph could not be everywhere at once, it was always necessary for him to delegate his authority in these matters. Meanwhile, over time, his power and authority diminished in the world, and rivals emerged. Furthermore, jihad was acknowledged to be not only a collective activity: it was also a matter of concern and choice for the individual, of great consequence for his or her personal salvation. Thus the jihad became the site of an argument over authority, and it has remained one right down to the present day.

We have already mentioned the insistence, in many writings of our own day on jihad and Islam, on continuity. First of all, continuity in time: today's historical actors are often seen to be repeating or reenacting things that happened long ago. Second, continuity between doctrine and practice: so for instance, calls to warfare and martyrdom in Quran and Tradition are thought to provide explanations for today's violent behavior. This claim to continuity requires critical examination. However, there is no doubt that Muslims have often expressed a strong desire for continuity with their own past. In this case, does performing jihad establish continuity with the Prophet Muhammad, through literal imitation of the actions he took during his military campaigns in Arabia? Or does it involve immersion in the study of the divine law? Or does it mean identifying oneself with the organized authority, the Islamic state—which in the language of early Islam often means the caliph/imam himself? Or does performance of jihad establish continuity with that other great protagonist of early Islam, the community, which did, after all, forge its place in the world through warfare and campaigns?

Other themes of debate in this book can be expressed in the form of binary oppositions that recur in the writings of medieval and modern authors, jurists and nonjurists, Muslims and non-Muslims. These include the following.

"Real" Jihad versus "Mere" Fighting

In the Hadith or Tradition (see chapter 3), as well as in some other sources, a distinction is often made between, on the one side, militant activity (usually called *jihad*, or *ribat*, or both) that has authentic status and, on the other side, fighting undertaken with no concern for divine commandments, divine reward, and so on. It is often stated that some people act in accordance with jihad, while others fight only for the sake of worldly things such as glory, plunder, and power. The distinction is polemical, and perhaps applied arbitrarily or unfairly on some occasions.

External and Internal Jihad

Most accounts of the jihad agree that it has both an external and an internal aspect. The external jihad is an activity in the world, involving physical combat against real enemies in real time. The internal jihad, sometimes called the "greater jihad," is a struggle against the self, in which we suppress our own base desires, purify ourselves, and then rise to contemplation of higher truth. Most modern Western writings on the jihad consider that the external jihad, the physical combat against real adversaries, was the first to arrive in history and has priority in most ways. In this view, the internal jihad, the spiritualized combat against the self, is secondary and derivative, despite all the importance it eventually acquired in Muslim thought and society.[23] However, much of contemporary Muslim opinion favors the opposite view. As a question of first

[23] Ibid., 291–336 (chapter on "Le ğihâd interne," the internal jihad).

origins, we can argue that elements of the internal jihad were already present at the beginning, including in the Quran itself, and that jihad has often been, in equal measure, a struggle against both the enemy within and the enemy without.

Collective and Individual Jihad

This is a central issue in the classical doctrine of jihad. As we shall see, it corresponded to real problems that confronted Islamic governments, rulers, and military commanders, together with a wide array of individuals who, in their quest for salvation and religious merit, became involved in the activities of the jihad. The most original modern treatment of this ancient problem came in the doctoral thesis of the late Albrecht Noth. In Noth's analysis, warfare against external enemies is a concern for the entire Muslim community, under the leadership of its imam/caliph. This warfare requires resources and organization on a scale that only the state can provide. At the same time, this warfare may be holy, as it fulfills religious objectives by protecting and, where possible, expanding the community and its territory. Then, on the other hand, we have the individuals who volunteer to participate in this activity. They too are carrying out divine commands. They receive a religious reward for their activity; their motivation (the sincerity of their intention) is often a source of concern. However, even if their intentions are pure, these individuals are likely to be less concerned with public goals (warding off enemy invasion, conquering new territory for Islam) and more interested in achieving religious merit for themselves. Noth identified these two elements as "holy war" and "holy struggle"—both of them components of what I am seeking to identify as the jihad, and at odds with each other much of the time.[24]

Historiography and Origins

Presentations of the jihad, and indeed of Islam itself, most often have as their starting point a historical narrative that begins with

[24] Noth, *Heiliger Krieg und heiliger Kampf in Islam und Christentum*. I disagree with Noth where he states that the "private" heiliger Kampf is the dominant mode, and that true "holy war" almost never occurs in jihad (pp. 87–91). The distinction remains valuable nonetheless.

Muhammad in Mecca at the beginning of the seventh century and reaches a culminating point when Muhammad establishes his community in Medina in 622 CE, year 1 of the Hijra. When questions such as "What emphasis does Islam place on fighting and conquest?" or "What is jihad?" are asked, the answer most often takes the form of this master narrative about the rise of Islam, continuing from Muhammad's life through the great Islamic conquests that took place in the seventh-century Near East and beyond.[25] We are told how Muhammad first received divine Revelations and how a community gathered around him in Mecca; how then, in Medina, Muhammad and his community began to wage war; and then afterward, how Islam grew, in part through conquest, into a comprehensive system of belief and doctrine and, at the same time, into a major world power.

More than in any other major religious or even cultural tradition, the narrative thus contains the answer to the question. This approach is shared by those who are sympathetic to Islam and those who are hostile to it. The matter is complicated further by the fact that the Quran, the Islamic scripture, is not a connected narrative in the sense that, for instance, much of the Old Testament presents a sequential history of the world and of a people. Somewhat paradoxically, a fundamentalist attitude in Islam—which is to say, a radically decontextualized attitude—usually bases itself not only on the sacred text of the Quran but also on a narrative of origins, a narrative that is, strictly speaking, exterior to the sacred text.

The rise of Islam was indeed an astonishing event, with tremendous consequence for world history. Moreover, narratives of the first origin were vividly present to Muslims of all later generations, especially those who found themselves acting within the broad sphere of jihad. However, as we have already seen, this search for an origin immediately leads into complex arguments about the reliability of the sources for earliest Islam, arguments that are not about to be resolved any time soon. Above all, the focus on a single narrative of origin can lead us to forget that any act of founding becomes obscure in retrospect, because it necessarily includes an element of myth—even in cases where the course of events and

---

[25] For instance, Firestone's *Jihad: The Origin of Holy War in Islam*, which does not venture far beyond the Quran and the life of Muhammad.

the actors' identities and roles are not particularly in dispute, as for instance in the founding of the American republic.

In this book I speak of the origins of jihad, in the plural. There is no need to challenge the primacy of the first beginnings. However, speaking of origins allows us to look afresh at each historical instance, and at Islamic history as a whole. It also encourages us to look at how the jihad has been revived and reinterpreted in many historical contexts, right down to the present day. It may also help us to integrate the jihad into the history of "real" armies and warfare, from which it has largely been divorced in modern historical scholarship.

Much of this book, especially its early chapters, is devoted to modern debates over the sources for early Islam. Writing already existed in Arabia when Islam first arose, and many Muslims of the first generations wrote, most often in the Arabic language. However, for a number of reasons, writings from that earliest period of Islam have survived only sporadically and by accident. (Here, as so often, the Quran constitutes the great exception.) The compendious Arabic works on which we rely for most of our knowledge of the events, ideas and doctrines of the earliest Islam were written in later times (beginning around 750 CE, and in most cases considerably later than that). These works were based on earlier works, but those earlier works have since disappeared and it is difficult or impossible for us now to establish their texts. The matter grows even more complicated because of the intertwining, within the oldest Arabic sources, of oral and written techniques of transmission, itself very much a matter of dispute among modern scholars. The modern arguments over the old Islamic sources have raged mainly on two battlegrounds, one regarding the formation of Islamic law and the other regarding early Islamic historical writing. Both of these will be mentioned as we go along.

Many of these modern arguments over historiography, and over the rise of Islam and the origins of jihad more generally, began in the nineteenth and the earlier twentieth centuries among European academic specialists in the study of the East, often referred to as the orientalists. Their involvement in the colonial project has been much discussed.[26] What will come back over and again in the

---

[26] Said, *Orientalism*, followed by a large literature; see also Rodinson, *Europe and the Mystique of Islam*.

present book is their relation to the classic Islamic narrative of origins. For origins were precisely what many of the orientalists liked best. Their approach was predominantly textual: finding the manuscripts, establishing the texts, understanding what the texts mean, and then sifting and combining all this information so as to produce a more "scientific" narrative than what the "native" sources had to offer. In many cases, the orientalists' interest in origins had the further, and unfortunate, result of encouraging them to see the social practices of Muslim countries—in their own time and also for earlier periods—as outcomes or expressions of the text. In this view, the norms of doctrine and religion dictated everyday behavior; the texts, especially the texts concerned with origins, became all the more precious as a result.

At the same time, other scholars, some of them in the orientalist tradition and some not, have posed different kinds of questions and inserted different kinds of protagonists into their narratives. I have tried to put emphasis on at least some of these, and on the other options available to us today. It is noteworthy, in any case, that there have been few successful attempts to apply the methods of the modern social sciences to these questions. This is partly because of the burden that such an attempt imposes (a combination of textual and linguistic expertise together with profound knowledge of the social sciences) and partly, no doubt, because of the difficulties inherent in the primary evidence itself.

I portray the origins of jihad as a series of events, covering all of the broad extent of Islamic history. Of course, I only have room for a few representative instances. However, I hope to show that many people have used the notion of jihad creatively in the construction of new Islamic societies and states. For this they have employed a shared idiom, derived from the Quran, from the various narratives of origins, from the classical doctrine of jihad, and from their own shared experience. However, their ways of doing this, and the Islamic societies they have constructed, have been quite diverse: not mere repetitions or reenactments of the first founding moment but new foundations arising in a wide variety of circumstances.

Questions regarding the jihad and its origins resonate loudly in our world today, when jihad has become the ideological tool of a major, and substantially new, political actor. I see no choice but to ask whether today's "jihadists" are in continuity with their own tradition and past. The answer, not surprisingly, is that in some ways they are and in other ways, quite radically, they are not. But here the emphasis on origins, both among Muslim believers and among many non-Muslim observers, should not lead us to think that the same thing merely happens over and over, that Islam—and now, all of us—is doomed to repeated cycles of violence and destruction.

For as long as we deal with this subject matter, it is our destiny to speak "of war and battle," as Socrates, arriving late, is informed by his host.[27] We must account for many debates over debating and fighting, and describe numerous intellectual, spiritual, and physical techniques of contention. All the more reason to leave room at the end of the book for the often-discredited claim that jihad and Islam are both really about peace. For peace is the true goal of all righteous contention and war, both in the *bellum iustum* of Augustine, Gratian, and Grotius and in the *jihad* of the Quran, al-Shafi'i, and Saladin.

Readings

The comprehensive survey by Alfred Morabia, *Le Ǧihâd dans l'Islam médiéval: Le "combat sacré" des origines au XIIᵉ siècle* (Paris: Albin Michel, 1993), includes a thorough summary of the doctrine of the jihad and its role in Islamic history. Since this work was published after the author's premature death in 1986, it does not include more recent developments. The recent article by Paul L. Heck, "*Jihad* Revisited" (*Journal of Religious Ethics* 32 [2004]: 95–128), covers much of the ground covered in this book from a somewhat different perspective. Important terrain is mapped out in "The Idea of *Jihad* in Islam before the Crusades," by Roy Parviz Mottahedeh and Ridwan al-Sayyid, in *The Crusades from the Perspective of Byzantium and the Muslim World*, 23–29, edited by Angeliki Laiou and Roy Parviz Mottahedeh (Washington, D.C.: Dumbarton Oaks Research Library and Collection, 2001). Another valuable contribution has just appeared, too late for me to incorporate into this book: *Understanding Jihad* by David Cook (Berkeley and Los Angeles: University of California Press, 2005).

[27] Plato, *Gorgias*, 447a.

This book covers much of the same ground as the present one, but also from a different perspective. It includes a full and well-informed survey of the jihad as conceived and deployed by modern-day radical Islamist groups. Just war and holy war are studied in comparative perspective in two volumes edited by John Kelsay and James Turner Johnson, *Cross, Crescent and Sword: The Justification and Limitation of War in Western and Islamic Traditions* (Westport, Greenwood Press, 1990); and *Just War and Jihad: Historical and Theoretical Perspectives on War and Peace in Western and Islamic Traditions* (Westport: Greenwood Press, 1991). Albrecht Noth's *Heiliger Krieg und heiliger Kampf in Islam und Christentum* (Bonn: Ludwig Röhrscheid Verlag, 1966), already mentioned, provides a comparative synopsis of the notions and practice of holy war in Islam and Christendom. Noth began by remarking that until then (the 1960s), Western treatments of the jihad tended simply to recapitulate the Islamic juridical doctrines; history was seen as a mere application or outgrowth of these doctrines. With Noth's book, this situation began to change. However, historical treatments of armies and warfare in the Islamic world, such as Hugh Kennedy's excellent *The Armies of the Caliphs* (London: Routledge, 2001), still tend not to devote large amounts of attention to the jihad and its practitioners. A few of the many books on jihad in contemporary thought and society are mentioned in the notes to the beginning of this chapter. Rudolph Peters, *Jihad in Classical and Modern Islam* (Princeton, NJ: Markus Wiener, 1996) provides a general introduction, essays, and translated texts.

In addition, see the recent book by John Kelsay, *Arguing the Just War in Islam* (Cambridge, MA: Harvard University Press, 2007). Ibn Khaldun's views on jihad and warfare are discussed by Malik Mufti in a paper titled "Jihad as Statecraft: Ibn Khaldun on the Management of War and Empire," presented at the November 2007 meeting of the Middle East Studies Association.

CHAPTER TWO

The Quran and Arabia

The Quran has always been the most important source of inspiration for the doctrine and practice of jihad, but never the only one. Limited in its length but boundless in its subject matter, the Book does not account for every single possibility that can occur to individuals and to the community of believers over the course of the generations. Accordingly, when we put together the various passages of the Quran that deal with warfare and jihad, we find that these are not so very numerous. The themes of warfare and jihad take up the greater part of only two *suras*, or chapters of the Quran (the eighth and the ninth); we also find these themes scattered in other places throughout the Book. These passages on warfare are certainly vivid and memorable, but they do not, in and of themselves, constitute a coherent doctrine. Moreover, on close examination of these passages, we also find what seem to be contradictions among them, or differences in emphasis, at any rate. Resolving these differences requires interpretation on our part, which in turn means the application of principles and source materials taken from outside the text of the Book.

Above all, while the Quran does include many short narratives, it contains no consecutive narrative of the earliest Muslim community and the life of the Prophet. In all fairness, this is a point of controversy.[1] However, there is no doubt that the narratives through which people have usually understood the Quran are

---

[1] See Watt, *Muhammad's Mecca*; and Rippin, "Muhammad in the Qur'an."

mainly to be found in other books, which will be described in the following chapter. For it so happened that from the very beginning, the Islamic community loved narratives, and for many reasons—political, legal, rhetorical, moral, emotional—it felt a need for that narrative of origins, which the Quran, on its own, did not provide. The community found this narrative about itself in several genres of Arabic writing, which included *maghazi* (campaigns), *sira* (biography of the Prophet), *tafsir* (formal interpretation, or exegesis of the Quran, much of it narrative in character), *hadith* (reports of sayings and deeds, with normative force, attributed to the Prophet and to those around him), and *akhbar* (reports, historical accounts in general). While these writings, in the form in which we have them, are generally quite old, all of them are more recent in date than the Quran itself.

Many approaches have been taken, both in medieval and modern scholarship, to the study of the Quran. However, in this chapter we can only concentrate on two contrasting approaches to the Quranic materials regarding warfare and jihad. The first of these is what we find most often among modern scholars, in both Muslim and Western environments. This approach involves taking the various passages in the Quran that relate to jihad and warfare, and correlating and comparing these passages with narratives about the early community and its wars, as these narratives occur in books of maghazi, sira, and other genres. Analysis of various kinds is applied, and a new, more complete, perhaps more "scientific" narrative emerges. The second approach involves setting the sequential narrative aside altogether and searching the Quranic material for patterns and structures that reflect or constitute coherent doctrines, sources of motivation, and worldviews. Each of these two projects has its strengths and its drawbacks.

Combat in the Quran

Jihad occurs in the Quran, but not quite in the form and sense that are most familiar to us now. To begin with, where the Arabic word *jihad* literally occurs, it appears to refer not to warfare, but rather to disputation and efforts made for the sake of God and in his cause. "So obey not the unbelievers, but struggle with them thereby mightily" (*wa-jahidhum jihadan kabiran*);[2] "Struggle for God as is His due" (*wa-jahidu fi llahi haqqa jihadihi*).[3] More broadly, Arabic words deriving from the root *jhd*, which denotes "effort," occur forty-one times in the Quran, including these two instances, just cited, of *jihad*. Of these, only ten refer clearly and unambiguously to the conduct of war.[4] In all these places—involving *jihad* and other words derived from its root—the Quran calls for devotion to God, righteous conduct, utter dedication and indeed, sacrifice of oneself ("striving with one's person and one's wealth" for the sake of God, see below).[5] Such an attitude may, of course, involve physical combat, but in most of these cases this is not obviously what is meant.

All the same, fighting and warfare do constitute a major theme in the Quran. These activities are most often described there with a vocabulary derived from Arabic roots other than *jhd*: these roots include especially *qtl* (fighting, killing), and *hrb* (fighting, making war). These Quranic passages relating to warfare include exhortations to take up arms; outright commands to fight or to desist from fighting; the distribution of military duties and of exemptions from these duties; rulings on the distribution of spoils of war and the treatment of noncombatants and prisoners of war; and other matters. Strictly speaking, they do not seem to constitute—and most likely were not meant to constitute—a coherent doctrine in and of themselves.[6]

For reasons that are not entirely clear to us today, the Quranic word *jihad* became associated with a full, complex doctrine and set of practices relating to the conduct of war. This development seems to have taken place sometime after the revelation and collection of the Quran itself. It is important to remember, however, that the concept of jihad was not, in the Quran, primarily or mainly about fighting and warfare. The "internal," "spiritual" jihad can thus claim to be every bit as old as its "external," "fighting" counterpart.

[2] 25:52 (*Furqan*), Arberry translation.
[3] 22:78 (*Hajj*), Arberry translation.
[4] Ella Landau-Tasseron's article "Jihad," in *EQ*, 3:35–43.
[5] Heck, "*Jihad* Revisited," 96–98.
[6] Landau-Tasseron, "Jihad," 3:38–39. See also Reuven Firestone's article "Fighting," in *EQ*, 2:208–210.

Before we proceed any further, we should mention a few general points that are already familiar to many readers. The Quran is, both in Muslim dogma and in the general understanding of Muslims in all times and places, literally the Word of God, as this was transmitted to the world through the person of Muhammad, who died in 632 CE. Being the most complete, direct, and final message that humanity has received from its Creator, the Quran is the first source for the divine law of Islam. At the same time, however, what we may call the historical Quran, the book between two covers that is available to us now, is the product of a complex process of editing or collection. This process has always been the object of disagreement among scholars, but by most accounts it was completed, or nearly so, during the reign of the caliph 'Uthman (644–656 CE). The editing principles governing this "'Uthmanic recension" are now largely obscure to us. Verses—often in rhyming prose, rarely in poetry—are arranged in *suras* (chapters). The order in which the suras are presented, and the placement of verses within each sura, do not always have a logic that we can easily ascertain or appreciate. What is sure, in any case, is that the verses, as we read them now in the Quran, do not appear in the order in which they are thought to have been revealed to Muhammad during his career as a prophet in Mecca (ca. 610–622) and then in Medina (622–632).[7]

One of the traditional tasks of Quranic exegesis has been to establish a chronological order among the verses. In other words, as soon as Muslim scholars began to concern themselves with the detailed interpretation of the Quran, they sought to situate the verses of the Quran within a narrative or narratives about the early community and its Prophet. However, as we have already seen, the Quran itself does not provide these narratives on its own, at least not in a connected way. The exegetes—together with historians, jurists, and others—found these narratives about the early community in the extra-Quranic genres of Arabic literature called *maghazi* (campaigns) and *sira* (Prophetical biography), as well in the literary genre of Quranic exegesis (*tafsir*) itself. As all this work grew more refined, it resulted eventually in an exegetical subgenre called *asbab al-nuzul* (the circumstances of revelation). Here it be-

---

[7] For a more nuanced and detailed treatment, see de Prémare, *Aux origines du Coran*.

came possible, at least in principle, to take any verse from the Quran and identify precisely when it was revealed to Muhammad and on what occasion.

At the same time, the task of placing the verses of the Quran within a chronological order has always had more than narrative significance. Since the Quran is the primary source for knowledge of the divine law, or *shari'a*, jurists and lawyers have always had to confront the apparent contradictions within it. One of their intellectual tools for this task has been the doctrine of abrogation, for which they have relied, in turn, on a well-developed chronology of the narratives. So, for instance, the narratives may report that on some occasion God revealed a certain teaching or ruling to Muhammad. This teaching or ruling became expressed in a verse or verses, which later on, during the collection of the Quran, become included within one of the 114 suras of the Book as we have it now. Years later, as Muhammad faced different circumstances, God sent him another revelation, which provided a different ruling from the first revelation, thereby abrogating and superseding it. This second revelation then became included in the Book, through the same process as the first one. Thus, where two (or more than two) revelations conflict with each other, the later trumps the earlier. Where the two revelations are located within the text matters little. What does matter is their place within the chronology of Muhammad's life.

Abrogation was only one of several intellectual tools available for dealing with this problem—though it was certainly one of the most important—and not all jurists made use of it. But in any case, despite all the learned and abstruse treatises that the jurists wrote on abrogation and related topics, they needed constantly to reach out to sources (both narrative and nonnarrative) beyond the text of the Quran itself. For no master chronology, relative or absolute, ever succeeded in imposing itself completely. Nor could it: any such effort inevitably becomes bogged down in difficulties of interpretation and detail. Meanwhile, people who used the divine text for inspiration and encouragement—composers and reciters of narratives, preachers, recruiters for the armies, solitary worshippers—certainly did not think of their scripture as a welter of mutually opposing doctrines, each one canceling another.

Seen from this point of view, the broad thematic area of warfare and jihad in the Quran presents a number of difficulties. Before we come to the problem of historical and chronological context, we have the even greater problem of apparent contradictions. To put it more precisely, a number of discrete themes relating to fighting and jihad appear in the Quran that are not, at first glance, easy to reconcile with one another. A recent study by Reuven Firestone can help us to identify some of the most important of these themes.[8]

(1) Injunctions to self-restraint and patience (*sabr*) in propagating the faith, inflicting punishment only in accordance with injuries already suffered. "Call thou to the way of thy Lord with wisdom and good admonition, and dispute with them [your adversaries] in the better way. . . . And if you chastise, chastise even as you have been chastised. . . . And be patient."[9]

(2) Permission to engage in defensive war. "Permission [to fight] is granted to those against whom war has been made, because they have been wronged."[10]

(3) Permission to wage offensive war, but within certain limits, especially those of the "sacred months" and "sacred mosque" (a time and a place where war is not allowed), unless the enemy is the first to violate these limits.[11]

(4) The lifting of some or all of these restrictions, as in the famous "sword verse": "But when the Sacred Months have passed, then kill and capture the infidels wherever you find them. Lie in wait for them with every stratagem."[12]

(5) Patience with the "People of the Book," that is, Jews and Christians, and calls for reconciliation and peacemaking. "But if they incline to peace, then incline to it also, and trust in God."[13]

(6) Loss of this patience, accompanied by the requirement to subdue the Jews and Christians. The classic example is known as the other "sword verse," or the "*jizya* verse": "Fight those who

[8] Firestone, *Jihad: The Origin of Holy War in Islam*. See also Donner, "The Sources of Islamic Conceptions of War," 46–48.

[9] 16:125–128 (*Nahl*), Arberry translation.

[10] 22:39–41 (*Hajj*).

[11] 2:194, 2:217 (*Baqara*).

[12] 9:5 (*Tawba*).

[13] 8:61 (*Anfal*).

believe not in God and the Last Day and do not forbid what God and His Messenger have forbidden—such men as practise not the religion of truth, being of those who have been given the Book—until they pay the tribute (*jizya*) out of hand and have been humbled."[14]

(7) Evidence of internal tension and reluctance to fight: "Fighting has been prescribed for you, though you dislike it."[15]

The most common procedure among historians, jurists, preachers, and others has been to correlate these themes, in a sequence more or less like the one just presented, to a chronological narrative derived from sira, maghazi, and other extra-Quranic texts. The result is compelling. At first Muhammad and his community in Mecca, in a position of weakness, avoid the use of violence, though they do not "turn the other cheek." With the *hijra*, or Emigration to Medina, in 1/622 and the founding of a new state there, organized violence becomes an option, but practiced sparingly and within traditional restraints. In time, as Muhammad gains in strength and his conflict with Mecca grows more bitter, these restrictions are cast away. At the same time, Muhammad's relations with Scriptuaries (Christians and Jews), especially the Jews within his home city of Medina, deteriorate. As all these adversaries are won over or eliminated, internal disagreement becomes more noticeable: certain members of the community become reluctant to fight and prone to disagreement over warfare and other matters.

For many of the medieval jurists, the divine rulings that counted the most out of all these were the ones that came at the end of the story, thus abrogating the earlier ones. In this way, it was often claimed that the two "sword verses" (9:5 and 9:29) superseded other verses that might have supported different principles. From the point of view of literary narrative, however, the verses relating to fighting and warfare are especially difficult to place within the context of the Prophet's life.[16] Firestone claims, and with good reason, that the strict application of a chronological scheme such as the one just described actually encounters severe difficulties. In other words, it is actually quite difficult or

---

[14] 9:29 (*Tawba*), Arberry translation.
[15] 2:216 (*Baqara*), and much of Sura 9 (*Tawba*).
[16] Rizwi Faizer's article "Expeditions and Battles," in *EQ* 2:143–152, esp. 145.

even impossible to reconcile the broad narrative we have just outlined with a precise, detailed examination of the Quranic verses
that deal with warfare and jihad. Here Firestone goes not only
against the medieval Islamic exegetes and jurists, but also against
the modern academic orientalists, especially those who, from the
mid-nineteenth to the mid-twentieth century, painstakingly re-
worked the Quranic verses into ever more "scientific" chronolo-
gies. As an alternative, Firestone proposes to read the verses relating to jihad not diachronically, but synchronically, so that they
represent tensions that occurred within the Muslim community
over a prolonged period of time, both during and after the life of
its Prophet. One problem with this solution is that the Quran
contains yet other themes relating to warfare that do not fit easily
into either reading.[17]

Gift and Reciprocity

Now we propose to take a different look at warfare and jihad
in the Quran. Here we will set aside the supporting sequential
narratives about Muhammad and the earliest Muslim community,
which are to be found in the medieval Arabic books of maghazi,
sira, and other genres. Afterward, in chapter 3, we will return to
those narratives and consider them in their own right. Meanwhile, in the rest of this chapter, we will try to limit ourselves to
consideration of the Quranic text, alone and in and of itself. Of
course we may question whether this is really possible: can we
ever examine a text without some sort of context lurking some-
where in our minds? On consideration, however, the operation
seems possible, at least in a limited way: after all, we have just
described seven Quranic themes relating to warfare and jihad, at
first without any reference to the well-known narratives about
Muhammad and his community. The reason for doing this sort
of thematic analysis, without recourse to the narratives, is that
we need to discover the inner logic, the structural sense of these
Quranic teachings, even if these teachings sometimes appear to
be in contradiction with one another. For while the narratives of
sira and maghazi can and often do resolve the apparent contradic-

---

[17] For instance, the theme of war as "temptation" (*fitna*).

tions in the Quranic text, they do so, necessarily, in the realm of the particular and not of the universal.[18] A thematic analysis, on the other hand, may show that the contradictions are not really contradictions at all; or if this proves not to be so—if the contradictions remain contradictions—then a thematic analysis may still help us make sense of these teachings in such a way as to show why they have had such enormous appeal for so many nations and peoples over so many generations.

We have already noted that out of all the verses in the Quran, only a relatively small fraction deal directly with the thematic area of warfare and jihad. Before we study these verses, we will briefly consider another thematic area in the Quran for comparative and other purposes, this one relating to generosity and almsgiving. Again, at least for now, we will try to leave out all consideration of historical context, the well-known story of Muhammad and his nascent community in Mecca and Medina.

In the Quran, the act of feeding the poor identifies a person as one of the "companions of the Right Hand."[19] A person who rejects the orphan and "does not urge the feeding of the poor" is identical to one who denies the Day of Judgment.[20] The righteous are those who "give food, though it be dear to them, to the poor, the orphan, and the prisoner."[21] Alms are taken from the believers' possessions "so as to cleanse and purify them."[22] In other words, we must destroy a piece of our property (Bataille's famous "cursed share"[23]), in order to keep the rest intact. The Quran also provides a distinctive view of the circulation of goods in society, summed up in a passage of special interest to us, since it seems to regulate the division of spoils of war:

> That which God has bestowed (*ma afa'a llahu*) on His Messenger from the people of the towns is for God and His

---

[18] This remains so whether or not the narratives are historically true, i.e., whether they accurately describe events that took place in the world. The point here is that the Quran represents the Norm and the Ideal, aside from (or in addition to) its veracity as a representation of what actually happened. See Schöller, "Sira and Tafsir."

[19] 90:18 (*Balad*).

[20] 107:2–3 (*Ma'un*); 69:34 (*Haqqa*).

[21] 76:8 (*Insan/Dahr*).

[22] 9: 103 (*Tawba*).

[23] Bataille, *La part maudite*.

Messenger, and for him who is close [generally understood to the Messenger], for the orphans, for the poor, and for the traveler, lest it become something that circulates among the rich among you.[24]

Here "bestowal" was universally understood to include a notion of "return": *ma afaʾa llahu* literally means "that which God has returned." Bad circulation goes from rich to rich, good circulation from rich to poor. This notion of circulation of wealth is thus founded on acts of generosity toward the unfortunate and the poor.

Acts of generosity had enormous importance in Arabia before Islam, conventionally known as the *jahiliyya* (age of ignorance, or uncouthness). From the extant Arabic poetry of that time, and from the prose that provides context to that poetry, it appears that anyone in pre-Islamic Arabia who had any economic surplus (*fadl*) was expected to give this away to a social inferior, a "client" or "ally."[25] Translations of the Quran usually render *fadl* as something like "divine grace," but it can also carry a more concrete sense of "surplus wealth." "God will make you wealthy/give you surplus out of his *fadl*, if He wills."[26] On these occasions, we find exhortations to the believers to reciprocate God's bounty through their own generosity. So God addresses the Messenger: "Did he not find you in need, and make you wealthy/independent? . . . Therefore, do not treat the orphan harshly, do not rebuff the beggar, and proclaim the bounty of your Lord."[27]

God makes a gift to us of His *fadl*, His surplus, a gift that we can never reciprocate: in the Quran this gift is also called *rizq* (sustenance). In the relationship between God and believer, and between donor and recipient, there is no expectation that the gift will ever be restored to its original donor. Indeed, the believer cannot return the gift that God has made to him. However, he can and should imitate God's action by making his own gifts to the poor and needy, freely and unstintingly. These two relationships—between God and believer and between wealthy donor

[24] 59:7 (*Hashr*): *kay la yakuna dulatan bayna l-aghniyaʾi minkum.*
[25] See Bravmann, "The Surplus of Property."
[26] 9:28 (*Tawba*), *fa-sawfa yughnikumu llahu min fadlihi in shaʾa*; also 24:22 (*Nur*); 62:9–10 (*Jumuʿa*); 59:8 (*Hujurat*).
[27] 93:8–11 (*Duha*).

and needy recipient—thus form the basis of circulation of goods within society: this is the virtuous cycle or "return" of Quranic economics. In this way, the Quran transforms old Arabian economic and spiritual concepts.

Fighting and Recompense

Fighting, warfare, and jihad constitute another broad thematic area within the Quran, in several ways a counterpart to the previous one. In fact, warfare and generosity often overlap. The believers are exhorted repeatedly to give generously and to spend "in the way of God"—which, according to the consensus of the exegetes and, broadly speaking, according to the internal evidence of the Quran, has to do with fighting and military service. Some of the believers show parsimony and reluctance to give to the warriors; such behavior is reprehensible because "God is the wealthy/independent one, while you are poor/dependent."[28] The believers must expend both their lives (their persons) and their substance (possessions, money). This double expenditure is an identifying trait: "The Believers are those who have believed in God and His Messenger, and since then have never doubted. They have striven with their possessions and their persons (wa-jahadu bi-amwalihim wa-anfusihim) in the path of God. These are the truthful ones."[29] It would apparently be a good thing for wealthier members of the community to help those who wish to join the army but lack the means to do so. However, it is the sira and maghazi narratives that insist on this point repeatedly. In the Quran we find that such disadvantaged fighters have a legitimate excuse for not fighting, but that the Prophet is under no obligation to help them.[30]

We have already seen that with regard to generosity, God sets the example (we might say, in modern terms, that He sets the economy in motion) through gifts that man can never reciprocate, except indirectly by imitation. Something similar can happen when God directs a battle: "Remember God's bounty (ni'ma) upon you, when the armies marched against you, and We sent

[28] 47:38 (Muhammad).
[29] 49:15 (Hujurat).
[30] 9:91–92 (Tawba).

against them a great wind and armies that you did not see."[31] God's reward for the fallen in battle is sometimes called *rizq*, the "sustenance" which the recipient can never return,[32] or *fadl*, "bounty," here meaning much the same thing.[33]

However, where the Quran treats war, we more often find a rhetoric of requital and recompense, rather than of gift. First of all, those who fight may do so not only out of love for God, but also to seek redress for wrongs done against them. "Permission [to fight] is granted to those against whom war has been made, because they have been wronged. . . . They who were expelled from their homes, without any cause/right (*bi-ghayr haqq*), except for having declared, 'Our Lord is God.' "[34] Fighting in the path of God is a worthy response to the activity of oppressors (*zalimun*), especially when performed on behalf of the weak (*al-mustadʿa-fun*).[35] It is also appropriate to fight non-monotheist opponents (*mushrikun*) who have violated their covenants and oaths.[36] Insofar as these are all ways of reestablishing a balance that has become disturbed, they show continuity with what we know of bloodshed in ancient Arabia. For there, although some did glory in violence and killing, the prevailing attitude was a grim determination to set things right, through revenge or whatever else needed doing. Stubborn endurance (*sabr*), is a common point between the ethics of *jahiliyya* (pre-Islamic Arabia) and those of the Quran.

Recompense and requital also assume another form in the Quran, that of the divine reward (*ajr*). At times this is offered gratuitously, just like the sustenance and bounty/surplus just mentioned. More often, however, this reward comes out of a situation of tit-for-tat, of *do ut des*, where it is understood that someone who has received something must return the same object, or its equal in value, in exchange. This applies to goods as well as to persons: for whatever wealth you spend (*ma tunfiquna min shayʾ*) in the path of God, you will be amply repaid and not defrauded.[37] God calibrates the reward according to the effort and danger undertaken,

[31] 33:9 (*Ahzab*). The battle in question is universally thought to be Badr, 624 CE.
[32] 22:58–59 (*Hajj*).
[33] 3:169–171 (*Al ʿImran*).
[34] 22:39–41 (*Hajj*).
[35] 4:75 (*Nisaʾ*).
[36] 9:12–14 (*Tawba*).
[37] 8:61 (*Anfal*).

promising a better reward for those believers who fight than for those who sit safely at home.[38] The deal between God and those who fight in his path is portrayed as a commercial transaction, either as a loan with interest ("Who is there who will make a fine loan to God, which God will then multiply many times over?"[39]), or else as a profitable sale of the life of this world in return for the life of the next. How much one gains depends on what happens during the transaction: one obtains Paradise if slain in battle, or victory if one survives, either way a grand reward (*ajran ʿaziman*) and one of the two finest things (*ihda al-husnayayni*).[40]

Modern treatments of this commercial vocabulary in the Quran have commented, sometimes with an apologetic or patronizing tone, that Muhammad was, after all, a merchant and that commerce was second nature to the Meccans. What we stress here is that Quranic discourse includes, on the one hand, reciprocity and generosity, creating ever more solidarity among the community of believers in all their activities (in both war and peace), and on the other hand, an emphasis on reward and striving, giving the believers, *as individuals*, an unparalleled sense of confidence and entitlement. Albrecht Noth's distinction between holy war and holy struggle thus proves useful for understanding the Quran. In later generations, this dual heritage (reciprocity/generosity and reward/striving) will appear not only in military and militant activity, but also in ascetic practice (*zuhd*), based on the principles of both solidarity and individualism.

The Beggar and the Warrior

One of the most interesting debates of recent years over early Islam followed the publication in 1991 of Christian Décobert's *Le mendiant et le combattant: L'institution de l'islam*.[41] Décobert attempted—for the first time ever, at least on such a scale—to focus attention on poverty within a discussion of the beginnings of

---

[38] 4:95 (*Nisaʾ*).

[39] 2:245 (*Baqara*).

[40] 4:74 (*Al ʿImran*); 9:52 (*Tawba*).

[41] This book covers much more than Quran, but I bring it up here for several reasons.

Islam. He did this through a largely structuralist argument based on the twin figures of the beggar and the warrior. Here, two strands of continuity stand out: first, the survival of old Arabian notions, especially regarding poverty and warfare, into mature Islam; and second, the melting together of these two ubiquitous figures, the poor man and the fighter, in Quran, Tradition, and early Islamic culture in general. At a culminating point, Décobert says that the gift was universally necessary in this society: by giving alms, one's own wealth would eventually be restored; the recipient of alms therefore became rich so that he might then reimpoverish himself, in a never-ending eleemosynary chain. What the Muslim ate had ideally been produced by others: in this economy of alms (*économie aumônière*), gain was perceived as exterior to the activities of production and exchange.

Reaction to the book was mixed. However, the conversation nearly came to an end with the appearance of a devastating review article by Abdallah Cheikh-Moussa and Didier Gazagnadou.[42] They pointed out that a structuralist argument can only apply to the *longue durée*, and not to a historical transition. Above all, they demolished the supposed identity of the two central figures. Poverty and begging were shameful and scandalous among the early Muslims, as among the ancient Arabs. Although the fighter in the early Islamic armies received a pension or allowance called '*ata*' (literally, "gift"), which might have associated him with the poor, he actually enjoyed status, wealth, and a measure of independence. Other reviewers pointed to other problems, including the credibility of the Arabic sources for early Islam. For, while Décobert constantly critiqued the so-called revisionist school, he did not show exactly how and how far we may use those Arabic sources.[43]

Despite all this demolition work carried out against it, this book made valuable contributions. Its influence on this chapter should be obvious. The poor man was not identical to the warrior, neither in Arabic texts nor in early Islamic society. These two are best thought of as symbols in any case, and not as historical actors. Where it is most useful to think about them is in regard to the Quran. For there, we find on the one hand the phenomena of

---

[42] "Comment on écrit l'histoire . . . de l'Islam!"
[43] Bonner, Review of Christian Décobert. On the "revisionists," see the following chapter.

almsgiving, generosity, and giftgiving and on the other hand those of fighting and striving. Whatever these things may be, they are much more than themes of rhetoric. Décobert was right to identify them as basic elements in the formation of Muslim identity. With the Quran, something new emerges in the world, at once transformational and deeply rooted in the Arabian past.

Readings

A good place to begin is Michael Cook's aptly named and incisive *The Koran: A Very Short Introduction* (Oxford: Oxford University Press, 2000), and the compact volume by Alfred-Louis de Prémare, *Aux origines du Coran* (Paris: Tĕraèdre, 2004). The new *Encyclopaedia of the Qur'an* (*EQ*), edited by Jane McAuliffe (Leiden: Brill, 2001–), contains useful articles, already cited in the notes to this chapter.

The summa of older European Quranic scholarship is the *Geschichte des Qorans*, originally published in 1860 by Theodor Nöldeke, and subsequently revised in three volumes by F. Schwally and others (Leipzig, 1919–1938; 2nd ed., Hildesheim: G. Olms, 1961). For a one-volume introduction, Régis Blachère's *Introduction au Coran* (Paris: Besson et Chantemerle, 1949) is serviceable, though inevitably outdated. Still useful and readable is W. Montgomery Watt's re-edition of an older work, *Richard Bell's Introduction to the Qur'an* (Edinburgh: Edinburgh University Press, 1970). Rudi Paret combined his German translation of the Quran with a useful commentary, *Der Koran: Kommentar und Konkordanz* (Stuttgart: Kohlhammer, 1977). These works (Nöldeke-Schwally, Blachère, Bell-Watt, and Paret) fall within the academic orientalist tradition, combining analysis of content and style together with a correlation of the Quranic data to detailed chronological schemes. Major concerns for orientalist Quranic studies include "the origin of the Quran" (this is the title of the first volume of Nöldeke-Schwally), and the extent to which Quran on its own can be used to constitute a narrative.

For warfare in pre-Islamic Arabia, the chapter in Morabia's *Le Ğihâd*, 35–50, provides a starting point, together with F. M. Donner, "The Sources of Islamic Conceptions of War." Here we still rely on an older literature, including the first volume of Ignaz

Goldziher's *Muhammedanische Studien* (Halle, 1889), translated as *Muslim Studies* (London: Allen and Unwin, 1967–1968); and the study of the "battle-days of the Arabs" by Werner Caskel, "Aijām al-ʿArab: Studien zur altarabischen Epik," *Islamica* 3 no. 5 (1930), 1–99. Warfare in the Quran has not received much study on its own. Again, the chapter in Morabia (119–44) provides a point of departure, together with the *EQ* articles on "Bloodshed," "Expeditions and battles," "Fighting," and "Jihad." Here, as elsewhere, scholarly energy has been invested in the interrelation of the Quranic text with the historical narratives. Within those historical narratives, warfare is a theme of high importance, as chapter 3 will show.

Here, it is worth mentioning the alternative view of the Quran and its place in history offered in John Wansbrough's *Quranic Studies* (Oxford and London: Oxford University Press, 1977), issued in a new edition, with notes by Andrew Rippin (Amherst, NY: Prometheus, 2004). This book argues, among other things, that the final collection (or redaction) of the Quran happened much later than is usually thought, in the early ninth century CE, when theological debates raged around the concept of Divine Word. Wansbrough also presents the Quranic material as basically liturgical in character: on this see now Angelika Neuwirth, "Du texte de récitation au canon en passant par la liturgie," *Arabica* 47 (2000): 194–229.

I have discussed poverty in the Quran, and early Islamic views of poverty and the circulation of wealth, in "Poverty and Charity in the Rise of Islam," in M. Bonner, M. Ener, and A. Singer, eds., *Poverty and Charity in Middle Eastern Contexts* (Albany: SUNY Press, 2003), 13–30; and in "Poverty and Economics in the Qur'an," *Journal of Interdisciplinary History* 35 (2005): 391–406.

Finally, two recent contributions deserve special mention. These are Andrew Rippin, ed., *The Blackwell Companion to the Qur'an* (Malden, Oxford, and Carlton: Blackwell, 2006); and Jane Dammen McAuliffe, ed., *The Cambridge Companion to the Qur'an* (Cambridge: Cambridge University Press, 2006). These two books together provide a comprehensive and scholarly introduction to the field of Quranic studies.

CHAPTER THREE

Muhammad and His Community

We have seen that the Quran does not provide us with a sustained, connected narrative about the early community and its Prophet, and that if we wish to have such a narrative, we must look for it in narrative sources—mainly sira, maghazi, and hadith—that are exterior to the Quranic text itself. Now we turn to those narratives, which tell us about the Prophet who served as the vehicle for the Revelation, and about the community that gathered around him. It is here, through these narratives, that jihad begins to emerge, both as a doctrine and as a pattern of behavior.

The first thing to note about these narratives is their close relationship to the Quran. For although in theological terms it is conceivable that there may once have been a divine discourse that no prophet communicated to humanity, in historical terms these two, Scripture and Prophet, arrive together at the same moment and are utterly inseparable. An example is the question of credentials. How were people expected to know that these words of Revelation were indeed of divine origin? One answer to the question was that the Prophet Muhammad, through whom the words came into the world, was a trustworthy man whose life and behavior conformed to established patterns of monotheist prophecy. The books of sira and maghazi provided what one needed to know about this exemplary life and behavior. Then what if someone wished to put Muhammad's credentials as a prophet to the test? In that case, one proof came in the Quran itself (the famous "challenge verses"): the doubters were challenged to produce Arabic words of similar quality and beauty; their failure to do this confirmed the authenticity of both the Messenger and the Message.

Within the literary genres of sira, maghazi, and hadith,[1] jihad and fighting constitute themes of high importance. Contention and controversy also characterize the modern discussions around these genres.

Sira and Maghazi: Sacred History

In the early years of Islam, many men of learning devoted themselves to research on the Prophet and the earliest Muslim community. They collected, shared and transmitted reports, combining techniques of oral and written transmission in ways that are not entirely clear to us now. One of these men, Ibn Ishaq (d. 767 CE), seems to have been the first to produce a lengthy, chronologically ordered account of Muhammad's life, in Arabic prose, which we usually call al-Sira (the Way). As often happened in medieval Islamic book production, Ibn Ishaq's Sira went through further editing; what we have now is the recension of a later scholar named Ibn Hisham (d. 834). However, the manuscript evidence shows that the original title of Ibn Ishaq's work was not al-Sira but rather Kitab al-maghazi (book of campaigns [or battles]).[2] The importance of warfare in Muhammad's life is even clearer in the second-best-known work in the genre, also called Kitab al-maghazi, a book devoted entirely to the campaigns and raids of Muhammad's lifetime, composed by al-Waqidi, an important scholar who died in 823.

Ibn Ishaq and al-Waqidi collected their information from the work of other, earlier scholars. Much, if not all of this previous work was already available to them in written form. However, with

---

[1] Quranic exegesis (tafsir), receives short shrift in this discussion. In fact, the tafsir uses many of the same materials as the other three genres; the boundaries among them are porous.

[2] Hinds, "Maghazi and Sira in Early Islamic Scholarship." Maghazi is actually one of the three main divisions of Ibn Ishaq's work, which are (1) Mubtada', (beginning, genesis), including old Arabian lore; (2) Mab'ath (calling, summoning), the early (Meccan) portion of Muhammad's prophetical career; and (3) Maghazi (campaigns), the later (Medinan) part of the same.

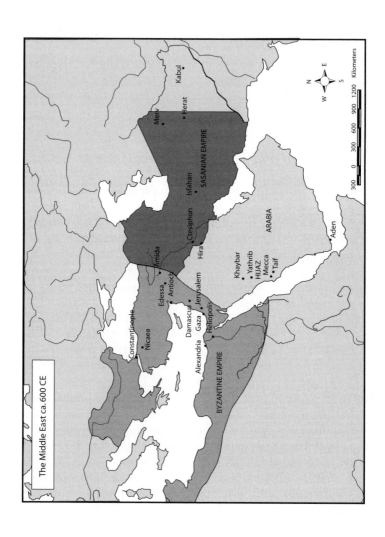

The Middle East ca. 600 CE

Constantinople
Nicaea
Edessa
Antioch
Amida
Damascus
Jerusalem
Gaza
Heliopolis
Alexandria

BYZANTINE EMPIRE

Merv
Herat
Kabul

SASANIAN EMPIRE

Isfahan
Ctesiphon
Hira

Khaybar
Yathrib
HIJAZ
Mecca
Taif

ARABIA

Aden

N
W E
S

300 0 300 600 900 1200 Kilometers

a few exceptions, these earlier writings have since then disappeared and are known to us now only by their titles, if that. So, on the one hand, we can confirm that there was a well-established genre of works of sira and maghazi that described, in considerable detail, the life of Muhammad and the history of the early Muslim community. On the other hand, the examples of these works that we have available to us now (beginning with Ibn Ishaq/Ibn Hisham and al-Waqidi) were written—again, in the form in which we have them—considerably later than the events in question. Even the earliest surviving fragments of sira and maghazi on papyrus do not bring us any earlier than the middle of the eighth century CE. Furthermore, no inscriptions, coins, original documents, or archaeological findings provide direct corroboration for any of this information, at least as it relates to the life and career of Muhammad in Arabia. This lack of external evidence for the sira and maghazi has added fuel to a modern debate over their historicity, which has generally meant over their reliability as bearers of the literal truth. In particular, some modern scholars have noted that these works of sira and maghazi, with all their profuse detail, are prone to contradiction, not only when compared with one another (for instance, Ibn Ishaq/Ibn Hisham compared with al-Waqidi), but also within each individual text. Others have replied that they show consistency in the broad structure of their narrative: though we may challenge any particular detail, the story as a whole remains trustworthy.

Here we may begin with a brief sketch of this commonly accepted narrative as it relates to jihad and warfare.[3] The earliest community, which formed in Mecca around Muhammad and his teachings from around 610 until 622, made no use of organized violence and warfare. The Emigration from Mecca to Yathrib (the oasis town soon to be known as Medina) in 622 (year 1 of the Hijra) changed all this, as Muhammad became a political leader overnight, and soon a military commander as well. Within the *Kitab al-maghazi* of Ibn Ishaq/Ibn Hisham, there is a section that stands out both for its content and its style. This is conventionally known as the Constitution of Medina, or, better, Covenant of the community—in Arabic

---

[3] Compare with the outline above in chapter 2. For full treatment, begin with Morabia, *Le Ğihâd*, 51–76 ("Du prophète avertisseur au prophète armé: naissance du ğihâd"), and any of the standard biographies of Muhammad.

ʿahd al-umma, an agreement (or agreements) among the allied groups in Yathrib, written down soon after Muhammad's arrival there.[4] The Constitution, or Covenant, is an early piece of evidence, written in an archaic, seventh-century Arabic, rather than the eighth- and ninth-century language of the sira and maghazi narratives. The community here is clearly founded more for war than for any other recognizable purpose, even though the text of the Covenant does not name the adversary in this war.

This last, Medinan part of Muhammad's life and career (622–632) was thus taken up largely by warfare. In year 2 of the Hijra (624), at a place near Medina called Badr, a raiding expedition against a Meccan caravan returning from Syria turned into a full, armed confrontation against Muhammad's kin and adversaries, the Quraysh. Divine intervention came in the form of angels fighting on the Muslim side: this is how the maghazi narratives interpret several passages from the Quran. Badr, the first battle of Islam, proved a great victory. In year 3 of the Hijra, the Meccans returned and inflicted a defeat on Muhammad's band at Uhud, but did not follow it up. In year 5 a large confrontation, known as the Trench because of the tactic used to defend Medina, proved inconclusive, but the Meccans and their allies finally withdrew. In the following year, Muhammad negotiated a truce with the Meccans at a place called al-Hudaybiya. Meanwhile Muhammad undertook other campaigns, seizing the Jewish oasis settlements of Khaybar and Fadak in year 7. In year 8, Mecca yielded and Muhammad entered his native town in triumph. Soon afterward, a tribal confederation challenged him at Hunayn and met defeat. Muhammad now began to send expeditions northward, against Byzantine frontier fortresses. In year 9 he personally led an expedition against one of these, at Tabuk, but obtained no result. At this point he may have been planning for a large-scale campaign against Byzantine Palestine and Syria. However, he died in 632, two years before such a campaign actually got under way.

This is, very broadly, what the narratives tell us. Again, we must emphasize the importance of warfare in this Medinan period (622–

---

[4] The text is translated by Alfred Guillaume in Ibn Ishaq, *The Life of Muhammad*, 231–233. See also Serjeant, "The Constitution of Medina"; and de Prémare, *Les fondations de l'islam*, 88–99, 401–402.

632), and the contrast with the earlier, Meccan part of Muhammad's prophetical career, where the dominant themes include the discovery of the transcendent God, the gathering of the first community, the appeals and injunctions for generosity toward the poor and unfortunate, and, yes, conflict with the hostile environment of Mecca—but never organized, armed conflict.

Now we turn to these narratives themselves, the works of sira and *maghazi*. We have already noted that there exists a tight link between these texts and the text of the Quran. This link takes a variety of forms. As a first example, we take a classic question of origins: What was the first revelation, the first piece of the Quran ever revealed to Muhammad? Ibn Ishaq's answer is that the angel Gabriel first came to Muhammad with a divine revelation while he (Muhammad) was asleep. Ibn Ishaq's narration has Muhammad speaking in the first person:

> He came to me while I was asleep, with a coverlet of brocade on which was some writing, and said: "Read!" [or "recite"] (*iqra*'). I said, "What shall I read?" (*ma aqra*') He pressed me with it so tightly that I thought it was death; then he let me go and said "Read!" I said, "What shall I read?" He pressed me with it the third time . . . and said, "Read!" I said, "What then shall I read?" . . . He then said: "Read [recite] in the name of thy Lord who created / Who created man of blood coagulated."[5]

These last words are the beginning of sura 96, *al-ʿAlaq* (the Bloodclot), which thus, by this account, was the first revelation, the first piece of the Quran that Muhammad ever received. The Quran by itself contains none of this story; its connection to Ibn Ishaq's narrative comes in the keyword *iqra*' (call, read, recite). Interestingly, we find this same keyword in another scriptural context, this time the Bible, in Isaiah 40: 6–8:

> A voice says, Cry! (in Hebrew, *qra*') And I said, What shall I cry? (*mah eqra*') All flesh is grass. . . . The grass withers, the flower fades . . . surely the people is grass. . . . [Yet] the word of our God will stand for ever.

[5] Ibn Ishaq, *The Life of Muhammad*, 106.

The similarity between the Arabic and Hebrew texts (*iqra'/qra'*, *ma aqra'/mah eqra'*) cannot be a coincidence. Interestingly, late antique Jewish and Christian exegesis on Isaiah shows a similar concern to what we find in Ibn Ishaq's narrative: in both cases we have the beginning of a prophetical mission and, at the same time and more broadly, the salvation of a people.[6]

This harkening back to older monotheist texts occurs constantly in the Arabic sira and maghazi literature, in a variety of ways. Here is another example, this time having to do with warfare and jihad. When Muhammad was traveling on the route that eventually led him to al-Hudaybiya, it seemed for a while that he would have to face yet another battle against the Meccans. In one version of the story, Muhammad asks his companions for advice on what to do. They respond as follows:

> By God, we shall not tell you what the Children of Israel told their prophet: "Go forth, you and your Lord, and do battle; we will remain sitting here." Nay, we say: Go forth, you and your Lord, and do battle; we will fight with you.[7]

These words refer clearly to Quran 5: 22–29 (*Ma'ida*). But behind both the Quranic passage and the maghazi narrative lies another biblical reference, this time to Numbers 13–14. This is where the Children of Israel lose their desire to conquer Canaan, after their spies have brought them discouraging news about the overwhelming strength of the country's inhabitants. As a result, they are punished with forty years of wandering in the desert. In the maghazi narrative, Muhammad and his companions risk repeating what happened long ago to the Children of Israel—except that they behave more courageously than their predecessors, and so avoid their fate. We should note also that this same narrative identifies striving in battle as the heart of Muhammad's

---

[6] In the Jewish Aramaic Targum to Isaiah, *qra'/mah eqra'* is interpreted as: "Prophesy! / What shall I prophesy?" (*ma ithnabi*). See Stenning, *The Targum of Isaiah*, 130–131. For late antique Christian exegesis, see Theodoret of Cyrrhus, *Commentaire sur Isaïe*, 2:398–401. Nöldeke et al., *Geschichte des Qorans*, 1:81–82, is apparently the only place in orientalist and Islamicist literature connecting this episode of the Sira with Isaiah 40.

[7] Rubin, "Muhammad and the Islamic Self-Image," 7, quoting Ibn Abi Shayba, *Musannaf*, 14:429–430 (no. 18686), and al-Muttaqi al-Hindi, *Kanz al-'ummal*, vol. 10, no. 30153.

mission, when he is reported to say: "By God, I will go on fighting (*ujāhidu*) for the mission which God has entrusted to me, until God makes me prevail."

The ancient paradigm of the exodus from Egypt—a people liberated from bondage, condemned for its sins to wander in the desert, then transformed into the warrior nation that conquers Canaan—reenacted here in an "exodus from Arabia"[8] whereby another wandering nation, living in uncouth ignorance (*jahiliyya*), undertakes emigration (*hijra*) and becomes transformed into the valiant, purposeful conquerors of, once again, Palestine (together with most of the Near East). The fit is imperfect, but striking nonetheless. Then is the entire story of the maghazi, of Muhammad and his community, merely an allegory of the Exodus? No, because, for one thing, it contains several other monotheist themes, tending in different directions. Above all, we must ask what these biblical references and recollections are actually doing in these texts of sira and maghazi. Are they really anything more than pious, literary embellishments around a solid core of fact? Two approaches to these questions stand out for us now.

Half a century ago, William Montgomery Watt wrote a two-volume biography of Muhammad that has since withstood the test of time.[9] Watt was quite aware that Ibn Hisham, al-Waqidi, and their colleagues offered parallel versions of events, with a proliferation of differing, overlapping, and even contradictory details. Watt maintained that even if particular details are suspect, the overall structure of the narrative about Muhammad at Mecca and Medina is not. Moreover, most of the episodes in these narratives seem rather plausible in themselves. According to Watt, historians may therefore sift through the sira and maghazi narratives, applying commonsense criteria, while remaining on their guard against tendentious storytelling. In this way, they can rescue or reconstruct a certain amount of detail, in addition to the broad structure of the narratives.

A vastly different approach came in John Wansbrough's *The Sectarian Milieu*,[10] which first fully identified the monotheist and

---

[8] Jacqueline Chabbi, "Histoire et tradition sacrée. La biographie impossible de Mahomet," 192.

[9] Watt, *Muhammad at Mecca*; idem, *Muhammad at Medina*.

[10] Wansbrough, *The Sectarian Milieu*.

biblical thematics of the sira and maghazi literature. Wansbrough located the origins of this literature, not in early seventh-century Arabia, but rather in the postconquest urban Near East, where groups of many persuasions (including Monophysite, Nestorian, and Chalcedonian Christians; Jews; Samaritans; and Manichaeans) had long been accustomed to arguing with one another over established monotheist themes (scripture, Christology, etc.), according to mutually agreed-on rhetorical principles and rules. Islam, in this view, was merely a newcomer to the "sectarian milieu." The Arabic sira and maghazi literature emerged, according to Wansbrough, out of these monotheist themes of contention. To what extent this literature describes what actually happened (that is, the earliest history of Islam) is beyond knowledge and inquiry. All we can do is to analyze these texts and their methods of composition. Furthermore, while everyone might agree that in some sense, these narratives constitute a sacred history, Wansbrough made this concept more precise: it is the "salvation history" (*Heilsgeschichte*) brought out in modern studies of the Old Testament. The salvation in question is collective in nature: what is at stake for individuals is their choice of community.

By all accounts, the Medinan period of the Prophet's life was a time of conflict, not only with the Meccans and other external adversaries, but also with the Jews of Medina, and with dissenters within the community itself, the "hypocrites" (*munafiqun*) mentioned so often in the Quran. In the maghazi narratives, the Prophet makes pronouncements on warfare and its conduct, especially toward the end of his life. These include maxims such as "war is trickery"; instructions on the allocation of spoils and the treatment of noncombatants and prisoners; and identifying warfare and jihad with the Prophetical mission itself (see above).[11] However, these dictates on war do not yet constitute an ordered doctrine: what stands out is the narrative about the Prophet and the community which finds salvation by following him.

In addition to battles such as Badr, Uhud, and Hunayn, the sira and maghazi literature describes countless raids (*ghazawat*) aimed at seizing plunder and inflicting minor damage on the enemy. These appear as a normal part of Arabian life: participation in them is praiseworthy but unremarkable. Whenever such a raid

---

[11] Morabia, *Le Ǧihâd*, 145–155.

becomes elevated into an enterprise of jihad, participation in it is, naturally, even better. A good indication that this has happened is an increase, in the maghazi texts, of allusion to or quotation from the Quran. Interestingly, the sira and maghazi texts show little of the tension and contrast, which was described in the introduction, between "mere" fighting and "authentic" jihad. They do, however, strongly condemn those members of the community who "stay behind" while others go off to fight. This theme, which we have already encountered, is well represented in the Quran, especially in the ninth sura (al-Tawba), where those who dodge their obligation to fight the enemies of God are called sitters (qaʿidun) and laggers (mukhallafun), subjected to snide remarks in this life[12] and to other, more lasting forms of punishment in the next.[13] The sira and maghazi literature illustrates this theme with many examples, linking these episodes closely to the text of the Quran.

Finally, the sira and maghazi literature makes little mention of the internalized "jihad against the self" (see introduction), the effort and struggle engaged against the self. In these texts, the Muslim warriors fight against real, external enemies, who are usually quite numerous. It is the hadith that will proclaim the importance and superiority of "the greater jihad" (al-jihad al-akbar, see below), or in other words, the internalized jihad. However, a strong emphasis on asceticism and mastery of the self is already present in the concept of maghazi itself: we will examine this in chapter 5, when we come to the concept of martyrdom. But now we must turn to the more contentious environment of the hadith.

Hadith: The Norm

We may briefly define the hadith, or Tradition, as reports of authoritative sayings and deeds attributed to the Prophet Muhammad, or to those around him (the Companions), or to respected persons of the following generations (the Successors). Among these three types, the first, the Prophetical hadith, has by far the

[12] 9:46 (Tawba).

[13] 9:35, 39 (Tawba). Firestone, in Jihad: The Origin of Holy War in Islam, discusses this quʿud or "holding back" from warfare, ascribing it to reluctance on the part of the tribesmen to injure their kin or allies on the other side.

greatest prestige and probative value. At first the reports were transmitted orally but then, at some point, also with the aid of written texts. As these written texts proliferated, the hadith emerged as a major branch of Arabic literature, of which the two most famous and revered examples (among Sunni Muslims) are the great collections, both called *sahih* (sound, true), produced in the later third/ninth century by two scholars named al-Bukhari and Muslim ibn al-Hajjaj. In formal terms, a hadith has two main parts: the *isnad* (support) which lists, in order, the persons who have transmitted the report, usually going back to the time of the Prophet himself; and the *matn*, the body of the report, usually rather short, often only a few lines or words. The topic of an individual tradition may be a precise point of legal or theological doctrine or else an argument of a more general, ethical character. Above all, the hadith provides the basis for knowledge of the Sunna, the Example of the Prophet, generally agreed to be the second great source for the divine Law, after the Word of God, the Quran itself.

In its content, in the stories that it tells, the hadith is often quite close to the sira and maghazi. However, the genres are not all identical. For whereas the works of sira and maghazi place their narratives squarely in the foreground, the hadith tends to reduce its narratives to mere context. It directs all eyes toward the Prophet who, with epigrammatic precision, dictates the Example through his actions and words. The hadith also differs from the sira and maghazi in being the site of enormous disagreement. If we look back at the sira and maghazi literature, we find that the many contradictions of detail within and between, for instance, Ibn Hisham and Waqidi, often do not seem to have tremendous consequence for legal or theological doctrine. This, after all, is why modern scholars (led by Montgomery Watt) have been able to harmonize or reconcile these sira and maghazi narratives with one another, by applying criteria of common sense. By contrast, in the hadith we will often find a particular doctrine enunciated in one tradition and then, in another tradition, contradicted outright or in part. In other words, we often find a hadith that says "A" and another hadith that says "not A." Since a normative principle is likely to be at stake, the listener or reader—especially if he holds a position of responsibility, such as a judgeship—must choose between the conflicting traditions and must state the reasons and methods that have brought him to his choice.

The hadith has been the site of considerable modern controversy in the West. Well over a century ago, the Hungarian scholar Ignaz Goldziher published an essay on the hadith that became one of the most influential pieces in all of orientalist scholarship.[14] Muslim scholars had always said that some of the hadith was the result of falsification and forgery. Goldziher went further and claimed that even though the hadith purports to derive directly from the early seventh-century environment of the Prophet and his inner circle, it actually has its origins in the lively quarrels over doctrinal, legal, and social issues that took place during the eighth and ninth centuries. It is thus all or mostly forged; if it does have a core of historical truth, this remains beyond our capacity to recover.

Two generations later, the German scholar Joseph Schacht went further, in building a counterintuitive theory of the origins of Islamic law.[15] Schacht began by identifying early regional "ancient schools" of law, which in the years following the Islamic conquest of the Near East functioned largely autonomously, with only loose connections to one another. Legal maxims and formulas circulated on the authority of important figures within these regional schools, or, in some cases, on the authority of the school itself. Then, as concern grew for consistency and conformity, the schools entered into competition with one another and deployed the hadith as one of their weapons. As they circulated their legal maxims and formulas in the form of hadith, they soon found that a hadith going back all the way to the Prophet could trump all others. The hadith, and especially the Prophetical hadith, then quickly became a growth industry and the vehicle of countless arguments.

According to Schacht, the intellectual hero of this drama of early Muslim jurisprudence is the great Arab jurist al-Shafi'i (d. 820), who formulated a comprehensive theory of Islamic law, in which he indicated a method for integrating the Example of the Prophet together with the Word of God. Shafi'i thought that it was possible to weed out the forgeries among the hadith—which were already numerous in his lifetime—and thus to identify the true, sound hadiths that form the basis of our knowledge of the

---

[14] Goldziher, *Muslim Studies*, vol. 2.
[15] Schacht, *The Origins of Muhammadan Jurisprudence*.

Example of the Prophet, and thus of the authentic *Sunna*. Eleven and a half centuries later, Schacht found himself differing from al-Shafi'i, despite his vast admiration for the great medieval jurist. Schacht thought that no hadith could be proved to date from before year 100 of the Hijra (718–719 CE). There is much more to Schacht's theory than this, but here it will suffice to point out that for several decades in the West, much of the argument over the hadith has been an argument over the theories of Joseph Schacht.

Nowadays Schacht's work, together with Goldziher's, is less favored than it was not very long ago. As more texts of hadith and early Islamic law have become available, several scholars have analyzed these materials, correlating the isnad (the supporting chain of authority for each hadith) together with the matn (the text of the hadith itself) in more painstaking and systematic ways than Schacht had done in his day. As a result of this work, we can perceive, often in rich detail, the activities of transmission of learning and production of written texts, going on in early periods, sometimes before the cutoff date of AH 100 that Schacht declared to be the outer limit. On the other hand, some scholars (a clear minority) have expressed even more skepticism than Schacht did himself over the reliability of this early juridical literature, claiming that the juridical texts attributed to such early masters as Malik, Abu Yusuf, and al-Shafi'i do not reliably represent their work.[16] Meanwhile, although we now have detailed studies of legal activity in individual locales—what Schacht would have called the ancient schools[17]—only a few scholars have tried to link all these local pictures together and to correlate them to the broader controversies and trends that marked Islamic society at the time, including and beyond the domain of law. For these and other reasons, al-Shafi'i and Schacht still provide the two methodological poles in the approach to the hadith.[18] The other arguments, though nuanced and complex, still do not offer a clear third alternative. We will return to this situation at the end of this chapter. Now we proceed to a brief consideration of the hadith regarding the jihad and its principal themes.

---

[16] Especially Calder, *Studies in Early Muslim Jurisprudence*.

[17] Motzki, *The Origins of Islamic Jurisprudence*; and Dutton, *The Origins of Islamic Law*.

[18] Cook, *Muslim Dogma*, 116: "The choice is between Schacht and Shafi'i: there is no methodological middle ground."

Themes of Jihad in the Hadith

We have already noted in the introduction that each of the major collections of hadith includes a section or chapter called *Book of Jihad* or something similar. Collections that are not arranged by topic usually contain materials relating to jihad nonetheless. Here we will briefly consider some of the main themes of these chapters, corresponding to the most prominent aspects of the doctrine of jihad.[19]

First of all, the hadith, like the sira and maghazi literature, is closely intertwined with the text of the Quran. For example, we have seen that in the Quran, God's generosity toward mankind takes the form of sustenance (*rizq*), which man cannot reciprocate except indirectly through imitation, by caring for the poor and unfortunate. In the hadith, we again find the Quranic *rizq*, but now with a difference. Here the Prophet says: "I have been sent [by God] to bear the sword at the approach of the Hour. My sustenance (*rizqi*) has been placed in the shadow of my spear; humiliation and debasement are the lot of those who oppose me."[20] Here, *rizq* may refer to the food and other things that the warriors seize during their campaigns, but it may also refer to their divine reward, achieved through fighting. The sword (*al-sayf*) that is so prominent here does not appear in the Quran, at least not when *rizq* and similar things are under discussion.

What emerges, from this and many other places in the hadith, is a central theme of the jihad, namely *the propagation of the Faith through combat*. Islam must be brought to the entire world, as when the Prophet says: "I have been sent to the human race in its entirety,"[21] and "I have been commanded to fight the people [or the unbelievers] until they testify: 'There is no god but God, and Muhammad is the Messenger of God.' "[22] This fighting and spreading of the faith will continue until the end of the world as we know it now.

---

[19] The following are brief samples from a large body of material. For a more complete introduction, see Morabia, *Le Ǧihâd*, 156–175; Peters, *Islam and Colonialism*, 9–38; idem, *Jihad in Classical and Modern Islam*, 9–26.

[20] Wensinck, *Concordance et indices de la tradition musulmane* (hereafter *Concordance*) 2:254, 3:50; Morabia, *Le Ǧihâd*, 162.

[21] Wensinck, *Concordance*, 1:194; Morabia, *Le Ǧihâd*, 160.

[22] Wensinck, *Concordance*, 5:298, with many variants; Morabia, *Le Ǧihâd*, 160.

Conduct of Warfare. This category includes, as we have seen, allocation of the spoils of war and treatment of noncombatants, including prisoners. Many of these traditions are reported on the authority of Successors and Companions, rather than of the Prophet. Likewise, some of the traditions of this kind are practical and this-worldly, while others bring in theological considerations. Declaration of hostilities is an important topic: in offensive operations, this requires summoning the adversary to Islam and allowing him either to convert to Islam or to pay tribute (*jizya*, see chapter 6). The ending of hostilities, whether through surrender or truce, also receives much attention.

Leadership. Closely attached to the preceding is the theme of leadership, good or bad. A topic of great importance is the Imam, the Caliph, the supreme leader of the Islamic polity, whose permission and supervision are needed for all expeditions of jihad. The hadith often poses questions that must have had real import. For instance, is it all right to go on a campaign "with any commander"—that is, even if that commander fails to meet the standards of morality and religion?[23] The answer is usually positive.

Jizya. This word, which means "tribute" or "poll tax," can stand for the entirety of relations between the Muslims and the non-Muslims whom they have subdued, discussed in chapter 6.

Asceticism. In one famous and much-quoted tradition, the Prophet declares against the ascetic practices of the Christians: "Monasticism has not been prescribed for you" (*inna al-rahbaniyya lam tuktab ʿalaykum*). Another version of this tradition says: "The monasticism of Islam is the jihad."[24] The hadith literature thus shows signs of controversy and disagreement over questions of this sort. It is clear that combat and ascetic practice were closely associated; it seems equally clear that some people found this assocation troubling.

Martyrdom. Many hadiths deal with this doctrine, discussed in chapter 5 below.

The Merits of Jihad. The numerous traditions of this kind are often rhetorical and without much doctrinal content. They are often about *ribat*, which here seems to mean nearly the same thing as jihad, but with emphasis on defensive warfare. Many traditions

---

[23] *Al-ghazw maʿa kull amir.* ʿAbd al-Razzaq, *al-Musannaf*, 5:283–284; Bukhari, *Kitab al-Jamiʿ al-sahih*, 2:238–239.

[24] Wensinck, *Concordance*, 2:312.

take the form: "A day of ribat in the path of God is better than
_____ ."[25] Other traditions describe the divine reward in store for
those who perform jihad or ribat.

The Place of Jihad and Ribat among Islamic Practices. The hadith
on this topic, which proceeds logically from the preceding, points
to considerable disagreement. Jihad is always considered a good
thing, but how does it compare to other religious duties such as
prayer, fasting, and pilgrimage? Is it a "pillar" of the faith? And if
so, what does that mean?

Correct Intention. Many traditions are concerned with the warrior's intention. Is he seeking only worldly glory or wealth? Or does
he truly have his mind set on God's will and commands? Many of
the traditions in this category are long and complex, making much
of the distinction between "mere" fighting and "authentic" jihad.
A well-known example comes when the Prophet is asked: "O Messenger of God! Men may fight out of a desire for booty, or for fame
and glory. Who is it that [truly] fights in the path of God?" To
which comes the answer: "Whoever fights so that the Word of God
may be highest is fighting in the path of God."[26]

The Internalized Jihad. Many traditions claim that the true,
"greater" jihad is not a fight against physical, external enemies,
but is rather a fight rather against the self (*nafs*).

These themes account, in a broad way, for much of the discourse in the hadith regarding jihad, though far from all of it.
Some of them are sites of considerable contention and controversy; others less so. To give a more precise sense of the hadith
regarding jihad, as well as of the juridical, theological, and political
debates it can convey, we end this chapter with a somewhat technical example.

Fighting with One's Money

We have already seen that the Quran expects that the believers
will "strive with their wealth and their persons" (*wa-jahadu bi-amwalihim wa-anfusihim*) in the path of God.[27] The Quran does not

---

[25] Ibid., 2:212.

[26] Wensinck, *Concordance*, 4:344; Morabia, *Le Ǧihâd*, 166.

[27] Quran, 49:15 (*Hujurat*) and several other places; see above, p. 22, 30. For the
following, see also Bonner, *Aristocratic Violence*, 11–42; "*Jaʿaʾil* and Holy War in
Early Islam."

give detailed instructions on how to carry out this requirement, although it is clearly related to the Book's many calls for generosity, beneficence, and almsgiving. It is the hadith that gives detailed instructions for "fighting with one's wealth and one's person." So, for instance, the hadith says repeatedly that giving weapons, supplies, and riding animals to a warrior who cannot afford these on his own is a meritorious act. Then does the person who makes these gifts receive the same reward (*ajr*) as the one who actually does the fighting? This theological problem receives different answers in different traditions, as we are about to see. However, practical questions also emerge, under the rubric of *siyar* (conduct of war). These include, among other things, the problem of whether shares of the spoils should be allocated to minors, women, slaves, non-Muslims fighting together with the Muslims, and other categories. Among these other categories we also find the *ajir* (hireling, camp follower).

> The *ajir* who accompanies a man in the Muslim army in enemy territory, serving him in return for a wage (*ajr*), without fighting, receives no share in the spoils, whether he is slave or free. . . . But if the *ajir* is a free man, and if he fights together with the Muslims, with the result that they obtain spoils, then he is allotted a share, as are the Muslims.[28]

This is the view of certain jurists, and is not ascribed to the Prophet. Here the hired man's *ajr* is simply a "wage," and not the "divine reward" that we find in the Quran. However, this passage raises the possibility that the hireling may also, on occasion, fight in the army. Then what if someone offers money or goods to a warrior, not only because the warrior needs these things to join the army, but so as to entice him into performing military service in the first place? Or what if—as actually did happen on occasion— a man who owes military service makes a payment to another man, who thereby becomes his substitute in the army? Such payments, called *juʿl* or *jiʿala* (plural: *jaʿaʾil*), arouse some controversy that is reflected in sayings ascribed to the Prophet, which is to say, in the hadith. Here we find the Prophet defending the practice:

---

[28] Tabari, *Ikhtilaf al-fuqaha'*, 20–21. The view is that of the followers of Abu Hanifa.

Those of my community who go on expedition and accept a wage (*ju'l*) with which to fortify themselves against their enemy are like the mother of Moses as she suckled her child while accepting her wage (*ajraha*).[29]

Other hadiths of the Prophet seem to be trying to make sense of the resulting confusion between the everyday, worldly wage and the divine reward promised in the Quran:

The warrior gets his reward (*ajr*), and the giver of the wage (*ju'l*) gets his reward (*ajr*), plus that of the warrior.[30]

However, the majority of the Prophetical hadith on this topic is adamantly opposed to the practice, and makes "hireling" (*ajir*) practically into a term of abuse. This seems to reflect a deep opposition among most Islamic jurists to any commodification whatsoever of military service. But in that case, what becomes of the Quranic requirement that we spend our substance, as well as our persons, in waging war in God's path? The jurists devoted considerable time and energy to this question of "fighting with one's money," *al-jihad bil-mal*. The soldiers, of course, worried about it less.

Can these conflicting traditions help us to understand what was actually happening in the early Islamic world? Is there any way to reconcile all these differences? Here, everything depends on our methodological preference in the study of the hadith. If we find Goldziher and Schacht convincing, then we may say that controversies raged over many issues—such as military substitution—in early Islamic society, and that the hadith allows us to pinpoint some of the elements in those controversies, and even to discern the general outline of how the controversies proceeded over time; in no case, however, does the hadith allow us accurate insight into what happened before the second century of the Hijra, and certainly not during the lifetime of the Prophet himself. On the other hand, if we follow the traditional Muslim view of the matter, as formulated by al-Shafi'i around the turn of the third/ninth cen-

[29] Bayhaqi, *al-Sunan*, 9:27.21–24; al-Muttaqi al-Hindi, *Kanz*, 5:336, no. 10779; Ibn Qudama, *Mughni*, 9:303.10–12; Morabia, *Le Ğihâd*, 166; Bonner, *Aristocratic Violence*, 35.

[30] Abu Da'ud, *Sunan*, 3:36–37, Jihad 31; Bayhaqi, *Sunan*, 9:28.20–22; Ibn Qudama, *Mughni*, 9:303.8–9.

tury,[31] then we may say that yes, there are contradictions in and among these traditions, as Muslim scholars have always freely conceded; the task that lies before the community of believers is to separate the true from the false, the sound from the forged. No matter how difficult this task may be, it will always be possible to arrrive at a sound core of Tradition, which will convey what is necessary to know about the norms that God has imposed on His community through the agency of His Prophet.

Recent research on these matters—much of which has been hostile to Goldziher and Schacht—has concentrated on the networks of scholarship and teaching in which the hadith and early law emerged, and on the development and growth of coherent juridical methodologies, whether for proto-schools, ancient schools, mature schools (*madhhabs*), or for Islam as a whole. In these and other ways, we have acquired a richer knowledge of the workings and contexts of early Islamic law, and many of the conclusions of Goldziher and Schacht have indeed been shown to be faulty or outright wrong. What has been lost, however, is a sense of the close interaction between these hadith and legal doctrines, on the one hand, and the controversies that brewed within early Islamic society over such matters as the integration of non-Arabs into the community and empire of Islam, the claim to rule made by various competing actors, and, not least of all, the complex of issues and doctrines that this book is considering under the rubric of *jihad*, on the other. For this reason, we may still say that between the two positions that we have identified here with the work of al-Shafiʿi and Schacht, others have been proposed, but none has yet been proved to work, at least with regard to the jihad.

Readings

There are several biographies of Muhammad in Western languages, different in approach and well worth reading. One of the best is Maxime Rodinson, *Muhammad* (New York: Pantheon, 1971). W. Montgomery Watt's two-volume biography, *Muhammad at Mecca* and *Muhammad at Medina* (Oxford: Clarendon, 1953

[31] The assignment to al-Shafiʿi of the role as spokesman for this view is due in part to Schacht, and has come under attack.

and 1956), is still much cited. It is better to read these two volumes than Watt's one-volume abridgement, *Muhammad: Prophet and Statesman* (Oxford: Clarendon, 1961), which lacks the detailed argument. Michael Cook's *Muhammad* (Oxford: Oxford University Press, 1983) is incisive and original. A readable contribution, quoting generously from original sources, is F. E. Peters, *Muhammad and the Origins of Islam* (Albany: SUNY Press, 1994). An original analysis, closely based on the Quranic text, comes in Jacqueline Chabbi, *Le Seigneur des tribus: L'Islam de Mahomet* (Paris: Noêsis, 1997). Those who wish to confront original sources may consult the translation of the Sira by Alfred Guillaume, *The Life of Muhammad: A Translation of Ibn Ishaq's Sirat Rasul Allah* (Oxford: Oxford University Press, 1955).[32] The monumental history of al-Tabari (d. 922) has been translated, including the volumes covering the life of Muhammad (vols. 6 and 7, edited by M. V. McDonald and W. M. Watt, 1988 and 1987; vol. 8, edited by M. Fishbein, 1997; vol. 9, edited by I. K. Poonawala, 1990. Albany: SUNY Press). The essays collected by Harald Motzki in *The Biography of Muhammad: The Issue of the Sources* (Leiden: Brill, 2000) present a wide range of the views regarding the sources for Muhammad's life. *The Sectarian Milieu*, by John Wansbrough (Oxford: Oxford University Press, 1978), is discussed in the chapter and remains important.

For an introduction to the hadith, very different approaches may be found in John Burton, *Introduction to the Hadith* (Edinburgh: Edinburgh University Press, 1994), and Muhammad Zubayr Siddiqi, *Hadith Literature* (Cambridge: Islamic Texts Society, 1993).

---

[32] This rendition of the book's author and title is incorrect, for two reasons. First, the book as we have it is by Ibn Hisham, not Ibn Ishaq—Guillaume thought that he could isolate the "real" Ibn Ishaq, but this result is far from clear. Second, the book's original title was, as we have seen, *Kitab al-maghazi* (book of raids), and in any case not "The Sira of the Messenger of God."

CHAPTER FOUR

The Great Conquests

The early Islamic conquests are a transforming event in history. They are also difficult to explain. How could a people who had lived for so long on the margins of the civilized world rise suddenly to defeat the two superpowers of the day, the Byzantine (East Roman) and Sasanian (Persian) empires? Where did they find the manpower to invade and overrun so many lands? And, most surprising of all, how did they then keep control over these lands and ultimately transform them? For even in defeat, the empires had reason to believe that the alien conquerers would eventually ask for nothing better than inclusion in the conquered empire for themselves, just as the Germanic intruders in the west had once settled on Roman lands, adapted Roman law to their own use, and eventually taken Romance dialects and Latin as their speech and Catholicism as their religion. Yet not only did the Arabs continue to speak Arabic, but many of the conquered countries also became Arabic-speaking after two or three centuries, while the religion of Islam came to extend over a majority of the population. This does not mean that the new Islamic civilization was not the result of cultural and ethnic mixing. It was this indeed, just like its Christian, western European counterpart. However, its pattern is different, and calls for explanation. Much of the controversy over all this has revolved around the jihad.

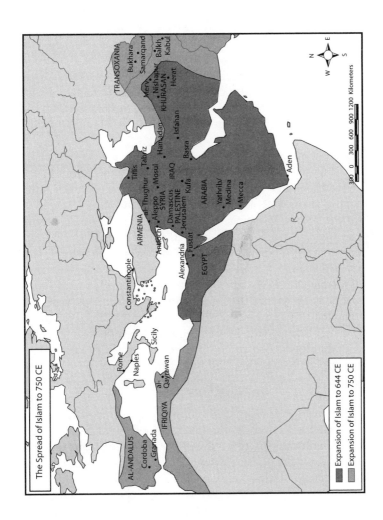

The Spread of Islam to 750 CE

Expansion of Islam to 644 CE
Expansion of Islam to 750 CE

TRANSOXANIA
Bukhara
Samarqand
Balkh
Kabul

Merv
Nishapur
KHURASAN
Herat

Tabriz
Isfahan

Tiflis
Mosul
Hamadan

ARMENIA
Aleppo
al-Thughur
SYRIA
Damascus
IRAQ
Basra
Kufa

Antioch
PALESTINE
Jerusalem
ARABIA
Yathrib/
Medina

Fustat
Mecca

Constantinople
Alexandria
EGYPT

Rome
Naples
Sicily

al-
Qayrawan

IFRIQIYA

AL-ANDALUS
Cordoba
Granada

Aden

300 0 300 600 900 1200 Kilometers

N
W E
S

The Course of Conquest

Military operations against the Byzantines and Sasanians did not begin in earnest until 634, two years after Muhammad's death. The intervening time (632–634) was taken up by internal conflict in Arabia, known as the wars of the apostasy (*al-ridda*). For at that time, upon the death of Muhammad, many Arabs renounced their loyalty to Islam. The Islamic leadership in Medina, under the first caliph, Abu Bakr, sent out armies that defeated these rebels, or "apostates." Now, for the first time in its history, the entire peninsula found itself unified and armed.

Meanwhile, things had been going badly for the two great empires (Byzantium and Sasanian Iran). After a long series of wars between them, they engaged in a final, devastating conflict in the second and third decades of the seventh century. The Persians conquered Syria, Palestine, Egypt, and much of Anatolia, but the Byzantine emperor Heraclius won these back and slogged on to decisive victory in 628. By this time, however, both empires had been bled white, with many of their cities and territories in ruins.

This mutual exhaustion worked to the advantage of the Arab newcomers. So too did the situation of the civilian populations. In Byzantine Egypt, Syria, and Palestine, a majority adhered to Monophysite Christianity rather than the Chalcedonianism that prevailed in Constantinople and among most of the imperial elite. When Heraclius reconquered these provinces from the Persians, he instituted harsh measures against Jews and dissident Christians, which led to disaffection and resentment. Iraq, the seat of the Persian Sasanian empire, was also Christian in its majority, with significant Jewish, Zoroastrian, and other minorities. Here the traditional Persian tolerance in these matters was offset by military defeat and political crisis. So it is not surprising that when the Arabs arrived in all these places, they met little resistance from local civilians. Many of the provincials must have thought that the newcomers would be no worse, and possibly better, than the previous governors, who had been squeezing them dry for the sake of their fruitless wars.

All this makes the Muslim Arabs' initial success easier to understand. As the *ridda* subsided, their movement of conquest got under way. It may have begun locally, as raiding expeditions met with unexpected success, followed up quickly by larger armies

under unified command. Fighting broke out more or less simultaneously in Byzantine Syria and Palestine and Sasanian Iraq. However, the evidence points to Syria and Palestine as the original
goal.[1] The Arabs fought in tribal units, with different groups pre-
dominating in the conquest of different areas.

The leadership in Medina passed in 634 to the second caliph,
ʿUmar ibn al-Khattab, who found himself conducting a war on
two fronts, or rather, two wars. At one critical moment, the commander Khalid ibn al-Walid crossed the desert from Iraq to Syria
to reinforce the Muslim forces there. For the most part, however,
the war on each side proceeded according to its own rhythm.
Many battles were fought, most of them Muslim victories. These
included the Yarmuk, in or around 636, where a large Byzantine
force was badly mauled, forcing Heraclius to withdraw from Syria;
and al-Qadisiyya, probably in 637, where the main Sasanian army
in Iraq was likewise smashed to pieces. ʿUmar left Medina to visit
Palestine and Syria, by most accounts in 638; while there, he is
said to have received in person the surrender of Jerusalem. Soon
afterward a small Arab force set off for Egypt, accepting, in 641,
the surrender of a Byzantine post, oddly named Babylon, near
what later became Cairo. The conquest of Alexandria, the Egyptian capital, took longer, but soon the Arab Muslims controled
Egypt and its fabulous wealth. Meanwhile, in 642 a victory at Ni-
havand, in western Iran, opened the Iranian plateau to the Muslim
armies. Here in the ethnic heart of the Sasanian empire, aggra-
vated by difficult terrain, resistance proved tough. Around fifteen
years were required to complete the conquest of Iran. The Muslims then kept going, more gradually, eastward into Central Asia,
westward into North Africa, and in other directions.

By the end of this initial phase of the conquests, the Sasanian
empire had ceased to exist altogether. However, despite repeated
raids by land and by sea and occasional large-scale expeditions, a
truncated Byzantine empire continued to hold out and resist, a
fact of great importance for the doctrine and practice of jihad as
these developed over the coming years.

Within a very few years, the Arab Muslims had conquered vast
territories, including fertile lands and wealthy cities. Now they
faced the question of what to do with them. As in all conquests,

[1] Donner, *The Early Islamic Conquests*, 96f.

the options included expropriating and expelling the natives, exploiting their labor from a distance, settling on the land as a new aristocracy, or merely concentrating on trade. The Quran and the young community's earlier experience in Arabia provided some guidance, but the disagreement seems to have been considerable. The caliph ʿUmar (ruled 634–644) is credited with the solution that prevailed. He decided that the Arabs should not settle in the countryside but should gather in towns, making themselves available for military service whenever required, while receiving stipends from the communal treasury. This treasury, in turn, would be constantly replenished by the native populations who would remain on their lands, paying taxes as before. New urban centers sprouted in Iraq (Basra, Kufa) and Egypt (Fustat), while older cities prevailed in Syria and Iran. In this way, for over a century the Arabs remained, ideally and also to a large extent in reality, a privileged, urban-dwelling warrior group. Chapter 6 will consider the fiscal regime that resulted, together with the treatment of non-Muslims.

Explanations

Most of the explanations that have been made for the great conquests fall into a few broad categories.[2] The single most important point of difference among them involves the role of religion and jihad. Put simply, were these conquests "Islamic" or "Arab"?

Islamic Explanations

In the centuries following the great conquests, extensive and detailed narratives of them were written in the Arabic language. Most of these sources present the events from an Islamic point of view that corresponds to the view of believing Muslims over the centuries, right down to the present day. While these medieval Arabic authors do not neglect the poverty of the Arabs before Islam and their love of fighting, they have no doubt regarding the events' true cause: the Arab Muslims fight and conquer because God has commanded them to do so, and has given them both

---

[2] In addition to the following summary, see Décobert, "Les méchanismes de la conquête arabe."

motivation and opportunity. Has not the Quran announced that God will cause the believers to inherit the lands, houses, and property of the People of the Book (Jews and Christians) in "a land where you had not set foot before"?[3] Enemy commanders are shocked to learn that the Muslims are "fighters by day and monks by night." While the Muslims take plunder and distribute it among themselves, they are not motivated by greed. Nor are they motivated by fear: the Arabic sources contrast their willingness to sacrifice themselves with the behavior of the opposing armies, frightened and unenthusiastic, even (in some stories) chained together in line of battle. Furthermore, these Arabic sources generally portray the campaigns of conquests as orderly and planned. Commanders take advantage of local opportunities, but the caliph in Medina dictates strategic movements and goals. Within the armies, though organization may be rough, discipline and morale remain high, maintained through prayer and sermons.

Anti-Islamic Explanations

In his monastery on the coast of Northumbria in the eighth century, the Venerable Bede learns that the Saracens have conquered much of Asia and Africa. Perplexed, Bede turns to biblical etymology to explain the relationship of Sarah and Isaac to Hagar and Ishmael, and the existence of a people known as Saracens, Ishmaelites, or Hagarenes. Here we have the beginning, in western Europe, of a thematics of misunderstanding that has survived to our own day. Much of this goes back to writings produced by Byzantines and by Christians living inside the early Islamic world. Here the conquests are a catastrophe calling out for explanation. Why has God taken dominion from the Christians and handed it over to these newcomers? An early and much-reiterated response was that the Saracens are the scourge of God, sent to punish the Christians for their sins. An apocalyptic literature described them as a sign of the end of time, and the invasions as a "testing furnace." Some writers inscribed Islam within the already-long list of Christian heresies. Others went on to claim that Muhammad was not really a prophet, because he could not foresee the future and because he pursued power, sensual pleasure, and other worldly goals. These and other themes then became enlarged and embroidered

---

[3] Quran 33:27 (*Ahzab*).

over the centuries. Generally speaking, these medieval Christian writings explain the early conquests through the will of a vengeful God, and focus upon the life of Muhammad, whom they vilify endlessly. They seldom ask what motivated the Saracens or Arabs, but rather dwell on the Saracens' love of violence—which, again, they often attribute to Muhammad himself.[4]

Modern Arab Explanations

Much (though not all) of modern orientalist scholarship on the early Islamic conquests, at least up until the Second World War, played down the idea of religion (and jihad) as a motivating force. Instead it explained these events through the history of Arabia and the Arabs, a history in which scarcity and poverty held sway. In this view, by the seventh century, long-term desiccation and desertification had reduced many of Arabia's centers of civilization to ruins. As the Arabs lost their habitations, their love of fighting and plunder only increased. Meanwhile, they had the good fortune of being less exposed to infectious disease than their neighbors in the plague-ridden Fertile Crescent. However, if Arabia was healthy, it was also poor, with its resources under increasing strain. The result was a Malthusian crisis of overpopulation, for which only the constant, murderous feuds and tribal wars provided any relief. Inevitably, the Arabs felt pressure to migrate into the rich lands under the control of the empires. And migrate they did: in the 630s the conquerors encountered many of their fellow Arabs in the borderlands, some of them allies and some of them fighting on the other side.

Many of these Arab explanations emphasize the Arabs' skill in fighting, which was real enough and certainly helped them against the imperial armies when the moment came. The northward migration of Arabs is also historical, part of a process of migration (in many directions) as old or older than the history of the Near East itself. However, desertification should make us suspicious. Ruins loom large in the imagination of the time, providing the best-known image in the pre-Islamic Arabic poetry and also appearing in the Quran.[5] Yet the abandonment of settle-

---

[4] Tolan, *Saracens*.
[5] See the treatment of this theme in Bamyeh, *The Social Origins of Islam*.

ments in western and southern Arabia was more a result of political turmoil, than of a spontaneous decline of the natural environment. The Arabs suffered from scarcity and want, but so too have other peoples who have not then undertaken the conquest of the world. The same might be said of the love of plunder, which was hardly unique to the bedouin. At any rate, the tendency of these Arab explanations is to view the conquests not as the product of the new teaching of Islam, but as the result of other, more material factors. Some even portrayed the early conquests as a mass migration, a *Völkerwanderung*; in this view, the Islamic view of the early conquests, and indeed Islam itself, was a later development, which historical tradition subsequently invented and retrojected to the early, formative period.

State Formation

Some recent treatments have emphasized the political aspect of the conquests. In particular, F. M. Donner has identified the fledgling Muslim state in Medina as the main protagonist in the story. This state and its leadership first showed their mettle by subduing the Arabian rebels of the *ridda* (war of apostasy) in 632–634. Then, as groups of Arab fighters achieved success, somewhat unexpectedly, against Byzantine and Persian garrisons and armies along the frontiers, the Medinan leadership intervened to maintain control and to make sure of the loyalty of the Arab tribesmen. The conquests thus resulted in a successful central state, against all the Arabs' historical precedent. In this view, the religion of Islam provided the new state with a secure ideological foundation.[6] Other contributions of recent decades have analyzed the internal situation among the Arabs before and immediately following the first wave of conquest, including the tensions between the Arab tribesmen who fought the battles of the first conquest and others who arrived later and demanded an equal share of the benefits.

Here we have a reconciliation of the "Islamic" and "Arab" views of the conquests. After all, why should the tribesmen not have been motivated *at the same time* by religious fervor and by hunger, want, and even—at least in some cases—greed? Likewise, all can

---

[6] Donner, *The Early Islamic Conquests*; idem, "The Origins of the Islamic State"; idem, "Centralized Authority and Military Autonomy in the Early Islamic Conquests."

agree that the weakness of the Byzantine and Sasanian empires in the 630s, and the resentment that many of their subjects felt against them, were of great, even decisive importance. However, this approach still begs the question of to what extent this ideology—including the jihad—was already in place. The Arabs believed fervently and fought hard, but what exactly did they believe in? Did the nascent structures of their army and society coherently express these beliefs?

Approaches to the Islamic Sources

We have seen that most modern accounts of the early conquests, whether Arab or Islamic in tendency, rely on the large body of medieval Arabic historical writings that describe these events in detail from an explicitly Islamic point of view. Here, for the critical period between the death of Muhammad and the first civil war (632–656), the situation resembles what we have found for the earlier period (ca. 610–632). Archaeology, epigraphy, papyrology, and numismatics provide some aid, but in the end we have no choice but to work with the literary tradition of Arabic historical writing. Everything thus depends on how we approach that tradition.

Some books about the maghazi, the campaigns of the early community (see chapter 3), included narratives about the great conquests, as did some collections of hadith. For the most part, however, conquest narratives—often referred to as *futuh* (conquests, openings)—were transmitted and collected separately from the maghazi narratives before being integrated into larger histories of the caliphate, of Islam, and of the world.

One interesting question that arises is whether these two genres, maghazi and futuh, express different conceptions of warfare and jihad. Here we can only begin to attempt an answer. In the futuh narratives, we are dealing with much larger units of fighters, moving over greater distances and facing more fearsome enemies than was the case in the maghazi. Accordingly, in the futuh, we learn less about the individual fighters, with the exception of the high commanders, than we do in the maghazi, where we have, for instance, detailed lists of the Muslims who participated in particular battles and of those who were slain in them. There is also considerable variety within the futuh narratives themselves: some of these focus on the spoils of war and accumulation of wealth in the course of military operations, while others put more emphasis on the acquisition of religious merit, on the necessity of having the correct intention (*niyya*) when performing jihad, and so on. But perhaps the single greatest difference between maghazi and futuh narratives has to do with their relation to the holy text of the Quran. We have seen that the Quran is often closely intertwined with the maghazi and sira narratives. After all, the story of the early community's progress, especially in the ten years from its founding in Medina in AH 1/622 CE until the death of Muhammad, is the story of the revealing of God's will, both through human action and through the arrival on earth of the divine Revelation. In the futuh, of course, the Prophet is no longer there and the Revelation no longer arrives through him; God's design is realized entirely through the actions of commanders and armies. The Quranic message is still present, but less vivid on the whole. Likewise, in the maghazi narratives, the Prophet leads his community in war, constantly issuing orders and soliciting strategic advice from his companions; at the same time, however, it is rare for him to appear with weapons and armor actually taking part in the fight. The commanders in the futuh, on the other hand, are military figures through and through.

The futuh, or conquest, narratives had considerable popularity among medieval audiences, and not surprisingly, for they show enormous literary and rhetorical skill. Once again, however, as in the case of the maghazi narratives, we face a gap. These narrative accounts of the conquests have survived in books that rarely date from before 800 CE. Furthermore, these accounts often contradict one another in detail, and where they do not do this, they overlap and repeat one another. As with the sira and maghazi, it is possible to draw a broadly coherent picture of the conquests on the basis of these narratives, but on close examination things tend to bog down in detail. Moreover, although the authors of these books of *akhbar* used the authenticating device of the supporting chain of authorities (*isnad*; see chapter 3), they seem to have been rather nonchalant or even sloppy about it, at least when measured by the more rigorous standards that were applied to the hadith.

It was Julius Wellhausen who, just over a century ago, established the prevailing consensus of orientalist scholarship regarding the Arabic narratives for the great conquests. Earlier in his career, when he specialized in biblical scholarship, Wellhausen had been the pioneer of the documentary hypothesis, according to which the Hebrew biblical narratives were actually the product of different authors (the Yahwist, the Elohist, the Priestly source), which a later redactor or redactors combined into the text of the Bible as we know it. Afterward, when Wellhausen turned his attention to the Arabic conquest narratives, he applied a similar technique and obtained broadly similar results.[7] He found that he could reduce the welter of conflicting and overlapping reports into bodies of work that he could ascribe to known authors of the early Islamic period. These authors, in turn, belonged to discrete, though informal schools of historical writing, located in Arabia (Medina), Iraq (Kufa and Basra), and Syria. Wellhausen then maintained that among these schools, the Medinans were to be preferred over the Iraqis, who, he claimed, were prone to exaggeration, regional bias, or even outright lies. (In Wellhausen's day almost all of the Syrian historiography was lost.) In this way, by privileging the Medinan narratives and scholarship to the detriment of the others, Wellhausen made the job of writing conquest history possible, if not easy. Other scholars refined this approach, with remarkably patient analysis of detail.[8]

The work of Goldziher and Schacht, mentioned in chapter 3, dealt with hadith and early Islamic law rather than with political and military history, and had rather different implications for students of Arabic historical writing. These, however, did not become clear until afterward.[9] Meanwhile, Wellhausen's theory of regional schools held considerable, though not universal, sway.[10] Then, in the late 1960s and early 1970s, Albrecht Noth opposed this theory of regional schools and, in the opinion of many, demolished it.[11]

---

[7] Wellhausen, "Prolegomena zur ältesten Geschichte des Islams."

[8] Especially the monumental *Annali dell'Islam* by Leone Caetani.

[9] Beginning with the work of John Wansbrough, mentioned in chapters 2 and 3.

[10] Note that Wellhausen and Schacht both developed theories of "local schools" of historiographical and legal activity, respectively.

[11] Noth, "Isfahan-Nihawand. Eine quellenkritische Studie zur frühislamischen Historiographie"; idem, "Der Charakter der ersten großen Sammlungen von Nachrichten zur frühen Kalifenzeit"; and with Conrad, *The Early Arabic Historical Tradition: A Source-Critical Study* (1994), which first appeared as *Quellenkritische*

Noth argued that the Medinan authors were just as prone to inconsistency and exaggeration as the Iraqis. More important, Noth claimed that the entire mass of narrative traditions (*akhbar*) relating to the conquests had many characteristics in common. They all emerged from an enormous process of telling, retelling, collecting and compiling, which we can trace back in time, but never to where the narrative traditions were first composed. Thus, how those traditions originated—and, so, whether or not they are literally true—is beyond our knowing. Noth further found that certain basic themes permeate the Arabic historical tradition as a whole, together with transferable, often-repeated elements of narrative content (literary topoi). Many of these involve religious motivation in fighting. Were these themes and topoi authentic—that is, do they extend all the way back to the 630s? For example, with regard to the summons to Islam (*daʿwa*), did the Arabs, on the eve of battle, really call upon their opponents to assume Islam or else to face the consequences of battle and defeat—as the Arabic narratives say they did and as Islamic law would have required them to do? In general terms, Noth's approach leads to the conclusion that the *daʿwa*, and other such themes, correspond to primary concerns in the tradition as whole: that is, *for as far back as we can see*, elements of the jihad were indeed present in the narratives.

The study of early Islamic historical writing has flourished in the last few decades. Now, however, we turn to another piece of the puzzle.

Approaches to the Non-Islamic Sources

We have seen that biased and fantastical views of the Islamic conquests, and of Islam itself, prevailed in the Christian West during the Middle Ages and afterward, and that these views owed much to earlier works written by Christians residing in the Byzantine empire and in the Islamic lands. This is one reason why modern historians of the early Islamic conquests have treated non-Islamic primary sources for the conquests gingerly and have often avoided

---

Studien zu Themen, Formen und Tendezen frühislamischer Geschichtsüberlieferung. I: Themen und Formen (Bonn: Selbstverlag des Orientalischen Seminars der Universität, 1973).

them altogether. Another reason for their caution in this matter has to do with the peculiarities of their own field of study. For, after the First World War, the formation of specialists in late antique and medieval oriental or Near Eastern studies increasingly meant a concentration in either the Islamic languages and cultures (principally Arabic, Persian, and Turkish) or else the non-Islamic ones (Hebrew, Aramaic-Syriac, Coptic, Armenian, Greek, etc.). As a result, few scholars were competent to judge the validity of writings in languages other than Arabic for the study of the Islamic conquests, while not all students of Arabic were eager to hear about these "exotic" writings in any case.

Nonetheless, at least some of these sources seem to have much to offer. Unlike the Arabic literary sources, which were written (in the form in which we have them) two or more centuries after the events in question, some of the non-Arabic ones come quite close. We have an anti-Jewish tract written in Greek ostensibly in North Africa in 634, at the very time of the beginning of the conquest of Syria and Palestine. The author mentions a prophet who has emerged among the Saracens and their violent takeover of Palestine. The writings of Sophronius, patriarch of Jerusalem in the 630s, include a sermon describing the Christians of Jerusalem, cut off from Bethlehem on Christmas day by the invaders and their siege. A few fragments of writing in Syriac may be literally contemporary with the early conquests, describing the death and enslavement of tens of thousands. Several chronicles, including one written in Armenian in the later seventh century, also mention the rise of Islam.

In the mid-1970s, two young scholars in London, Michael Cook and Patricia Crone, proposed to set the Arabic historical tradition aside altogether and to rewrite the history of early Islam entirely from the non-Islamic sources. The result: a book called *Hagarism*,[12] based itself on texts and studies that had been largely ignored by scholars of Islam ever since the First World War. Its

---

[12] Cook and Crone, *Hagarism: The Making of the Islamic World*. The title refers both to the biblical Hagar, concubine of Abraham and mother of Ishmael, and to the Quranic and early Islamic *muhajirun* (emigrants, "those who perform *hijra*"). The ambiguity (or pun?) appears in seventh-century documents and literary sources, where the newcomers are called *mahgraye* in Syriac and *moagaritai* in Greek.

argument was complex. The earliest phase of Hagarism ("Islam" in its familiar sense does not appear until toward the end of the story) involved an alliance between the Jews of Palestine and the Arabs of northern Arabia, who appeared, armed, under the leadership of their Prophet. (Some of these Christian and Jewish sources describe Muhammad as a participant in the conquest of Palestine, whereas in the Islamic tradition he dies, like Moses, before this event takes place.) The alliance's initial goal was to take Jerusalem from the Byzantines and to restore the Temple there. (Mecca does not enter the story at all, at least at this point.) However, the alliance did not last. Early Hagarism also went through a messianic phase, where Muhammad figures as a kind of John the Baptist preparing the way for a Messiah. There are hints that this Messiah's identity is none other than ʿUmar ibn al-Khattab, known to Islamic tradition as the second Caliph, and bearer of the Arabic epithet al-Faruq, rather like the Christian Syriac term *paroqa* which means "savior." Ensuing phases are set out in a discrete, though unaccustomed chronological order, before we arrive at a world that corresponds to what we can recognize as classical Islam.

The controversy over *Hagarism* was fierce. Some scholars accused its authors of rejecting the Islamic tradition outright, which was not quite fair: what they did was to point to its internal "dilemmas," as had already been discussed by Goldziher, Schacht, Wansbrough, and Noth.[13] Many objected that even if some of these non-Muslim sources fall closer in time than the Muslim ones to the era of the great conquests, their authors were blinded by polemical passion and could not possibly have had accurate knowledge of the Muslims and their affairs. Yet others maintained that the narrative motifs in these sources were all, in equal measure, polemical, and that a chronological reconstruction of the earliest Islam on the basis of these sources, whether Arabic, non-Arabic, or both, made little sense.[14]

More recently, the full range of these non-Islamic sources for the rise of Islam has become more accessible to nonspecialists, thanks especially to the work of Robert Hoyland and Alfred-Louis

[13] Ibid., 3.

[14] See Wansbrough's review of *Hagarism* in *Bulletin of the School of Oriental and African Studies.*

de Prémare.[15] Hoyland, in his long, careful study of these sources, seems to vindicate the overall picture of the early conquests that we have from the Arabic Islamic sources themselves, although he also supports several of the conclusions of *Hagarism*. A similar, cautious affirmation of the picture of the conquests that we have from the Arabic sources also emerges from the work of Albrecht Noth and some of those who have followed him. Again, this means that for as far back as we can see—which can never be back to the very event itself at the beginning—the events of the early conquests are inseparable from certain primary themes. Several of these themes, in turn, are inseparable from the jihad, as we are trying to understand it here. So, while a process of state formation is certainly at the heart of the rise and early expansion of Islam—as it will be in many more historical manifestations of the jihad (see chapter 8)—this process does not, by itself, explain the astonishing event of the early Islamic conquests.

This means that we must do full justice to the "Islamic" explanations for the conquests. Something new happened in early seventh-century Arabia, something greater than hunger and the desire for domination, something that brought about a transformation of social and spiritual life, in part through participation in combat. In chapter 2 we began to try to discern just what that transformation was all about through the study of our single most important source, the Quran.

Meanwhile, attention is increasingly paid to another, related argument, this one over the origins of Islam more generally. Here we may identify the opposing camps as "Arabian" and "Near Eastern." Did Islam emerge in the seventh-century Hijaz, a harsh, isolated environment where social life was dominated by tribal forms and, to a great extent, by violence? Or was it yet one more expression of the perennial civilization of the Fertile Crescent, the Mediterranean, and Iran? Questions of this sort turn our attention away from the astonishing military success of the early Islamic armies which can, after all, be explained through conjunctural elements such as battlefield tactics and the momentary (though fatal) internal weakness of the Byzantine and Sasanian empires. Instead we find ourselves asking to what extent Islam brought a break with

---

[15] Hoyland, *Seeing Islam as Others Saw It*; de Prémare, *Les fondations de l'islam*.

the past; and whether we ought to view this past as primarily Arabian, Near Eastern, Mediterranean, or all of these.

Readings

One of the most vivid accounts of the early conquests is Carl Heinrich Becker's "Die Ausbreitung der Araber," *Islamstudien* vol. 1, 66–145 (Hildesheim: G. Olms, 1967). This appeared in English as chapters 11 and 12 in volume 2 of the *Cambridge Medieval History*, ed. H. M. Gwatkin and others (Cambridge: Cambridge University Press, [1913] 1967). Francesco Gabrieli's *Muhammad and the Conquests of Islam* (New York: McGraw-Hill, 1968) is highly readable but now out of date. The close and careful analysis by Fred McGraw Donner in *The Early Islamic Conquests* (Princeton: Princeton University Press, 1981) carries considerable authority. There is now an English translation of the single most important source for the early conquests, *The History of al-Tabari* (Albany: SUNY Press, 1993 [vol. 11, ed. K. Y. Blankinship]; 1992 [vol. 12, ed. Y. Friedmann]; 1989 [vol. 13, ed. G.H.A. Juynboll]; 1994 [vol. 14, ed. Rex Smith]). Modern approaches to the Arabic sources are outlined in this chapter and its footnotes. In addition to Albrecht Noth and Lawrence Conrad's *The Early Arabic Historical Tradition* (Princeton: Darwin Press, 1994), the series in which it was published, Studies in Late Antiquity and Early Islam, includes several volumes of interest, especially Fred M. Donner, *Narratives of Islamic Origins: The Beginnings of Islamic Historical Writing* (Princeton: Darwin Press, 1998); and the book by Robert G. Hoyland, already mentioned, *Seeing Islam as Others Saw It: A Survey and Evaluation of Christian, Jewish and Zoroastrian Writings on Early Islam* (Princeton: Darwin Press, 1997).

In addition, see the new book by Hugh Kennedy, *The Great Arab Conquests: How the Spread of Islam Changed the World We Live In* (Cambridge, MA: Da Capo, 2007).

Chapter Five

Martyrdom

One point on which most observers of the early Islamic conquests agreed was the extraordinary motivation of the Muslim fighters. An official Chinese source of the tenth century put it this way:

> Every seventh day the king [of the Arabs] sits on high and speaks to those below, saying: "Those who are killed by the enemy will be borne in heaven above; those who slay the enemy will receive happiness." Therefore they are usually valiant fighters.[1]

Though the scenario is inaccurate, it captures the essence of the matter, at least as non-Muslims saw it: the Muslims' self-sacrificing zeal came from a promise of heaven made to those who fell in battle. For the Muslims themselves, their religion did indeed promise ample rewards to those who fought on its behalf. For whoever survived the battle, this reward consisted of victory and spoils, as we have seen in chapter 3. For those who fell, the reward meant a privileged place in Paradise. Here we have the heart of the Islamic doctrine of martyrdom, which both connects Islam to the other monotheist traditions and sets it apart from them.

---

[1] Ou-yang Hsiu. *Hsin T'ang shu*, trans. by Isaac Mason as "The Mohammedans of China," *Journal of the North China Branch of the Royal Asiatic Society* 60 (1929): 66–69, cited by Hoyland, *Seeing Islam as Others Saw It*, 250–251.

Martyrdom before Islam

Orientalist scholars of the nineteenth and early twentieth centuries often identified common Semitic origins for the practices of Judaism, Christianity, and Islam. In this way, J. A. Wensinck described martyrdom as a common heritage going back to the very beginnings of Near Eastern settled society and literature, where the epic of Gilgamesh assigns a privileged place in the afterlife to the slain in battle.[2] In a more specific way, martyrdom begins with the philosophical schools of antiquity, Stoicism above all. The philosopher demonstrates the superiority of reason over emotion, and his own superiority to this corrupt and corrupting world, by putting an end to his life or allowing others to do this. Like Seneca slitting his wrists in the bath, he may direct his gesture against the holders of power. Out of such gestures comes the role of the philosopher and the holy man in the later Roman Empire, as the symbol and embodiment of resistance against unjust authority.[3]

From here, it was not far to the precepts and practices of monotheism. What is to be done when a pagan ruler demands that the Jews do repugnant things, such as eat the flesh of swine? The response comes in the second book of Maccabees: "We are ready to die rather than transgress the laws of our fathers."[4] Going further, in Fourth Maccabees, the Jewish heroes endure the tortures and executions inflicted on them by King Antiochus, all the while delivering discourses on the superiority of reason, the truth of the God of Israel, and the futility of the tyrant's efforts.

To the extent that this drama involved demonstration and proof, it made sense to call the victims "martyrs" (in Greek *martyres*; sing. *martys*), which meant witnesses in law. However, early Christianity transformed this term, in close association with another juridical term, *homología* in Greek, *confessio* in Latin. (It may be recalled that Roman judicial inquiry involved the systematic use of torture.) Together, the Christian "confession" and "martyrdom" extended over broad, new semantic fields, never laid out with entire precision for the understanding but all the more fertile as a result. Furthermore, a prime characteristic of the early Chris-

---

[2] Wensinck, "The Oriental Doctrine of the Martyrs," 7.
[3] Bowersock, *Martyrdom and Rome*.
[4] 2 Maccabees 7:2.

tian martyrs, through the persecuting reign of Diocletian (284–305), was their passivity. Even though some of them had once served in the Roman army, as Christian activists they refused to employ violence to defend themselves or their cause. In their executions, which were highly theatrical affairs, their deeds became known (to their admirers) as struggles (*athloi*), and the martyrs themselves as "soldiers of the arena" and "athletes of God."

Martyrdom in Quran and Tradition

Like the Greek *martys*, the Arabic word *shahid* (plural: *shuhada'*) means "witness." In this sense it appears numerous times in the Quran. Often the witness is the Messenger (Muhammad), bringing testimony of God's truth to a recalcitrant people, as when God addresses him: "One day We shall summon among each nation (*umma*) a witness against them, from among themselves; and We shall bring you as a witness against these."[5] *Shahid* as "witness" also appears as an attribute of God: so on the Day of Resurrection, God will distinguish among the followers of all religions (and judge them), "for God is witness (*shahid*) of all things."[6] Elsewhere, however, the Quranic *shahid* seems compatible with early Christian teachings regarding martyrdom, as in the procession-like list: "Those who obey God and the Messenger are in the company of those who receive God's bounty: the prophets, the just (*al-siddiqin*), the martyrs (*al-shuhada'*), and the righteous (*al-salihin*). . . ."[7] There is no direct indication anywhere in the Quran that the *shahid* is one who dies in battle, although some Muslim exegetes do identify him this way. On the other hand, we have already seen that the Quran describes the reward awaiting those who die in combat in the path of God. They are alive with God,[8] enjoying the delights of Paradise. These delights include marriage to dark-eyed maidens, although in this respect the Quran does not distinguish the fallen in battle from the other righteous in Heaven. Thus the core of the doctrine of the divine reward for the fallen

[5] 16:89 (*Nahl*).

[6] 22:17 (*Hajj*), among many examples.

[7] 4:69 (*Nisa'*).

[8] As at Quran 2:154 and 3:169f. At 4 Maccabees 7:19, the fallen Jewish heroes likewise "do not die to God, but live in God."

in battle is already present in the Book, but only the core; they are not yet called *shahid*s.

The Islamic Tradition, specifically the hadith, makes this connection and spells out the doctrine with abundant detail. Here, as in the Christian doctrine of the martyr, *shahid* signifies a person who, through suffering and death, has achieved high reward in the hereafter. Descriptions of the martyrs in the Tradition include their ability to intercede for the faithful on the Day of Resurrection, otherwise a prerogative reserved for the Prophet Muhammad himself. Their souls have the shape of white birds, feeding on the fruits of Paradise; or alternatively, they are held in the craws of green birds that feed in Paradise and drink from its rivers. These birds also nestle in golden lamps suspended underneath the divine throne.[9] These traits, setting the martyrs apart from the rank and file of the blessed, also occur in early Christian descriptions of the martyrs, and again point to a close connection between the two traditions. Indeed, the Arabic word *shahid* may plausibly be thought to derive from the Christian Syriac for "witness" and "martyr," *sāhdā*.[10]

Nonetheless, the underlying idea is different. No longer do we have the Christian insistence on passivity and nonviolence. Instead of metaphorical soldiers of God, we have fighters who literally take up arms and use them. The Muslim texts of Tradition and Law repeatedly affirm that the martyrs (*shuhada'*) are those who die while fighting for the faith. Their sins are forgiven, though not their debts. They go immediately to Paradise, skipping the long wait for Resurrection and the "tortures of the grave" that others must undergo. One who dies at sea receives twice the reward (whatever that means) of one who dies on land. Similarly, one achieves extra reward for death and burial deep in enemy territory. The martyr should be buried with his body unwashed—unlike the practice for ordinary dead—and still in his bloodstained clothes, since the mode of his suffering and death has already purified him. There is some disagreement among jurists over the question of the prayer that is recited over the dead: since the martyr is "alive with God," does the prayer need to be recited for him? In many

---

[9] Wim Raven's article "Martyrs," in *EQ* 3:281–287, esp. 284, citing various hadiths. Many of these traditions insist that the souls of the martyrs do not actually enter Paradise, although they receive provisions from there.

[10] Ibid.; Wensinck, "The Oriental Doctrine of the Martyrs."

narratives, the family, especially the mother of the slain hero, express gratitude at the news of their son's martyrdom and forbid any mourning. In this we see an element of continuity right down to the present day. There are many traditions of the hortatory type, where the martyrs, once they see the delights in store for them, ask to be sent back to earth so as to fight and be killed again. (This is the only request denied them.) Also occurring frequently is the story of the fighter who has just barely survived a wound in battle: he reports that he saw his dark-eyed spouse approaching, only to leave abruptly when she saw that he wasn't yet dead; now he longs for the opportunity to rejoin her for ever.

As in the other monotheist traditions, the connection between martyrdom and "witnessing" was not crystal clear. Muslim scholars tried to explain it as "bearing witness by one's blood,"[11] which makes some sense in and of itself. Nonetheless, the act's fundamental meaning seems to lie elsewhere. In hadith after hadith, what sets the martyr apart is the abundance of his divine reward (*ajr*). It has been remarked that this focus on individual spiritual reward could and often did result in a disregard for the actual outcome of war.[12] For indeed, in military history, we encounter army commanders who find themselves hindered and frustrated by the presence, under their command, of heaven-seeking volunteers (*muttawwiʿa*). Sometimes these commanders marginalize these disorganized, unreliable troops in order to rely on their more dependable and better-trained regulars, who may be all the more effective for their greater prudence and their reluctance to die. At any rate, what concerns us here is the individualist aspect of the doctrine. If the Christian Church was built over the bones of its martyrs, the Islamic community admired its martyrs as models of physical courage, relentless striving (*jihad*), and the individual internalization of norms.

Contexts of Martyrdom in Islam

Views differed regarding the status of those who die in combat against rebels (*bughat*) or other miscreants in conflicts among

---

[11] Morabia, *Le Ǧihâd*, 251–252, citing al-Sarakhsi and al-Shaybani.
[12] Noth, *Heiliger Krieg und heiliger Kampf*.

Muslims. Shi'is and Kharijites were generally willing to concede the status of martyr to these; Sunni opinion was mixed.[13] However, it became generally accepted that the martyrs' ranks include those who perish—outside of warfare—in the service of God and for the sake of their beliefs. For Sunnis these prominently include the early caliphs 'Umar (d. 644) and especially 'Uthman (d. 656), whose murder set off the first great inner conflict (*fitna*) of Islam. In this way, a great variety of groups established models of comportment for themselves: these included those Sufis, or mystics, who considered the mystic theologian al-Hallaj, executed in Baghdad in 922, as a great martyr.[14]

Martyrdom is especially important to the Shi'a. Here, where the emphasis falls on suffering, death, and redemption, the act of martyrdom itself may or may not take place on the battlefield. In the eyes of the Shi'a, the martyrs par excellence are the members of the family of the imams, descendants of the Prophet's cousin and son-in-law 'Ali ibn Abi Talib, who died at the behest of oppressive and illegitimate rulers. They especially revere 'Ali's son al-Husayn, killed in 680 CE at Karbala', in southern Iraq. They consider al-Husayn the "martyr of martyrs" (*shahid al-shuhada'*) and commemorate his death each year on its anniversary, the tenth day of the month of Muharram. The tombs of al-Husayn and the other slain imams are the major shrines within the Shi'i world. The Shi'a also attribute the status of martyr to those who died while fighting the enemies of the imams, and to others slain for the preservation of the Shi'i faith and community.

Martyrdom presented problems to Muslim thinkers and authorities. The problem of correct intention (*niyya*), which drew much attention in the general doctrine of jihad, had a sharp application here. The general consensus was that since only God has full knowledge of the fighter's intention, the slain in battle must be buried in the fashion of martyrs. If they went to war without true intention—for the sake of booty or without true belief—they will be deprived of the status of martyrs in the next world. And what about the fighter who recklessly exposes himself to danger, seeking Heaven without creating any palpable advantage for his

[13] In addition to the articles on martyrdom by Etan Kohlerg (see bibliography and the last section of this chapter), see Abou El Fadl, "*Ahkam al-Bughat.*"

[14] Massignon, *The Passion of al-Hallaj.*

own side on the earthly battlefield? Does not such seeking of martyrdom constitute suicide?

The Quran declares that too great a love of life can be an obstacle to salvation, and it praises those who "sell themselves"—apparently on the battlefield—in return for a divine reward.[15] However, the Islamic jurists tended to caution in this area, usually arguing against, for instance, a self-sacrificing charge made by an individual fighter or small group against a powerful enemy force unless such an action might lead to some positive military outcome. In any case, such self-sacrificing activity on the battlefield was not identified with suicide, which was condemned in the Quran and in Islamic doctrine.[16] Murderous attacks by individuals against political leaders, made with the certain knowledge that they would result in the attacker's death, were most famously and spectacularly carried out in the late eleventh and twelfth centuries CE by the Isma'ili (Sevener) Shi'i sect known as the Assassins.[17] Otherwise, self-destructive attacks took place only rarely, especially in Sunni Islam, until recent times, when this part of the doctrine of martyrdom and jihad has been the site of much rethinking and controversy.[18]

In addition to the martyrs who die in battle, the Islamic jurists recognized several categories of noncombatant martyrs. These included women who die in childbirth, persons who die of accident or of diseases such as pleurisy or plague, and those who die of natural causes while engaged in meritorious acts, pilgrimage above all, but also travel in the pursuit of learning (talab al-'ilm). Such cases as these were considered martyrs of the next life only: they do not receive the particular burial treatment of the slain in battle, who are considered martyrs of both this life and the next.

With this swelling of their ranks, the martyrs risked losing some of their distinctively high place. But for many thinkers, martyrdom was above all the status of those who overcame their base desires in the struggle against the self, frontline combatants in the greater jihad (al-jihad al-akbar) and the jihad against the self (jihad al-nafs). To become such a martyr, one needed perhaps to undergo a spiri-

---

[15] Quran 2:96, 207 (Baqara).
[16] Quran 2:195 (Baqara), 4:29 (Ma'ida); Rosenthal, "On Suicide in Islam."
[17] Lewis, The Assassins.
[18] Cook, Understanding Jihad, 142; see below, chapter 9.

tual death, but not necessarily a physical one. This was a spiritualization of the doctrine, but not necessarily a later, secondary development. For martyrdom in Islam had been close to ascetic practice and belief from quite early on. One indication for this comes in the word *maghazi*, which was originally used for the genre of early Islamic and Arabic literature concerned with the life of Muhammad and with the history of the earliest community and its raids and battles (chapter 3). The Arabic root from which this word derives connotes effort and striving, just like the root of *jihad*. A century ago, Eduard Sachau suggested that the word originated among Christian converts to Islam. These were already accustomed to describing their great men, their saintly miracle-workers, and their martyrs as "athletes of God" and their actions as struggles (*athloi*) of suffering in the arena. Once they had converted to Islam, they would have spoken of Muhammad's life and deeds in the same way, only now in Arabic: this life and these deeds would have constituted struggles, campaigns, or in Arabic, *maghazi*.[19] This observation has not been widely accepted (or noticed), but it seems to point to a truth that goes well beyond mere etymology, namely the inseparable quality of the "internal" and "external" jihad.

Nonetheless, at least for Sunni Muslims, armed struggle has most often been at the heart of the matter. Popular sentiment, reflected in many works of popular literature, has always yielded pride of place among the martyrs to the slain of Badr in 624 CE; to the Prophet's uncle Hamza, the "lord of the martyrs" killed at Uhud in 625; to Abu Ayyub, buried before the walls of Constantinople around 672; and to other early heroes.

Martyrs and Neomartyrs

Islamic martyrdom comes out of a common Near Eastern and monotheist experience and expression. It differs from its Christian and Jewish counterparts in its insistence, as a famous hadith says, that "Paradise is in the shadow of the swords." From time to time,

---

[19] Sachau, "Das Berliner Fragment des Musa Ibn Ukba," 448, n. 2; cf. Hinds, "Maghazi and Sira in Early Islamic Scholarship," 197, n. 55. See also von Grunebaum, *Medieval Islam*, 276.

some Christians attempted to institute doctrines among themselves that had some points in common with the Islamic teaching
regarding martyrdom. We can probably never know for sure if
they were then consciously imitating the Islamic doctrine, in the
hope of repeating Islam's success. What is sure is that Christians
who thought this way had to confront the rigorism of their own
Church Fathers and the ancient Christian ban against the use of
violence.

In the Latin West, Saint Augustine laid the foundations of a
Christian theory of just war, in a doctrine of considerable complex-
ity.[20] Afterward, however, in the aftermath of the pillaging of Rome
and Ostia in 846 by the Saracens, Pope Leo IV expressed the hope
of a heavenly reward for those who would die while fighting them.
The idea resurfaced over the next two and a half centuries, especially in Spain. Then came the Crusades, where the promise of
forgiveness for sins helped to motivate many participants. For
Latin Christian thinkers, the matter still remained controversial.
At any rate, while Crusading doctrine had a certain amount in
common with Islamic martyrdom and jihad, no direct link has
been found between them. The Latins must have taken this step
for their own reasons, and not merely through imitation of their
Islamic foe.[21]

The Eastern Orthodox Christians of the Byzantine Empire,
who for centuries bore the brunt of Christendom's fight against
Islam, remained devoted to the memory of the old martyrs of the
Christian Church and to the ideal of abstinence from violence.
While it was necessary to wage war to preserve the Roman empire
and to regain territories that the empire had lost, no martyr's palm
awaited those who died in the effort. Byzantine writers expressed
disgust at the Islamic notion of martyrdom (as they understood
it).[22] The great exception came in the reign of the warrior-emperor

[20] Russell, *The Just War in the Middle Ages*, 16–39.
[21] Riley-Smith, *The First Crusade and the Idea of Crusading*, esp. 22–23; Noth,
Heiliger Krieg und heiliger Kampf, esp. 139–146; Canard, "La guerre sainte dans le
monde islamique et dans le monde chrétien."
[22] The chronicler Theophanes (ed. de Boer, 334, A.M. 6122), in his account of
the rise of Islam, says (inaccurately) that Muhammad taught that Paradise was as-
sured to anyone who killed or was killed by an enemy. Like other Byzantine writers
on Islam, Theophanes describes the Muslim paradise as a place of purely carnal
pleasure.

Nicephorus Phocas (963–969), the high point of Byzantine military success against Islam. Nicephorus attempted to institute a kind of crusade, granting the martyr's halo to the soldiers of Christ who had "sacrificed their lives to serve the holy emperors and to liberate and avenge the Christians." But the ecclesiastical authorities nipped this effort in the bud, citing a fourth-century canon of Basil the Great that recommended that Christian Roman soldiers who had killed in war be excluded from the sacraments for a period of three years. The Byzantines persisted in their old ideas, afterward finding the Latin Crusaders, with their fighting priests, at least as dangerous and barbarous as the Saracens.[23]

The great age of the Christian martyrs had ended in the early fourth century with the conversion of the Emperor Constantine. Those who wished to imitate the martyrs might seek an ascetic life; martyrdom in the old style became rare. One exception was the pre-Islamic desert borderland between Syria and Arabia, where monks sometimes died at the hands of bedouin marauders. Another was the wilds of northern Europe, where missionaries such as Saint Boniface (d. 754) could meet a martyr's death. Christian martyrdom received some new impetus, however, with the arrival of Islam.

As far as we can tell, instances of Christians dying as martyrs at the hands of Muslim armies or political authorities are actually rather rare during the first centuries of Islam.[24] However, in the middle of the ninth century, the flourishing city of Cordova, capital of the independent Islamic amirate of al-Andalus, saw a brief but intense series of what, depending on one's point of view, were either martyrdoms or public suicides within the Christian community. In a series of episodes, a Christian, usually an ecclesiastic, would convert to Islam, and then openly and publicly renounce it—an act for which Islamic law requires death. The Muslim *qadi* (judge) would try unsuccessfully to change the apostate's mind; execution then took place. Comparable events took place in Palestine and Syria at approximately the same time. It is clear, even in the Christian narratives, that the Muslim authorities did not want

[23] Canard, "La guerre sainte dans le monde islamique et dans le monde chrétien," 616–618.

[24] For a possible episode, see Woods, "The 60 Martyrs of Gaza and the Martyrdom of Bishop Sophronius of Jerusalem."

this outcome and tried to prevent it. These events created storms within the Christian communities, where the authorities soon put a stop to them. They seem to have attracted little notice from the neighboring Muslims, though eventually they did receive attention from Christians in northern Europe. These willing victims, often known as "neomartyrs," were martyrs in the old, passive style, not the new, aggressive fashion of the Crusaders. The larger context was an increase of tension and isolation among Christian communities that, having adopted the Arabic language among themselves, and having come to realize that the rule of Islam was definitively there to stay, found their own numbers decreasing through peaceful conversion to Islam.[25] In the next chapter we look, among other things, at the regulation of intercommunal relations, closely tied to the jihad.

Readings

Morabia, *Le Ğihâd*, 251–255, provides a starting point, together with the *EI²* article "Shahid" by Etan Kohlberg, and Kohlberg's article "Medieval Muslim Views on Martyrdom" in *Mededeelingen der Koninklijke Akademie van Wetenschappen* (Amsterdam), Afdeeling Letterkunde, Nieuwe reeks, 60, no. 7 (1997): 279–307. On martyrdom for the Shiʿa, see M. Ayoub, *Redemptive Suffering in Islam: A Study of the Devotional Aspects of ʿAshuraʾ in Twelver Shīʿism* (The Hague: Mouton, 1978); and W. R. Husted, "Karbalaʾ Made Immediate: The Martyr as Model in Imami Shiʿism, *Muslim World* 83 (1993): 263–278. For a comparative view, see the article "Märtyrer" in *Religion in Geschichte und Gegenwart*, vol. 5 (Tübingen: Mohr, 2002), 861–873, and the classic study by Jan Arent Wensinck, "The Oriental Doctrine of the Martyrs," *Mededeelingen der Koninklijke Akademie van Wetenschappen* (Amsterdam), Afdeeling Letterkunde 53, serie A (1922). Marius Canard, "La guerre sainte dans le monde islamique et dans le monde chrétien," *Revue africaine* (1936): 605–623 = *Byzance et les musulmans*, no. 8, is still

---

[25] There is a fairly large literature around the martyrs of Cordova, including Wolf, *Christian Martyrs in Muslim Spain*. For Palestine and Syria, see Griffith, "The Arabic Account of ʿAbd al-Masīh an-Nağrānī"; Dick, "La passion arabe de S. Antoine Ruwah."

interesting. See especially Jean Flori, *Guerre sainte, jihad, croisade: violence et religion dans le christianisme et l'islam* (Paris: Le Seuil, 2002). Byzantine notions were discussed by Paul Lemerle in "Byzance et la Croisade," *Relazioni del X Congresso Internazionale di Scienze Storiche* (Florence) 3 (1955): 595–620; and recently, but less critically, by Geoffrey Regan in *First Crusader: Byzantium's Holy Wars* (Houndmills: Sutton, 2001). For an introduction to Crusading ideology, including its possible relation to Islamic jihad, see, as always, Noth's *Heiliger Krieg und heiliger Kampf* (Bonn: Ludwig Röhrscheid Verlag, 1966); and Jonathan Riley-Smith, *The First Crusade and the Idea of Crusading* (Philadelphia: University of Pennsylvania Press, 1986); Paul Alphandéry and Alphonse Duprout, *La Chrétienté et l'idée de croisade* (new ed., Paris: Albin Michel, 1995); and Jean Richard, *L'Esprit de la Croisade* (collection of texts) (Paris: Editions du Cerf, 2000).

Please note also the recent publication of David Cook, *Martyrdom in Islam* (Cambridge: Cambridge University Press, 2007).

CHAPTER SIX

Encounter with the Other

Conquest Society and Fiscal Regime

The early expansion of Islam set in place what we may call a conquest society.[1] When the dust settled, the Arab Muslims found
themselves scattered over great distances, clustered together in old
cities and new garrison towns. They continued to fight against
non-Muslim adversaries along the ever-receding frontiers and
also, at times, against each other. Their activity as fighters was not
a question of paid service. Rather, it had to do with identity and
status, of being Arab Muslim males—even if, in reality, some of
the fighters looked for ways to avoid their duty to serve in the
army (see end of chapter 3). The fighters received a fixed stipend,
called *ʿataʾ*, which literally means "gift," an indication that the
notions of reciprocity and gift, so important in the Quran (chapter
2), still had their importance. The fighters received their stipends
from a treasury staffed by bureaucratic specialists who kept the
recipients' names inscribed on a register (*diwan*).

Funds flowed into this treasury from taxes levied on the population. How much that population had suffered during the early
conquests is not entirely clear: there seems to have been much
movement because of enslavement and other reasons, while some
elite groups—such as the great landowners of formerly Byzantine
Syria—picked up and left altogether. For the most part, however,

[1] Crone, *Slaves on Horses*, 29–57.

the same hands cultivated the soil as before the arrival of the Muslims. The system of taxation also remained broadly similar to what had been in effect previously under the Byzantines and Persians. The most important tax, on the land, became known in Arabic as *kharaj*. Another tax, a poll tax "on the heads," was levied on individuals (and households), and became known as *jizya*. The relatively small elite of Arab warriors were thus recipients of tax money amidst an enormous, taxpaying majority. As Muslims they were expected to pay a communal alms tax (*zakat* or *sadaqa*), but this was lighter than the burden of *kharaj* and *jizya* imposed on non-Muslims. This distinction between recipients and taxpayers corresponded rather neatly to distinctions in religion and in occupation: those who received were Muslims, while those who paid were Christians, Jews, and Zoroastrians; the Muslims spent their time as warriors, the others as producers.

Of course this outline of a conquest society corresponds only roughly to what actually happened. And in any case, things soon changed. To begin with, some members of the larger group tried to join the elite. In order to do this, conversion to Islam was necessary but not enough. For the Arab Muslims disagreed among themselves over what to do with the new converts. Although the Quran's language was "clear Arabic,"[2] its message was just as clearly directed toward the entire world. Yet to admit non-Arabs into the inner group meant altering the lopsided balance between recipients and payers of taxes. Now, the armies often needed recruits, and many non-Arab converts were eager to enlist, on the condition that they receive the same treatment—including the stipend—as their Arab coreligionists. Nonetheless, some of the Arabs insisted on keeping these newcomers out. Tensions of this kind became a major preoccupation, going far beyond the armies. Ultimately, the Arab fighters lost their privileged position, and the conquest society came to an end. By then, however, it had created several results of lasting consequence.

One of these regarded the armies. During the Umayyad period (661–750), some non-Arab converts did manage to get their names inscribed on the register as fighters in the army and as recipients of stipends. Others failed but continued to press forward anyway, going on campaign with little or no compensation other than a

[2] 16:103 (*Nahl*).

share of the spoils of battle. These volunteers (*muttawwi'a*) formed units that set a precedent for the future practice and theory of jihad, as the following two chapters will show.

Another result regarded the fiscal regime of classical Islam, which took some time to emerge. During the Umayyad period, as people converted to Islam and claimed exemption from their heavy tax burden, the ruling elites faced a threat to their fiscal base, together with severe disagreement among themselves. Eventually these controversies gave birth to the classical theory of Islamic taxation. The kharaj, the tax on the land, was to be paid regardless of the religious status of the land's owner. (This had become a bone of contention because of the conversion of landowners to Islam, and because of the alienation of land through inheritance and sale.) The jizya (poll tax) was demanded only from non-Muslims living under the protected status of "People of the Book" (to be described shortly). One's obligation to pay jizya thus ended on conversion to Islam. In reality, it seems that in some circumstances, the treasury tried to recoup its loss of revenue from jizya by making the zakat or sadaqa, the alms tax on Muslims, into a heavier tax.[3] In theory, meanwhile, the entire system became based on a right of conquest, through the principle of *fay'* (return) deriving from Quran 59: 7 (see above, chapter 2). The conquered lands—or most of them—were now seen as a kind of trust in perpetuity for the benefit of the Muslim conquerors. Non-Muslim landholders retained title to their property, but the Muslim community as a whole had a residual right of ownership.

This system of taxation weighed heavily on the countryside and the land. Urban and merchant wealth were also taxed, but by comparison they got away nearly unscathed. This imbalance provided a boost to the tremendous commercial expansion of the eighth and ninth centuries, but it also led to problems. For by now the archaic structure of the conquest polity had become, irrevocably, the fiscal system of Islamic law. Over and again, rulers and governors, finding themselves strapped for cash, would resort to extra-canonical fiscal measures, at times including outright confiscation. And over and again, the jurists and other spokesmen for the divine legislation (*shari'a*) would oppose these measures. The rulers might then grant a "reform," canceling the extra-canonical taxes,

[3] Sijpestijn, "The Collection and Meaning of *Sadaqa* and *Zakat*."

until once again they found it impossible to proceed with the limited resources available to them.[4] The fiscal law of Islam was destined to conflict with political and economic realities or else to become a body of ideal norms, observed selectively when at all. Meanwhile, the fiscal and landholding structures themselves changed profoundly, as the caliphate went into political decline and as the old *levée en masse* of fighters receiving stipends became replaced by a variety of professional, specialized military units.

Treatment of Non-Muslims

Like the fiscal regime, the treatment of non-Muslims in Islamic law grew directly out of the ancient conquest society. It differed from the fiscal regime in that it was actually observed in most times and places in the premodern Islamic world, at least in its broad outlines and general spirit.

The Arabic sources for the early conquests report the texts of numerous agreements made between conquerors and conquered on termination of hostilities. These texts exist only in chronicles and legal compendia; not a single original document survives and, as before, we must rely entirely on a long process of literary transmission. The treaty texts take the form of contracts, often in the form of a letter sent by the Muslim commander in the field, addressed to "the inhabitants of such and such a place and their dependents." In some cases a specific person, often an ecclesiastic, is named as the representative of the city in question. In the simplest contracts, the Muslim commander stipulates that the inhabitants of the place will have safe conduct (*aman*) for themselves, their religion, and their property. In return they must pay jizya "out of hand" for every adult male, according to his capacity. They must show goodwill and avoid deception; they must accommodate Muslim travelers in their houses for a day and a night. The arrangement is called *dhimma* (protection); those who benefit from it then become known as *dhimmi*s (protected persons).

The most famous of these arrangements is the one the caliph ʿUmar is said to have granted to the residents of Jerusalem, sometime between 636 and 638. The different versions of this text show

[4] Halm, *The Empire of the Mahdi*, 356–357.

considerable variety. The Christians are allowed free practice of their religion, but in some versions, Jews are debarred from residence in the city.[5] In several versions, the Christians are forbidden to build new churches and monasteries. They must refrain from making noise during their services, and they must not display crosses prominently. They may not "mount on saddles," and they may not carry swords or weapons of any kind. They must dress differently from the Muslims, and in particular they must wear a sash around the waist known as the *zunnar*. Their houses must be lower than those of the Muslims. They are also forbidden to teach the Quran to their children.

This "pact of ʿUmar" (ʿahd ʿUmar) has attracted much attention.[6] Some have pointed to its anachronisms: how, for instance, were the Jerusalemites to teach the Quran to their children in the 630s, when most of them knew no Arabic? This clause may relate to circumstances of a later time, when Palestinian Christians were becoming Arabic speakers and might have used the Quran as a model of literary style.[7] The document's historicity thus remains a problem. Most important, however, is that the two parties named in the contracts include all future generations. And for many centuries, these agreements were indeed seen as binding on all sides. For the pact is built to last. There are very few ways for its "protection" to come to an end; one of these is conversion to Islam on the part of the "protected." Here the jurist al-Shafiʿi raises a question: what about a Jewish dhimmi who wishes to convert to Christianity (or vice versa)? Al-Shafiʿi argues that he may not do this. The original agreement granted him protection, but only in the religious status of his forebears. He always has the right to convert to Islam if he likes—though no one may compel him to do this. His only other options are to remain in his current religion or else to leave the Abode of Islam altogether.

The fundamental obligation of the dhimmis is payment of the jizya. At first—including in many of the surrender agreements—

[5] Tabari, *Taʾrikh*, 1:2404–2406. This seems to be a concession to the Christians who, previously under Byzantine rule, had sought to prevent Jews from residing in Jerusalem.

[6] See the summary in Cohen, *Under Crescent and Cross*, 55–74; and idem, "What Was the Pact of ʿUmar?"

[7] See end of chapter 5.

jizya meant "tribute," a sum paid collectively by an entire community. Soon, however, it came to refer to the poll tax levied on individuals and households. All discussions of jizya turn on Quran 9:29 (*al-Tawba*):

> Fight those who believe not in God and the Last Day and do not forbid what God and His Messenger have forbidden—such men as practise not the religion of truth, being of those who have been given the Book—until they pay the tribute out of hand (*al-jizyata ʿan yadin*) and have been humbled. (Arberry translation)

The protected persons are monotheists, "People of the Book." This obviously applies to Jews and Christians. Zoroastrians presented some difficulty to the Muslim authorities, but the jurists soon agreed that these were monotheists of a kind, and that they even had a book. Conquests in "pagan" lands, especially India, afterward presented problems, but the solution was often similar. Jizya was due from the People of the Book every year, its amount graded according to their ability to pay. The sums in question were not trivial, but the Muslim authorities agreed that the significance of jizya had to do first and foremost with the "humiliation" prescribed in Quran 9:29: their paying "out of hand" (*ʿan yadin*) symbolically represented their state of subjugation.

At the beginning, when the ideal of the conquest society bore some relation to reality, the settlements of Arab Muslims amounted to no more than small islands scattered over the vast ocean of the People of the Book. We have seen that many of these Arab Muslims, jealous of their status and their stipends (*ʿata*ʾ), had incentives for keeping the outsiders at bay. But as the old structures broke down, especially under the ʿAbbasid caliphs (from 750 onward), conversion became freely allowed. In most of the great provinces, it appears that the proportion of Muslims reached half or more of the population by roughly 900 CE. After that it only increased.

This meant that the dhimma henceforth governed relations with minorities—although some later conquests, such as those of the Ottomans in eastern Europe, did restore demographic preponderance to the dhimmis, at least at a local or provincial level. But to a remarkable extent, the basic principles of the dhimma were actually observed in most times and places. To begin with, there was no forced conversion, no choice between "Islam and the sword." Islamic law, following a clear Quranic principle,[8] prohibited any such thing: dhimmis must be allowed to practice their religion. When Muslim armies encountered non-Muslims outside the lands already under the rule of Islam, they were supposed to offer them the choice of conversion to Islam; payment of jizya and acceptance of *dhimmi* status; or trying the fortunes of war. If the adversaries chose the last of these three and then lost, they faced expropriation, slavery, or even death. Even then, however, they must not be converted forcibly. And in fact, although there have been instances of forced conversion in Islamic history, these have been exceptional. Furthermore, the protection accorded to People of the Book meant that they—like the Muslims themselves—could not be enslaved. Since medieval Islamic societies made considerable use of slaves, especially for domestic labor, these had to be acquired from outside the Abode of Islam altogether. This combination of circumstances provided an incentive for constant raids by sea and on land, as well as for long-distance trade.

We have seen that the People of the Book were prevented from dressing in the same style as the Muslims, from bearing arms, and from riding. These sumptuary laws were taken seriously, but at the same time it is clear that they were often observed in the breach: we see this in the reforming zeal that accompanied their reintroduction from time to time. After all, it was difficult to maintain such distinctions in a world where patronage, business partnerships, scientific collaboration, and indeed friendship, often crossed confessional lines. Likewise, much ingenuity went into circumventing the prohibition against building new churches and synagogues and restoring old ones. The picture that emerges is thus endlessly variable, and serves to remind us that identity in the premodern world was itself often flexible. At the same time, this picture of the dhimma must also include shocking instances where it was flouted or abandoned, as in the massacre of the Jews of Granada in 1064,[9] or the reign of the Fatimid caliph al-Hakim, which lasted from 996 until 1021. In his capital of Cairo, this unbalanced (and, in the view of most, mad) caliph raged against the Christians in particular, preventing them from performing their

---

[8] 2:256 (*Baqara*): "Compulsion in religion is not allowed."
[9] Cohen, *Under Crescent and Cross*, 165–166.

rites and processions, exaggerating the sumptuary laws, and ordering a long series of confiscations and destructions of monasteries and churches, culminating in the razing of the Church of the Holy Sepulchre in Jerusalem in 1009. On the whole, however, such episodes remained exceptional, like the episodes of forced conversion to Islam.

The realities of this area are complex and often confound any attempts at generalization. One observation, however, seems to hold: that it was along the outer fringes of the Islamic world, especially in the presence of an urgent menace coming from outside, that Muslim tolerance wore thin, and local Christian or Jewish communities found themselves most in danger.[10] This helps to explain Granada in 1064, certain episodes in the age of the Crusades (when Syria became a frontier province), and a deterioration of the condition of non-Muslims at the beginning of the modern era, in many Muslim countries. But in most epochs, in the heartlands of Islam, dhimmis lived mainly unmolested, their numbers slowly dwindling over time. Even in theory, their situation was far from that of a minority in a modern state, especially since they absolutely did not enjoy equality of status with their non-Muslim neighbors. All the same, there is no doubt that the history of the dhimma compares favorably with the treatment of non-Christians in Europe during most of the premodern era.

The People of the Book did not, of course, constitute a single group, but were divided instead into many different confessional units. Christians in particular comprised several groups, often in intense rivalry with one another. Leadership within these confessional groups was religious (bishops, rabbis, etc.). The confessional groups within a locality had considerable autonomy in legal matters, and were collectively answerable to the fiscal authorities. These confessional groups (today often referred to by a Turkish word for them, *millet*) are often thought of today as solid blocs, rather like medieval Western corporate bodies, standing firm in solidarity vis-à-vis the Muslim authorities and one another. This picture derives mainly from the Ottoman Empire. In reality things were often far less neatly defined, including in the Ottoman Empire itself.

---

[10] Lewis, *The Jews of Islam*.

Abode of Islam, Abode of War

The early Islamic conquest society provides one of the first images (if that is the right word) of the community in relation to the world around it. Here the critical relationship was between the believers, who were consumers and warriors, and the far more numerous nonbelievers all around them, who were producers and taxpayers. In geographical terms this polity was already vast, and its pursuit of further conquests provided an outward extension for a center that already controlled an enormous part of the known world.

Soon afterward, Islamic jurists began to represent the world according to a different scheme, dividing it between an Abode of Islam *(dar al-islam)* and an Abode of War *(dar al-harb)*.[11] As the vocabulary indicates, these two are in a permanent condition of war. Since the only legitimate sovereign is God, and the only legitimate form of rule is Islam, the various rulers and states within the Abode of War have no legitimacy, and their rule is mere oppression or tyranny. The Muslim state—in the classical theory, the imam—may conclude a truce with those rulers and states, but for no longer than ten years. Individuals from the Abode of War who wish to visit the Abode of Islam, especially for purposes of trade or diplomacy, may be granted safe conduct *(aman)* for a limited period of time. However, in reality, Muslim states did often live in peace with their non-Muslim neighbors for prolonged periods. Some jurists therefore recognized the existence of an Abode of Truce or Treaty *(dar al-sulh, dar al-ʿahd)*, in addition to the Abodes of Islam and of War.[12] However, this addition of an intermediate category did not fundamentally change the territorial character of the doctrine of jihad. This doctrine requires warfare for the defense of lands under Islamic control and encourages the acquisition, through conquest, of new lands. It does not aim at the conversion of populations or individuals, but rather at the extension of God's rule over the world: "Fight them, till there is no persecution and the religion is God's entirely."[13]

---

[11] Mottahedeh and al-Sayyid, "The Idea of *Jihad* before the Crusades," 28, identify the first emergence of Realm of Islam/Realm of War in the later eighth century, in Muhammad al-Nafs al-Zakiyya.

[12] Beginning with al-Shafiʿi himself: see ibid., 29; H. Inalcik's article, "Dar al-ʿAhd," in *EI²*, 2:116.

[13] Quran 8:39 *(Anfal)*, Arberry translation.

At the same time, this territorial outlook did not dominate everything and everywhere. Islamic law also had an intense interest in the personal status of individuals, so much so that it tied this status to the historical conditions of the early conquests. In all these ways, the juridical and historical roots of dhimma were inseparable from those of *jihad*. This may help to explain the presence, in some Islamic texts, of what we might call both an internal and an external Other. The internal Other, the non-Muslim native of the Abode of Islam, has juridical characteristics that include both a long-term contractual relationship with the Muslims and the inability to carry arms. This means that he is destined to participate in never-ending negotiations, over his status, obligations, and rights.[14] But if the internal Other is a figure of constant negotiation, the external Other is not. We see this in the often-stereotyped view of early Islam's most stubborn enemy, the Byzantine empire. Characteristics of Byzantium, in Muslim eyes, included considerable worldly power; the identification of its ruler, the Byzantine emperor, as the paradigmatic tyrant (*taghiya*); skill in the arts, crafts, administration, and warfare; an alleged lack of generosity; and, surprisingly, women associated with immorality and prostitution.[15] Above all, the empire figures as Islam's main antagonist and rival, its archenemy until the end of time.[16] Even though many of the people in question—Christians living on either side of the border between Byzantium and Islam—were actually quite similar in their customs and beliefs, this external Other had an utterly different set of characteristics from the internal Other, a figure of constant negotiation and, on occasion, an object of condescension or even contempt.

Convivencia

Convivencia, "getting along together," has been a preoccupation of much modern scholarship on medieval Spain. And there is no

[14] Robinson, *Empire and Elites*, 1–32.
[15] Shboul, "Byzantium and the Arabs"; El-Cheikh,"Describing the Other to Get at the Self."
[16] Miquel, *La géographie humaine du monde musulman*, 2:384: "D'où viens-tu, qui t'as mis sur mon chemin, lequel de nous deux fut créé pour la ruine de l'autre?" ("Where do you come from, who put you on my path, which one of us was created so as to destroy the other?")

question that it did take place there under Muslim rule, as Muslims, Christians, and Jews coexisted and collaborated in some of the great cultural productions of the age. Of course, Islamic Spain was not the interfaith paradise that some have thought: we have already mentioned the terrible events of Granada in 1064. But when convivencia ultimately failed in Spain, this happened in the wake of the Christian *Reconquista*, after centuries of coexistence under Islam.

The history of the Reconquista includes a series of agreements between conquerors and conquered, going back to the occupation of Toledo by King Alfonso VI of Castile and León in 1085. Muslims who found themselves living under Christian rule became known in Spanish (at least at some point) as *mudéjares*. Their status paralleled that of Christians and Jews living in Islamic territory under the regime of dhimma: in return for payment of a tax, they enjoyed protection of their persons and property and were allowed to practice their religion with certain restraints. As more Islamic territory fell to the Christians, the numbers of Muslims living under this regime increased. Their status was not viewed favorably in Islamic law: most jurists outside Spain who were consulted on the topic agreed that Muslims residing in lands that had fallen under the control of the infidels ought to emigrate to the Abode of Islam.[17] Yet the *mudéjares* mostly stayed put, eventually forgetting their Arabic but not their Islam.

Unlike the dhimma of Islam, these arrangements all failed. The best-known part of the story is its tragic end. In January 1492, the last Muslim ruler of Granada, known to the Spanish as Boabdíl, handed over the keys of the Alhambra to Ferdinand and Isabella. Boabdíl had negotiated an agreement allowing the Muslim inhabitants of the province to remain both Muslim and Granadan. But soon this agreement fell apart. By 1526, the practice of Islam was outlawed in all of Spain. An exodus of Muslims took place, like the previous Jewish exodus of 1492. Some won the right to stay in Spain by converting to Catholicism. Yet in the end, this too was not enough and the converts, known as Moriscos, were expelled between 1609 and 1611. The existential absurdity of the situation appears in the *Don Quixote*, composed right at this time.[18]

---

[17] Salgado, "Consideraciones acerca de una fatwà de Al-Wanšarisi."
[18] Menocal, *The Ornament of the World*, 253–265.

Within Islamic history, Spain is unusual as a large piece of the Abode of Islam that became permanently lost to the faith. But whatever we may think about tolerance in Spain, the central Islamic lands on the whole practiced convivencia much more often than not. Though far from perfect, a practical system of tolerance prevailed in the central lands of Islam, right down until the modern era. That modern era is another story, less fortunate in many ways.

Readings

Morabia again provides a point of departure in Le Ǧihâd, 263–289. The fiscal regime of early Islam used to be hotly argued, including the idea that relief from taxes provided an incentive for conversion to Islam. Daniel C. Dennett, *Conversion and the Poll Tax in Early Islam* (Cambridge, MA: Harvard University Press, 1950), is still worth reading. A series of articles in the *Encyclopaedia of Islam* by Claude Cahen, Dominique Sourdel, and others, is still valuable.[19] An interesting approach to conversion may be found in R. Bulliett, *Conversion to Islam* (Cambridge, MA: Harvard University Press, 1979).

The position of non-Muslims in Muslim societies has provoked many writings, ranging from the myth of an interfaith paradise to the highly negative views expressed by Bat Ye'or in *The Dhimmi: Jews and Christians under Islam* (East Rutherford: Fairleigh Dickinson University Press, 1985). For a balanced summary of the question, see Mark Cohen, *Under Crescent and Cross: The Jews in the Middle Ages* (Princeton: Princeton University Press, 1994), esp. 3–14. The chapter "Islam and Other Religions," in Bernard Lewis, *The Jews of Islam* (Princeton: Princeton University Press, 1984), 3–66, also provides a balanced view. For the Christian communities, see now Anne-Marie Eddé, Françoise Micheau and Christophe Picard (eds.), *Communautés chrétiennes en pays d'Islam, du début du VIIᵉ siècle au milieu du Xᵉ siècle* (Paris: Sedes, 1997). Older treatments include K.A.S. Tritton, *The Caliphs and Their Non-Muslim Subjects: A Critical Study of the Covenant of 'Umar* (1930; reprint, London: F. Cass, 1970), and the more technical

---

[19] *EI*² articles on 'Ata', Bayt al-Mal, Diwan, Djaysh, Djizya, Fay', Kharadj.

work by Antoine Fattal, *Le statut légal des non-musulmans en pays d'Islam* (2nd ed., Beirut: Dar El-Machreq, 1995). For the Ottoman empire, F. W. Hasluck, *Christianity and Islam under the Sultans*, 2 vols. (Oxford: Oxford University Press, 1929) is still highly regarded; and see especially Benjamin Braude and Bernard Lewis, eds., *Christians and Jews in the Ottoman Empire: The Functioning of a Plural Society* (New York: Holmes and Meier, 1982). For medieval Egypt, there are useful chapters on the Jews and Copts by N. Stillman and T. Wilfong in Carl F. Petry (ed.), *The Cambridge History of Egypt*, vol. 1 (Cambridge: Cambridge University Press, 1998), 175–210. For an illustration of how the spirit of the dhimma, though not its strict letter, was observed in Crete under Ottoman rule in the seventeenth century, see Molly Green, *A Shared World: Christians and Muslims in the Early Modern Mediterranean* (Princeton: Princeton University Press, 2000).

In addition, see Yohanan Friedmann, *Tolerance and Coercion in Islam: Interfaith Relations in the Muslim Tradition* (Cambridge: Cambridge University Press, 2003).

CHAPTER SEVEN

Embattled Scholars

As Islam became rooted in societies that were separated by vast distances, from the Atlantic coast of Africa and Europe far into Central Asia and India, these societies acquired characteristics in common. One of these was the phenomenon of men of religious learning (often called *'ulama'*) taking it upon themselves to perform the jihad in person. This involved them, at various times, as legal functionaries or advisers, preachers, combatants, specialists in ascetic and mystical practice, experts in the history of the community and its wars, or any combination of these. Their activity had a largely symbolic value: by associating themselves with the conduct of war, the scholars affirmed their own sincerity, together with the values of the jihad and Islam. At the same time, they showed a desire for participation in the here and now, in the real world of conflict and combat.

One of them is 'Ali ibn Bakkar, who went to live along the Arab-Byzantine frontier in the early ninth century. Once 'Ali was wounded in battle, so that his entrails came spilling out onto his saddle. He stuffed them back, used his turban as a bandage to bind them in place, and then proceeded to kill thirteen of the enemy. Elsewhere, however, 'Ali makes a less warlike impression, as when we find him sitting in the wilderness with a lion sleeping in the fold of his garment, and when we are told that he wept until he went blind.[1] This combination is fairly typical. Here, however, we

[1] Ibn al-Jawzi, *Sifat al-safwa*, 4:267.

will dwell not on picturesque elements, but rather on the embattled scholars' role in the growth and development of the jihad in several regions of the Islamic world. Their presence along the great frontiers will help us to map out the jihad, while giving us a more accurate sense of the origins, in the plural, of the jihad.

Syria and the Byzantine Frontier

Among the frontier zones of the early Islamic world, the one facing the Byzantine Empire, known as al-Thughur (the passageways, mountain passes) was often considered the most important and prestigious. So according to the early tenth-century Iraqi administrator and geographical writer Qudama ibn Jaʿfar, since the Rum (Byzantines) are Islam's greatest and most stubborn enemy, "it behooves the Muslims to be most wary and on their guard against [them], from among all the ranks of their adversaries."[2] It is here, in northern Syria and south-central Anatolia, that we first find the warrior-scholar phenomenon on an appreciable scale.[3]

This begins during the caliphate of the Umayyads (661–750). A few chronicles tell us that in the great expeditionary force that besieged Constantinople unsuccessfully in 717–718, several scholars were in attendance. One of these, Khalid ibn Maʿdan al-Kalaʿi (d. ca. AH 104/722–723 CE), a Syrian from Hims, had a reputation as a student of the history of the early Islamic conquest of Syria. It is later biographical sources (from the tenth century onward) that describe him as an actual warrior. This progression is typical: early biographical notices drily note a thematic, scholarly interest in matters of warfare, while later sources, often of a more hagiographical nature, make the subject into both a swashbuckling hero and a model of pious conduct. Another Syrian scholar of the Umayyad period, Makhul (d. AH 113/731 CE) is also said to have taken part in expeditions. The details of this are vague. What is beyond doubt, however, is Makhul's role in the production of maghazi: the historical narratives about the early community and

---

[2] Qudama ibn Jaʿfar, *Kitab al-kharaj wa-sinaʿat al-kitaba*, 185.

[3] For the following, see Bonner, "Some Observations Concerning the Early Development of Jihad on the Arab-Byzantine Frontier"; idem, *Aristocratic Violence and Holy War*, esp. 107–134, 157–184; Heck, "*Jihad* Revisited," esp. 99–103.

its wars (above, chapter 3). Again, the study of past wars is connected with participation in present ones. To this we must add
Makhul's interest in the obligation of the jihad, and the statement
attributed to him, to the effect that this obligation is incumbent
upon every individual (able-bodied male) Muslim.[4]

The Umayyads fell from power in 750 and were replaced by
the caliphal dynasty of the 'Abbasids who ruled, from 762 onward,
from their new capital of Baghdad. It was in the following decades
that warrior-scholars began to congregate in large numbers along
the Arab-Byzantine frontier. The leading figure among them, in
this first generation, was Abu Ishaq al-Fazari (d. after AH 185/802
CE), whom we know both from biographical notices and from the
surviving parts of a book attributed to him, the *Kitab al-siyar* (book
of the law of war).

The literary genre of *siyar* (law or conduct of war) was already
established by this time: we have at least fragments of books on
siyar by al-Fazari's master, the great Syrian jurist al-Awza'i (d.
AH 157/774 CE) and the Iraqis Abu Yusuf (d. AH 182/798 CE) and
al-Shaybani (d. AH 189/805 CE). These books are devoted to practical questions relating to the conduct of warfare (treatment of
noncombatants, division of spoils, etc.). They make little mention of the themes of the merit of jihad and the fighter's divine
reward. Furthermore, these early siyar works tend to derive their
normative principles from terse statements about the Islamic
past, with minimal narrative context. Here Fazari seems original:
he intertwines normative statements regarding siyar, together
with maghazi narratives. We find a somewhat similar combination in the great compendia of hadith (see chapter 3) and in some
of the comprehensive manuals of Islamic law. These, however,
come later, and al-Fazari is among the first jurists to make this
combination.

What emerges in al-Fazari—both in the biographical notices
about him and in what survives of his book—is a distinctive view of
imitation of Muhammad. Because the Prophet fought wars, the way
to imitate him is through study of both the norms of warfare and
the history of the community and, at the same time, through taking

---

[4] 'Abd al-Razzaq, *Musannaf*, 5:172–173, nos. 9275, 9276, 9278. On al-Kala'i
and Makhul, see Van Ess, *Theologie und Gesellschaft im 2. und 3. Jahrhundert
Hidschra*, 1:75f., 111–113.

up arms against the enemies of Islam, thus literally reenacting what the Prophet did. At the same time, significantly, al-Fazari's attitude toward the 'Abbasid governmental authorities along the frontier seems to have been ambiguous at best. He certainly was not a political rebel, but in several accounts he is said to have been flogged for disobedience or some other offense. Above all, al-Fazari represents and embodies the authority of the religious and legal scholar, looking back to the precedent of the Prophet and the earliest Muslim community as this has been transmitted to him by other religious scholars in the intervening generations. Al-Fazari thus stands at the frontier—in every sense—of the Islamic state.

In al-Fazari's work, the word *jihad* occurs rarely, *ribat* even less so. It is in his eastern Iranian friend 'Abdallah ibn al-Mubarak (d. AH 181/797 CE) that we find these twin concepts flourishing. Ibn al-Mubarak's many achievements included several sojourns on the Byzantine frontier, and the composition of a *Book of Jihad*, apparently the oldest surviving work on this subject. Unlike al-Fazari's book, this is a work of hadith. It also differs in other ways. Whereas al-Fazari recalls the early community of Islam by recreating the Prophet's campaigns in study and in deed, Ibn al-Mubarak recreates the community here and now through internalization of the norm by each individual. Many of the narratives in Ibn al-Mubarak's book are accounts of the martyrdom of heroes in the early wars of Islam. Many of these narratives also place much emphasis on the fighter's intention (*niyya*) in jihad. The community thus takes form through the striving (*jihad*) and volunteering (*tatawwu'*) of the many individuals who comprise it. The Islamic state and its goals have little to do with all this: Ibn al-Mubarak shows little interest, if any, in the issues of obedience to the imam, and of the role of the imam in the conduct of military campaigns.

Biographical notices of Ibn al-Mubarak emphasize his personal strength and self-control: when he read from his own Book of Asceticism (*Kitab al-zuhd*), he bellowed like a bull being slaughtered.[5] These biographical accounts also describe a close bond between him and his comrades-in-arms on campaign, modeled on relations among the Companions of the Prophet. Similar themes abound in Ibn al-Mubarak's *Book of Jihad*, which also contains much *targhib* (exhortation), as we see in the title that circulated

[5] Khatib, *Ta'rikh Baghdad*, 10:167.

for this book in Muslim Spain, the *Book of the Merit of Jihad* (*Kitab fadl al-jihad*).

In addition to these two founding figures of the Arab-Byzantine frontier and of the jihad we may include a third, Ibrahim ibn Adham (d. AH 161/777–78 CE), another Iranian who, in biographical tradition, is said to have come to Syria and to have taken part in military campaigns. This activity may well be largely legendary; but in later generations we see Ibn Adham's lasting legacy among those radical ascetics of the frontier district whom the sources call *al-ʿubbad al-khushn* (the devotees of harsh practice). Their activities included extreme fasting, ingesting dust or clay, and a rigorous insistence on working for a living (*kasb*). Such people and practices were known, if not universally approved of, along the Arab-Byzantine frontier district for many years. Here the concern with purity of intention and conduct—already quite pronounced in Ibn al-Mubarak—goes that much farther: not only do Ibn Adham and his disciples ignore the imam/caliph—and with him, the public concerns of the Islamic state—but they even leave behind the Islamic community itself, in their uncompromising quest for absolute ritual purity (*al-halal al-mahd*) and their confirmation of the individual and his religious merit. What remains is obedience to and emulation of the ascetic master, Ibn Adham and others like him. This will all be characteristic of ascetic groups along the Byzantine and other frontiers, and later on, of mystical or Sufi groups.

Much of the information that we have on these three men and their many colleagues has been retrojected from later times and embellished. Nonetheless, they are useful to us because they represent three distinctive attitudes toward imitation and authority, precisely at the time when jihad first emerges as a comprehensive, coherent doctrine and set of practices. At the same time, there is evidence that many scholars did actually go to the frontier, from the later eighth century[6] until the reconquest of the district by the Byzantines in the mid-tenth. Typically they were transmitters of hadith, reciters of the Quran, and so on. A few accepted employment with the ʿAbbasid state, notably as qadis (judges). Some of them led contingents of volunteers for the wars, always arriving from Iraq and the Iranian East.

---

[6] See the debate over this point in Chabbi, "Ribat," and Touati, *Islam et voyage*, 247f.

Arabia

Although Arabia was neither a front line combat area nor a center of political power after the 650s, its two major centers of religious and intellectual life, Medina and Mecca, long held leading roles in the debates over warfare and jihad.

Medina

Yathrib, later known as Medina—*al-Madina*, "the city" of the Prophet and the first capital of the Islamic state—boasted many of the most famous specialists in maghazi narratives, including Ibn Ishaq (d. 767) and al-Waqidi (d. 823). These men did not seek to combine their teachings on past wars together with active participation in present ones in the way that Abu Ishaq al-Fazari had done. Of course, this does not mean that they disapproved of such active participation. However, there are indications that participation in jihad was a matter of some controversy in early Islamic Medina.

Medina was the original home of one of the four great Sunni *madhhab*s (schools of law), the Maliki School, named after its founding figure Malik ibn Anas (d. AH 179/795 CE). The most famous book of this school is the legal compendium called the *Muwatta'*, originally composed by the eponymous founder, Malik himself. As is typical for Islamic books of this and later times, we do not have a single, authoritative version of the *Muwatta'* which everyone agrees in ascribing to the master. Instead the *Muwatta'* exists in several recensions, which have come down through separate chains of scholarly transmission. The recension which is generally best known is the work of a man named Yahya ibn Yahya al-Masmudi, who died in Cordova in AH 234/848 CE.[7] Not surprisingly, this book—the *Muwatta'* of Malik in the recension of Yahya al-Masmudi—has a chapter on jihad (*Kitab al-jihad*).[8] This chapter opens with hadith of the *targhib* (exhortation) type, encouraging people to perform jihad, just as we find in Ibn al-Mubarak's *Book of Jihad*—and indeed, many of the traditions in the two books are

---

[7] F. Sezgin, *Geschichte des arabischen Schrifttums*, 1:459–460
[8] Malik, *Muwatta'*, 2:443–471.

nearly identical.[9] The chapter then moves on to siyar topics: division of spoils, treatment of prisoners, and so on, followed by sections on martyrdom and more exhortation. None of this seems particularly remarkable. However, when we examine another recension of the *Muwatta'*, that of the great Iraqi jurist al-Shaybani, we find something different. This recension is said to date from al-Shaybani's visit to Medina during his youth, roughly around 150/767 (when he came to attend Malik's lectures). Here we find a short chapter on siyar and otherwise nothing at all about jihad. Notable for its absence is the material that we find in Yahya's recension of Malik's *Muwatta'*, on exhortation, reward, martyrdom, and so on.[10] This is the case also in the famous *Ktab al-siyar* composed afterward by the same al-Shaybani: in its original form, al-Shaybani's *Siyar* is "neither an exhortative nor an apologetic treatise, and jihad is not evoked."[11]

What may we deduce from this? Perhaps the Medinan jurists in the middle of the eighth century, including Malik himself, were as yet unfamiliar with the notion of jihad as this was expressed afterwards in Yahya al-Masmudi's recension of the *Muwatta'* and in Ibn al-Mubarak's *Book of Jihad*. Or perhaps it was certain Iraqi jurists—al-Shaybani and the emerging Hanafi madhhab—who disapproved of this concept and excised it from their version of the *Muwatta'*. Either way, we have basic disagreement over the jihad.[12]

Ever aware of its status as the home of the Prophet and the earliest community, early Islamic Medina was at once a conservative place, concerned with maintaining older values, and the home of some quite distinctive views. For instance, regarding poverty and almsgiving, at least some Medinan scholars believed that we should place no limit on the amount we give in alms, that we may give to the point of impoverishing ourselves, and that we must give to anyone who asks, regardless of his status and wealth. Above all, they believed that if any group of poor are especially meritori-

---

[9] The exhortations to jihad from Malik's *Muwatta'* are translated in Peters, *Jihad in Classical and Modern Islam*, 19–26.

[10] As noted by Bonner, "Some Observations," 25.

[11] Chabbi, "Ribat," 495. Chabbi notes the presence elsewhere in the Shaybani *Muwatta'* (55–56, no. 95, s.v. "Prayer") of material on the "merit of jihad."

[12] See the discussion in Mottahedeh and al-Sayyid, "The Idea of *Jihad* before the Crusades," 25f.

ous, it is those who desire to fight in the army but lack the means to do so. Such donations should be made as a kind of alms. Here the Medinans seem to have opposed some teachings of Iraqi and Syrian jurists, as well as certain practices that were current in the early Islamic armies whereby military service became, to some degree, commodified.[13] Fighting in the wars is, for the Medinans, a matter of belonging and identity.

We have already noted the close connection between warfare and almsgiving in the Quran (chapter 2). And not by chance: for the early Medinan scholars seek to build their doctrine on solid Quranic ground. They want to send a Quranic fighter to war by making Quranic gifts to him. And here we come to a basic problem in the origins of jihad. Most of the jihad's basic elements are already present in the Quran, including the doctrine of martyrdom, the divine reward, and exhortations to take up arms for the sake of religion and God. Yet there is a practical difficulty. In the stateless condition in which Islam first arose in Arabia, and even to a large extent afterward under the caliphate, there was often no way to enroll all the warriors required for a campaign, and no agreed method of providing for their needs and transporting them to the battlefield. The Quranic solution to this problem amounts to a system of gift. However, the realities of conquest and empire—including the sudden arrival of unimaginably huge amounts of money—soon made this Quranic system of gift impractical in most ways and in most places. It survived in the fiscal vocabulary, and even in the fiscal practice of the Islamic state for some time (above, chapter 6). All the same, Medina, the city of the Prophet, positioned on the margins of power and events, continued to insist on and to refine the original, archaic Quranic system over several generations.

Mecca

Even more remote than Medina from the centers of power and the theaters of war, Mecca continued to attract immigrant scholars and ascetics, as well as an endless stream of visitors coming to take part in the pilgrimage (*hajj*). Of course, most of these scholars and

---

[13] See above, end of chapter 3. For the views of some of the early Medinans on poverty, see Bonner, "Definitions of Poverty and the Rise of the Muslim Urban Poor," 339–341.

ascetics did not take part in the wars. However, we are fortunate to have an early source that gives the views of some important Meccan scholars on these matters, together with the views of some other early Islamic jurists who lived in other places. The Meccan Ibn Jurayj (d. AH 150/767 CE) is reported to ask the elder Meccan scholar ʿAtaʾ ibn Abi Rabah (d. AH 114 or 115/732–733 CE), as well as ʿAmr ibn Dinar al-Makki (d. AH 126 or 127/743–745 CE) if fighting (*ghazw*) is an obligation incumbent on everyone. ʿAtaʾ gives an answer of admirable frankness: "I don't know." Ibn Jurayj himself also seems to be at a loss. By contrast, in this same chapter, the Syrians, led by Makhul (see above), think that the answer to this question is a clear "yes," and that such activity is called "jihad." Afterward, when the conversation turns to such topics as the "merit of jihad" and martyrdom, the Meccans do not take part, except very marginally.[14] Thus in Mecca we again detect the presence of something new and controversial. The main stumbling block is the nature of the obligation of fighting in the army: is it universal, and on whom does it fall?

Meccan reticence in jihad, like its Medinan counterpart, might possibly be explained by conservatism. Another explanation has to do with a rivalry between the advocates of the jihad and of the pilgrimage, or more accurately, between the advocates of sustained devotion to these two activities over long periods of time. The practices in question are called *jihad* and *ribat* for the fighters, and *jiwar* and *mujawara* (both of which mean dwelling nearby) for the enthusiasts of *hajj*. A partisan poem on the theme is ascribed to none other than Ibn al-Mubarak:

Worshipper of the two sanctuaries, if you could only see us,
You would know that in your worship you are merely
    playing games.

For some it may be fine to tinge their necks with tears;
But our breasts are dyed in our own life's blood.

They tire out their horses in some vain enterprise,
While our steeds grow tired on the Day of Brightness.

For you the scent of perfume, but the scent that we prefer

---

[14] ʿAbd al-Razzaq, *Musannaf*, 5:171–173, nos. 9271–9278; 5:255, no. 9543; 5:256, no. 9536; 5:271, nos. 9576, 9577.

Is the hooves' burning and the most delicious dust.

A true and trusted saying has reached us from our Prophet,
Out of his sayings, one that cannot be called a lie:

"The dust of God's cavalry, as it covers a man's face,
Will never be found together with the hell-smoke of
    the Fire."[15]

Ibn al-Mubarak's poem is addressed to his fellow Iranian, Fudayl
ibn 'Iyad, a famous practitioner of jiwar. However, in the biographical sources, the rivalry between these two does not seem
bitter at all. This is not really a conflict between two different
groups: some people, including Ibn al-Mubarak himself, have
associations with both. The intent here may be not to devalue
other acts of devotion, but rather to associate the jihad with these
practices.[16]

Iraq: The Synthesis of al-Shafiʿi

We see now that there was disagreement among the major intellectual centers of the early Islamic world over the jihad. We cannot
map this disagreement precisely, because it has been overshadowed
by the consensus achieved afterward. Nonetheless it was there, and
it seems to have its origins in the difficulty of reconciling the requirements of the Quran, with its economy of gift, together with
the practical demands of conquest and empire. Much of the argument bears on the nature of the obligation of jihad: is it universal;
on whom does it fall? This problem is inseparable from that of the
leadership provided by the imam/caliph or the state.

Early Islamic Iraq, like Arabia, was not a site of warfare against
the external enemies of Islam, though it did see much internecine
violence. Iraq's importance came from its place as the seat of empire and, increasingly, as the home of many of the most influential
juridical thinkers in Islam and as the original seat of three of the

---

[15] Al-Dhahabi, *Siyar aʿlam al-nubalaʾ*, 8:364–365; Ibn Taghribirdi, *al-Nujum al-
zahira*, 2:103–104; al-Harawi, *Guide des lieux de pèlerinage*, 149; Touati, *Islam et
voyage*, 244f. For the hadith paraphrased in the last verse, see Wensinck, *Concordance*, 4:45; al-Muttaqi al-Hindi, *Kanz al-ʿummal*, 2:261.

[16] Touati, *Islam et voyage*, 244; Noth, "Les ʿulamaʾ en qualité de guerriers."

four Sunni schools of law. Fittingly, it was in Iraq that a solution was found to the problem of the obligation of jihad, in the form of a doctrine known as *fard ʿala l-kifaya*: we may translate this as "collective obligation" or else as "obligation bearing on a sufficient number." This doctrine declares that the obligation of jihad may be considered fulfilled at any time if a sufficient number of Muslim volunteers undertake it and perform it. In this case, the obligation does not fall on each individual. However, if a military emergency occurs and the enemy threatens the lands of Islam, then the obligation falls specifically on any or each individual. In that case it becomes *fard ʿala l-ʿayn*, an individual obligation. This obligation bears especially on residents of the frontier district where the enemy invasion has taken place.

The great jurist al-Shafiʿi (d. 820), whom we have already met, had a key role in the emergence of this doctrine: he gives what is apparently the first full definition of *fard kifaya*.[17] Where he speaks about these matters,[18] al-Shafiʿi is not primarily concerned with the activity of volunteers for the jihad, and even less concerned with the ambitions of martially inclined scholars of the law. What impels him most of all is the role, in the allocation of resources, of something that we are tempted to identify as the state, an entity that al-Shafiʿi calls the *sultan* (constituted authority).[19] For al-Shafiʿi, the context of all this activity is defensive warfare, where Islam is threatened by invasion from its external enemies. It is interesting to see that the "classical" doctrine of *fard ʿala l-kifaya*, as it appears in many legal works written later on, often approaches the problem more from the point of view of the individual Muslim and less from that of the state or the imam. The political nature of the question is clear nonetheless, as al-Shafiʿi showed at the beginning.

The articulation of this doctrine of fard ʿala l-kifaya did not put an end to all these tensions. We see this in a wide variety of what we sometimes call the "successor states," the Islamic polities that

---

[17] Chabbi, "Ribat," 497.

[18] Al-Shafiʿi, *Umm*, 4:84–90; idem, *Risala*, 362–369. Discussion in Bonner, "Jaʿaʾil and Holy War," 59–61; *Aristocratic Violence*, 39–40; Chabbi, "Ribat," 497.

[19] The formal office or function of sultan did not come about until much later. In Shafiʿi's day, the word still maintains its sense of "authority," even though it is also applied, by metonymy, to caliphs and other representatives of the government.

arose and flourished over a wide geographical range from the third/ninth century onward, upon the decline of the central caliphate. In the remainder of this chapter, and in much of the next one, we will look at a selection of these.

North Africa

The former Roman province of Africa, corresponding to modern-day Tunisia and parts of Algeria and Libya, was conquered for Islam in the late seventh century and became known, in Arabic, as *Ifriqiya*. As they had done earlier on in Iraq and Egypt, the Arab conquerors congregated in a new garrison city, al-Qayrawan. Before very long, this became the site of quarrels and tension between the urban population and its political and military leadership. Under the independent Aghlabid amirate of Ifriqiya (800–909), jurists of the Maliki madhhab emerged as the prime spokesmen for this urban population. In 827, amid growing tension between these two sides, the Aghlabids called for jihad for the conquest of Byzantine Sicily, and received an enthusiastic response. The actual conquest of Sicily then required a good century, which worked to the advantage of both the Aghlabids and their successors, the dynasty of the Fatimids, who managed in this way to divert away from themselves an internal opposition that risked becoming quite fierce. For the ruling elite, the endless campaigning and turmoil in Sicily thus provided a much-needed escape valve.[20] Meanwhile, the coasts of Ifriqiya itself remained exposed to attack from the sea. The Aghlabid rulers and their subjects devoted considerable resources to fortified defensive structures, known as ribats, where volunteer garrisons of *murabitun*, people taking part in ribat (defensive warfare) could reside for long or short periods of time. Here the frontier faced the sea, even though the frontier life of the murabitun took place on land. This meant that often the enemy was not there: one reason why in the long run, North African ribat—both in the sense of the activity and of the physical structure—acquired a demilitarized character as time went by.

[20] Brett, *The Rise of the Fatimids*, 80.

It is in this context that scholar-warriors become a recognizable type in the Maghrib. Early in the series comes the great Maliki jurist Sahnun (d. AH 240/854 CE), who sojourned at ribats and encouraged wealthy people to provide endowments for them.[21] In Sahnun's son Muhammad, an important scholar in his own right, the association with ribat is already much stronger, or, we could say, more thematic. We see this in biographical accounts—which do indeed have a strong hagiographical character—such as the *Riyad al-nufus* of Abu Bakr al-Maliki (late fifth/eleventh century).

If, in the old days, the scholars of early Islamic Medina—the original home of the Maliki madhhab—had certain qualms about individual jihad, their intellectual descendants, the Maliki jurists of Aghlabid Ifriqiya, had few or none.[22] So, for instance, when the fourth/tenth-century Maliki jurist Ibn Abi Zayd al-Qayrawani takes on the topic of the obligation of jihad, he mainly cites Sahnun and Muhammad ibn Sahnun—both were local North African authorities, not far removed in time from Ibn Abi Zayd himself, and both were active practitioners of jihad and ribat. Here, as elsewhere, Ibn Abi Zayd does not much cite the earlier authorities of Medina, including the *Muwatta'* of Malik himself. Mathias von Bredow has argued that this mature Maliki doctrine of jihad actually originated with Sahnun and his son Muhammad ibn Sahnun, and that they borrowed it not from Malik and the old Medinan school, but rather from Iraq, and more specifically from the book of *Siyar* by the great Hanafi Iraqi jurist al-Shaybani (d. 805), which the North African Malikis acquired and used as a "systematic model."[23] One problem with this theory is that as we have just seen, al-Shaybani actually seems to have had little to say in his *Siyar* about the general nature of the obligation of jihad.[24] On the other hand, we see the gap between mature Maliki doctrine and early Medinan teachings when Ibn Abi Zayd does actually quote a few early Medinan sayings about participation in warfare, as-

[21] Noth, "Les ʿulamaʾ en qualité de guerriers," 188; Halm, *The Empire of the Mahdi*, 225.

[22] Maíllo, "La guerra santa según el derecho mâliki," 29–66; Bredow, *Der heilige Krieg* (Ğihād) *aus der Sicht der malikitischen Rechtsschule*.

[23] Von Bredow, *Der heilige Krieg*, 50–54.

[24] Above, p. 99 Bredow refers to Shaybani's *Siyar* only in the much later commentary, or expanded version of this work by Sarakhsi.

cribed to Ibn al-Musayyab[25] and to ʿAʾisha, the Prophet's wife.[26] These clearly date from before the time that the general consensus regarding *fard kifaya* took hold.

In the early tenth century, most of Muslim North Africa was conquered by the new Ismaʿili Shiʿi caliphate of the Fatimids. The (Sunni) Maliki doctors of the law led some of the resistance against them. However, they did not mobilize the networks and ideology of jihad and ribat against the new masters, at least not in an effective, concerted way. We see this in Jabala ibn Hammud, an ascetic and former student of Sahnun, who lived as a *murabit* in Qasr al-Tub. When the Fatimids came to power, Jabala, now in advanced old age, moved to Qayrawan. When people reproached him for abandoning his post against the Byzantines, he called on them to stand watch, no longer against the old enemy "from whom we are separated by the sea," but against this new, more dangerous foe. Now every morning Jabala took up his station on the outskirts of Qayrawan, facing the Fatimid center of Raqqada, holding his bow, arrows, sword, and shield. After sundown he would get up and return home.[27] The claim that many Maliki jurists suffered martyrdom at the hands of the Fatimids does not stand up to examination; it seems rather that, as Heinz Halm says, "retreat into the ribat" became for them "a kind of internal emigration."[28]

The Fatimids themselves made liberal use of the jihad in their propaganda during their campaigns of conquest. Beyond this, however, we are witnessing a long-term change. In Fatimid North Africa, we have on the one hand, tribal armies motivated by religious fervor and charismatic leadership, and on the other hand, military units that we may describe as, in some sense, professional. There is less room for the *mutatawwiʿ* (volunteer). The presence of scholars and ascetics continues, but as an increasingly abstract and ideological ribat.

---

[25] Von Bredow, *Der heilige Krieg*, p. 8 of the Arabic text of Ibn Abi Zayd's *Kitab al-jihad min kitab al-nawadir wal-ziyadat*, where Ibn al-Musayyab says, "It is an obligation on everyone, such that they must not neglect it."

[26] Ibid.: "If someone feels cowardice within himself, he should not go on campaign."

[27] Abu Bakr al-Maliki, *Riyad*, 2:37f.; Halm, *Empire of the Mahdi*, 239.

[28] Halm, *Empire of the Mahdi*, 246.

Spain

It now appears that considerable numbers of scholars in al-Andalus (Islamic Spain) participated in the wars.[29] Here, at the other end of the Mediterranean, the situation has much in common with the marchlands of Anatolia and northern Syria: an extensive land frontier zone (also often called the Thughur) lying between well-established adversaries. Here too, a caliphal government seeks the support of the doctors of the law, and at times comes into conflict with them.

We begin with the remarkable literary success in Spain of the trio of works that, in the late eighth century, had formed the basis of the ideology of jihad along the Arab-Byzantine frontier. These three books are the *Siyar* of al-Awza'i; the *Siyar* of al-Fazari; and the *Jihad* of Ibn al-Mubarak, known to the Andalusians as *Kitab fadl al-jihad* (Book of the merit of jihad). From the time of the introduction of these books in the peninsula in the later ninth century right down to the fourteenth, they enjoyed uninterrupted popularity,[30] even more than in their own homelands. The trio coexisted with native Spanish works such as the *Qidwat al-ghazi* (The fighter's exemplar), by Ibn Abi Zamanin (d. 1008). Above all, interest in historical narratives of sira and maghazi remained strong in al-Andalus, increasing whenever the struggle against the Christian adversary grew in intensity.[31] This helps to explain the lasting appeal, in al-Andalus, of al-Fazari and his attitude toward imitation of the Prophet. Thus the figure of the jurisconsult (*faqih*) who goes to the frontier to take up arms—of which al-Fazari remains a prototype—becomes naturalized in al-Andalus.

The Andalusian jihad also resembles its eastern counterpart in its use by ambitious rulers. As we shall see in the following chapter, Harun al-Rashid (r. 785–809) was the first true ghazi-caliph in

---

[29] Urvoy, "Sur l'évolution de la notion de ǧihad dans l'Espagne musulmane," thought there was little military activity by scholars. However, Cristina de la Puente has shown otherwise in "El Ŷihād en el califato omeya de al-Andalus y su culminación bajo Hišâm II." See also Philippe Sénac, *La frontière et les hommes*, esp. 127–134 ("Savants et hommes célèbres").

[30] De la Puente, "El Ŷihād," 28.

[31] Jarrar, *Die Prophetenbiographie im islamischen Spanien*

the East. In Spain, once the independent Umayyad caliphate was created in 929, the caliph ʿAbd al-Rahman III went on campaign in person, inciting to the jihad and recruiting volunteers all the while. The Andalusian ghazi-caliph then became most prominent, somewhat ironically, in the person of Ibn Abi ʿAmir al-Mansur, known in Spanish as Almanzor, the powerful regent and usurper (978–1002) who took great pains to appear as a fighter in the jihad, having himself buried, at the end, in his old fighting clothes. Almanzor attracted volunteers from among the scholars and ascetics and did whatever he could to keep them happy. This included enforcing hyper-rigorous orthodoxy, to the point of burning the "pagan" books in the library of his charge, the hapless caliph Hisham II.[32] However, even as he sought legitimation from the Andalusian ʿulamaʾ, Almanzor imported more and more Berber soldiers from North Africa. These contributed soon afterward to the final crash of the Umayyad caliphate in Spain.

Ultimately, this professionalization of the armies further marginalized the Andalusian scholar-volunteers. Nevertheless, they continued to fight. So we have the much-respected Abu ʿAli al-Sadafi, who died fighting "with the volunteers" in the Almoravid army at Cutanda in AH 514/1120 CE, a battle in which twenty thousand Muslim volunteers are said to have perished.[33] Meanwhile, with the arrival of the Almohads, the position of Sunni ʿulamaʾ in al-Andalus became increasingly strained. For many of them, ribat became a way of expressing or transcending their alienation;[34] and like its North African counterpart, this ribat had less and less to do with the actual conduct of war.

Central Asia

The early Islamic frontier zone of Khurasan and Transoxania was unlike its western counterparts in many ways. Here military operations took place over an enormous area, with territories and cities often changing hands. This eastern frontier was also different socially, in part because of the survival and flourishing of a local

[32] An early occurrence of this theme (the burning library) in Spanish history and literature.

[33] De la Puente, "Vivre et mourir pour Dieu," esp. 95–97.

[34] Maribel Fierro, "Spiritual Alienation and Political Activism."

landowning class or petty aristocracy, the *dehqan*s. Here, in the ninth and tenth centuries, the Tahirid and Samanid authorities went to great pains to construct systems of defensive fortresses, as well as walls, ramparts, and trenches to defend the great cities. Large numbers of "volunteers" served in these places; whether they did so out of religious motivation, or because of payment or coercion from the state, is still a matter of debate. For these and other reasons, it would be wrong to think of this eastern marchland as secondary or as less important than its Arab-Byzantine counterpart. The ideology and practice of jihad owed a great deal to it.

We have early instances of fighting scholars in this region: so for instance, Ibrahim ibn Shammas al-ghazi al-Samarqandi (d. AH 221 or 222/837–338 CE), was the owner of an estate (*day'a*) near Samarqand, and bequeathed one hundred thousand dirhams for the ransoming of prisoners from the Turks.[35] Significantly, Ibrahim ibn Shammas actually died in combat, unlike almost all his fighting colleagues along the Arab-Byzantine frontier. However, a number of these Central Asian scholars and ascetics left their own marches beginning in the second half of the eighth century, as Ibn al-Mubarak and Ibn Adham—both of them natives of Khurasan—established their ties with the Byzantine frontier region. During the following two and a half centuries, a significant proportion of the scholars who lived in the Arab-Byzantine frontier district came originally from Khurasan and Transoxania. Large masses of nameless volunteers moved along the same path, especially during the military crises of the tenth century. The scarcity of books expressing the ideas of Khurasan and Central Asia in the area of warfare and jihad (whether in the form of narratives, hadith, or legal works), books that might have played the role that al-Fazari's *Siyar* played for the Arab-Byzantine frontier, or that Ibn Abi Zamanin's *Qidwat al-ghazi* played for Spain, also points to a certain amount of "brain drain" toward other frontiers and other regions.[36]

During the amirate of the Samanids (892–1005) in Khurasan and Transoxania, religious scholars had a role in military as well

---

[35] Mizzi, *Tahdhib al-kamal*, 2:105–107.

[36] The well-known commentary by al-Sarakhsi (d. ca. 1090) on the *Siyar* of the Iraqi scholar al-Shaybani (d. 805) performs this role for the eastern frontier, but considerably later.

as political affairs. This consisted largely of preaching and exhorting, but there is also evidence for men of learning at the head of large units of *ghazi*s (fighters for the faith), units that do not seem to have been organized by the Samanid state. What we know about these men comes mainly from biographical notices about them in urban histories where they appear as ʿulamaʾ. Now to what extent do the categories of scholar and volunteer/ghazi overlap? If a ghazi rises to a position of leadership, does that not suffice to promote him to the category of scholar?[37] At any rate, this frontier ceased to have a military character by the eleventh century. From then on it has a central place in the history of asceticism and Sufism.[38]

The Embattled Scholars: Conclusions

When we speak of the jihad in history, we tend to generalize the various environments where it took place so as to obtain a more unified, composite picture. Here I have tried to give an idea of some of the variety among the frontier provinces of the early Islamic world. Of course, these provinces also had elements in common, including a shared idiom of expression relating to the jihad. However, we cannot always assume that this common idiom was present, in every case, from the very beginning. On the contrary, it sometimes took new forms and provoked new quarrels.

Volunteering, the participation of military nonprofessionals in the war against the enemies of Islam, has been a constant in Islamic history at all times. In a special sense—including the personal involvement of men of learning—it emerged first in Umayyad Syria, though perhaps also, simultaneously, on the northeastern frontier of Khurasan. The early Syrian jurist Makhul is said to have participated personally in the wars of his own time (which we may or may not believe); he had more than a passing interest in

---

[37] Paul, "The Histories of Samarqand," esp. 82–87; "The State and the Military: The Samanid Case"; *Herrscher, Gemeinwesen, Vermittler: Ostiran und Transoxanien in vormongolischer Zeit*, esp. 93–139.

[38] See the article in *EI²* on "Ribat" by Jacqueline Chabbi, and her "Remarques sur le développement historique des mouvements ascétiques et mystiques au Khurasan."

maghazi, which is to say, in historical narratives about the military campaigns of the Prophet and the earliest Islam; and he expressed the view that fighting against the enemies of Islam is a universal obligation incumbent on each able-bodied Muslim male. This combination, especially the idea of universal obligation, immediately became a matter of controversy. Two generations later, Abu Ishaq al-Fazari and his colleagues along the Byzantine frontier mixed these same elements into a far more potent brew, which many people in other environments, notably Islamic Spain, then found intoxicating. Al-Fazari combined his imitation of the Prophet Muhammad's martial activity together with a bold claim to authority for the religious scholar, at the expense of—and even in defiance of—the authority of the imam/caliph, which is to say, of the early Islamic state. At the same time, other scholar-ascetics along the frontiers, especially ʿAbdallah Ibn al-Mubarak and his followers, expressed the idea that volunteering for the jihad, and martyrdom, is the best way of constituting the community of Islam out of the striving and activity of many individual believers in search of their own religious merit and salvation.

Meanwhile, the classical doctrine of *fard ʿala l-kifaya* (collective obligation) first expressed by al-Shafiʿi, became widely (though not universally) accepted. This doctrine provided some resolution to tensions that had been breeding among various contending parties that included the imam/caliph and other representatives of the Islamic state, who needed to mobilize armies so as to defend and, where possible, expand the territory of Islam; scholars such as al-Fazari, who were making a claim to authority for themselves in matters of law and belief by looking back to the precedent of the Prophet and the early Muslim community; and those individuals who, following Ibn al-Mubarak and Ibn Adham, made the jihad into a vehicle by which one could join, constitute, or even (as in Ibn Adham's case) transcend the community of Islam itself. Nonetheless, this resolution of tensions through the juridical doctrine of *fard kifaya* is largely formal. Governments keep on having to solve the practical problems of recruiting and maintaining armies; while men of learning, in many later generations and in many different environments, find themselves taking up arms and confronting these questions all over again.

Houari Touati is right in saying that the activity of these fighting scholars is symbolic in its importance, and that its ultimate meaning is as a foundational act.[39] We may see this in the fact that among the hundreds of extant biographical notices of scholars and ascetics of the Byzantine frontier, only a handful are reported to have died in combat.[40] Yet in other places, such as Spain, plenty of them did fight and die. As symbolic actions go, this one is remarkably rooted in the here and now and can cause its practitioners to get their hands quite dirty. The question of real versus symbolic is not completely clear-cut.

The recurring phenomenon of the embattled scholars shows that the jihad does indeed have a plurality of origins. Each time a distinctive Islamic society emerges, it must work through a set of questions that regard the identity and meaning of volunteering and scholarship just as much as fighting against external or internal adversaries. In this way, these societies learn to express themselves creatively within the common idiom of jihad.

Readings

Once again, it was the late Albrecht Noth who first identified the phenomenon of men of learning, including *fuqaha'* or (jurisconsults), settling or sojourning in considerable numbers along the various military frontiers of the medieval Islamic world.[41] Since the early 1990s, the phenomenon has been taken up by Michael Bonner,[42] Jacqueline Chabbi,[43] Albrecht Noth again,[44] Cristina de la Puente,[45] Houari Touati,[46] Linda Darling,[47] Jürgen Paul,[48] Deb-

---

[39] Touati, *Islam et voyage*, 256–257.

[40] Bonner, *Aristocratic Violence*, 158; Noth, "Les ʿulamaʾ en qualité de guerriers," cites a few casualties.

[41] *Heiliger Krieg und heiliger Kampf in Islam und Christentum* (Bonn, 1966).

[42] Bonner, "Some Observations Concerning the Early Development of Jihad on the Arab-Byzantine Frontier," *Aristocratic Violence and Holy War*, esp. 107–134, 157–184.

[43] Chabbi, "Ribat."

[44] Noth, "Les ʿulamaʾ en qualité de guerriers."

[45] De La Puente, "El Ŷihād en el califato omeya de al-Andalus y su culminación bajo Hišām II"; idem, "Vivre et mourir pour Dieu, œuvre et héritage d'Abu ʿAli al-Sadafi."

[46] Touati, *Islam et voyage au moyen âge*, 237–258 ("Le séjour aux marches").

[47] Darling, "Contested Territory: Ottoman Holy War in Comparative Context."

[48] Paul, "The Histories of Samarqand"; idem, "The State and the Military"; idem, *Herrscher, Gemeinwesen, Vermittler.*

orah Tor,[49] and other writers, some of whom are cited in the notes to this chapter.

The identity and role of the 'ulama' in urban life and Islamic society as a whole has been much discussed. See the summary of the question in R. Stephen Humphreys, *Islamic History: A Framework for Inquiry* (Princeton: Princeton University Press, 1990), 228–254. To this we may add the highly interesting books by Jonathan Berkey, *The Transmission of Knowledge in Medieval Cairo: A Social History of Islamic Education* (Princeton: Princeton University Press, 1992); and Michael Chamberlain, *Knowledge and Social Practice in Medieval Damascus, 1190–1350* (Cambridge: Cambridge University Press, 1994).

Note the recent and much-anticipated arrival of the book by D. G. (Deborah) Tor, *Violent Order: Religious Warfare, Chivalry, and the 'Ayyar Phenomenon in the Medieval Islamic World* (Würzburg: Ergon Verlag and Orient-Institut Istanbul, 2007).

[49] Tor, "Privatized Jihad and Public Order in the Pre-Saljuq Period."

CHAPTER EIGHT

Empires, Armies, and Frontiers

Islam begins in Mecca in an encounter with the transcendent Other, with the God whose Word enters and transforms the consciousness of human beings. Out of this encounter there emerges an individual soul, acutely aware of itself and its precarious place in the cosmos.[1] At the same time, there emerges a new community, defined and held together by its faith in God. The activity that stands out as most characteristic of this early community, the activity that its Scripture calls for over and again, has to do with generosity and care for the poor and unfortunate. Though we may disagree over the historical details regarding this very earliest Islam, and some may even claim that these historical details are beyond recovery, we cannot doubt that all this involved a profound transformation, both spiritual and social, in Arabia.

Then comes what is usually presented as a new, separate stage involving the birth of an Islamic state and, simultaneously, of organized warfare in the path of that same transcendent God. This transition from Mecca to Medina, from the encounter with the divine to fighting and statehood, is described in the narratives about Muhammad and the early community (chapter 3). Again, some non-Muslim observers have had suspicions about the reliability of those narratives, as we have already seen. But the real difficulty, for some outsiders, may be in their underlying sense.

---

[1] Quran 81:14 (*Takwir*): "Then [on the Judgment Day] shall a soul know what it has produced" (Arberry trans.).

Why should the discovery of God, self, and community be linked so indissolubly to the waging of war? Why are these two nonetheless represented as separate stages, not only in the narratives but also, in some undeniable way, in consciousness? How does this combination then maintain such attraction over so many centuries and ranging so far beyond the original Arabian environment in which Islam first arose?

The best we can do for now is to confirm that things went this way. Islam transformed its early adherents through its spiritual and moral message, and through the activity of fighting on behalf of that message. The first results of this transformation included the early Islamic state. Here it is important to recognize the impassioned urgency of the early Arabic sources that describe these events. Modern treatments often tend to flatten or to avoid this urgency; one book that conveys it, together with a critical approach to the sources, is Hichem Djaït's *La Grande Discorde*.[2] Here the jihad is an indissoluble part of the transcendent, transforming Message—though at the same time, a part of the Message that has arrived somewhat later than the rest. The jihad provides motivation and pride; eventually, looking backward in time, it provides the basis of a criterion for establishing distinctions and degrees among the believers.

Now we proceed to outline a sketch of the jihad's trajectory in the political and military history of Islam down to the modern era. We have already traced the first and best-known episodes: the rise of Islam and its diffusion during the heroic period of the early conquests. Here, as in the previous chapter, we will examine the various contexts of the jihad through a series of frontier societies, linked together over time and space. We must also keep in mind that in this historical trajectory of the jihad, there is no neat, simple division between concrete, real experience on the one side and abstract, theoretical knowledge on the other.

The Umayyad Caliphate: Imperial Jihad

The most brilliant epoch of the great conquests was the thirty-year period following the death of the prophet Muhammad in 632.

[2] Djaït, *La Grande Discorde*.

Toward the end of this period came the first internal war of Islam, the *fitna* (great discord) eloquently described by Djaït in the book just mentioned. This war's arrival is not at all surprising. The Arabs had just vaulted from poverty and marginality into control over most of the territory and riches of the known world. However, their state rested on new foundations, and the juridical and moral status of their leader, the caliph, turned out to be precarious when the third caliph, ʿUthman, was murdered in Medina in 656. The ensuing struggle was, all at once, a quarrel over leadership, morality, and the allocation of resources within the nascent state. What concerns us now is the man who emerged as the winner of this first Muslim civil war, Muʿawiya (r. 661–680), together with the Umayyad dynasty (661–750) of which he was the founding figure.

Our textbooks of Islamic history still tend to describe the Umayyad caliphs as the rulers of an "Arab kingdom," eager for power and indifferent to religion, unlike the dynasty that eventually took their place, the more overtly pious ʿAbbasids who, according to this commonly accepted notion, held command over an "Islamic empire." This idea goes back, once again, to the orientalism of a century ago and, in particular, to the work of the German scholar Julius Wellhausen who, like so many others at the time, had great admiration for the *raison d'état*.[3] So where medieval Arabic writers had condemned the Umayyads for their alleged disregard for religion and their licentious behavior, Wellhausen and his followers could claim evidence for shrewd, Machiavellian statecraft on the part of those same Umayyads. Similarly, it was possible to dismiss the ostentatious piety of the ʿAbbasids as so much hypocritical display. More recently, however, it has been claimed, convincingly, that the Umayyads wished in fact to be portrayed as religious figures, ruling the earth as "God's deputy" (*khalifat Allah*).[4] It is clear, at any rate, that the Umayyads held the supreme power during a series of turbulent decades when the basic notions of Islamic rulership were first being invented, tested, and tried.

These early ideas of rulership definitely included leadership in the wars against the enemies of Islam. The first of the Umayyad

[3] Especially in his history of the Umayyads, *Das arabische Reich und sein Sturz* (Berlin, 1902), translated into English as *The Arab Kingdom and Its Fall*.

[4] Crone and Hinds, *God's Caliph*.

caliphs, Muʿawiya (r. 661–680), had already acquired considerable experience in warfare against the Byzantine empire, from having previously held the governorship of Syria for many years. Once he became caliph, Muʿawiya continued to reside in Syria, rather than in Arabia, which allowed him to maintain military pressure against the Byzantine empire. These campaigns did not bring much territorial gain, but they did reveal the imperial and Mediterranean scope of Muʿawiya's ambition: he would conquer Constantinople and occupy the seat of the Basileus, the Roman emperor. How Islam would have fared in the event that Muʿawiya had succeeded is beyond knowing: all we can say is that things would have turned out very differently from the way they did. But as it happened, neither Muʿawiya nor his dynastic successors achieved this imperial Mediterranean ambition. The expeditions sent against Constantinople in 669, 674, and 717 all failed, leaving thousands dead from wounds, hunger, and disease.[5]

The Umayyads fared better on other fronts, especially beginning in the 690s, as expansion resumed on a global scale. Muslim armies—we may no longer call them Arab armies, as many of their recruits were now not Arabs at all—conquered North Africa and then Spain, while in the East they advanced into the borderlands of India and China (see map 2). By this time, a full century after the Hijra, Islam securely occupied the largest single expanse of territory ever held under unified control in the history of the world until that time.

Territorial expansion was thus dear to the Umayyads' hearts. Was it an articulated, deliberate strategy? The lack of evidence makes it difficult to say. However, Khalid Yahya Blankinship has proposed that the Umayyad caliphate was indeed a kind of machine devoted to external expansion. With its huge armies, its expanding bureaucracy, and the conspicuous consumption of its central and provincial courts, the caliphate systematically lived beyond its means, placing its hopes in continuing conquest and in the acquisition of more and more spoils for distribution. This proceeded well enough until expansion met its inevitable limits, under the caliph Hisham (r. 724–743). Hisham, a serious and capable ruler, had to confront a near-catastrophic series of external

---

[5] See the article by Wellhausen, "Arab Wars with the Byzantines in the Umayyad Period," recently translated by Bonner.

defeats, internal rebellions, and fiscal crises. After his death, the Umayyad state split apart in civil war and then fell prey to its enemies. According to Blankinship, it was the jihad that provided the ideological basis to the entire Umayyad enterprise: "[The Umayyad] caliphate constituted the *jihad* state par excellence. Its main reason for existence, aside from maintaining God's law, was to protect Islam and to expand the territory under its control, and its reputation was strongly bound to its military success."[6] This argument has a certain shock value, in that it presents the jihad as an *imperial* ideology, and as the tool of rulers whom the Islamic tradition subsequently rejected, or at least found controversial. One possible flaw here is in the assumption of a neatly centralized empire, where one actor could pull all the right ideological, political, and military levers at once. Reality may have been otherwise: the Umayyad enterprise was vast, and its center in Damascus was often unable to compel the far-flung provinces (whose governors tended to behave like monarchs) to forward their fiscal surpluses; this center may thus have found itself isolated, overstretched, struggling to maintain control, and unable to benefit from the expansion taking place all the while on the frontiers of Central Asia, North Africa, and Western Europe.[7]

Nonetheless, there are arguments in favor of the imperial character of the jihad during the Umayyad century, especially in its later decades. Joseph Schacht, a modern historian of early Islamic law (see chapter 3), thought that the imperial legislation of the Umayyads provided much of the material basis for what eventually became Islamic law, especially in the area of the law of war (*siyar*). In other words, the Umayyad caliphs, through their governors, generals, and judges, began and developed much of what eventually became the Islamic law of war; only afterward was this law of war ascribed to more acceptably Islamic sources such as the Companions of the Prophet and, of course, the Prophet himself.[8] Though this point has been contested, like the rest of Schacht's work, it has much in its favor, especially in the figure of the important Syrian jurist al-Awzaʿi (d. 774), a specialist in siyar who was entirely sympathetic to the idea that the Umayyad caliphs

---

[6] Blankinship, *The End of the Jihâd State*, 232.
[7] Kennedy, "The Financing of the Military in the Early Islamic State."
[8] Schacht, *Introduction to Islamic Law*, 23–24.

might function as lawgivers.[9] Moreover, there is other evidence
that at least the later Umayyad caliphs promoted an ideology of
jihad which involved subduing all opponents to their rule, whether
these opponents lived outside the Umayyad domains (unbelievers)
or within them (heretics, rebels).[10]

It was in the later Umayyad period, in the metropolitan province
of Syria, that jurists such as Makhul began to preach the idea of
jihad as an obligation incumbent on each individual—an idea that
at first received a cool reception in the other provinces (chapter 7).
We do not know what effect this idea had on the "imperial jihad"
of the Umayyads, though from Blankinship's work we can clearly
see that the Syrian armies at the time were starved for men. It is
worth noting, in any case, that while the Umayyad caliphs sent out
countless military expeditions, they did not, as a rule, take part in
the fighting themselves. Those of them who, like Hisham, had
fought in their youth,[11] did not make this into a claim for legitimacy
or glory. At least not until the end: in the last years of the Umayyad
caliphate, we find that Hisham's sons were military men, and that
the last Umayyad caliph, Marwan ibn Muhammad (r. 744–750) was
a battle-hardened soldier who had fought all his life against Byzantines, Khazars, and a variety of Muslim opponents.

Even among the unloved Umayyads, Marwan has always been
one of the most unpopular figures. However, we have the text of
an epistle of thanksgiving, composed for Marwan by his chief
scribe on some occasion of victory.[12] Here we find the caliph acting
in matters of war as the divinely appointed head of the Muslim
community: he has inherited the legacy of the Prophet Muhammad, a legacy that allows him to endure the hardships now upon
him. Then, on the other side, we find warriors who acquire religious merit for fighting the enemies of Islam. God has caused
these warriors to inherit their enemies' lands and possessions; they
spend their blood in obedience to God, who has sold them Paradise in exchange for their lives. These warriors may or may not

[9] Abu Yusuf, *Kitab al-radd ʿala siyar al-Awzaʿi*, 1–2, 20.

[10] Heck, "*Jihad* Revisited," 106–108; al-Qadi, "The Religious Foundation of
Late Umayyad Ideology and Practice."

[11] Tabari, *Taʾrikh*, 2:1185; Baladhuri, *Futuh*, 186.

[12] The epistle is by ʿAbd al-Hamid, edited by ʿAbbas in *ʿAbd al-Hamid ibn Yahya
al-katib*, 273, no. 26.

include the caliph himself: the point seems not to matter. These two inheritances, of caliphate and jihad, are not closely linked, despite Marwan's lifetime of military service, and despite the Umayyads' long success in conquest and war. Afterward, sometime after the fall of Marwan and his dynasty, we will see an attempt to join these two inheritances together.

Revolution and Jihad

One of the most important things about the Umayyads in the history of Islam is the opposition they provoked. Whether or not it was fully deserved, this opposition extended over a broad spectrum of groups with very different interests and ideas, who had in common their hatred of the Umayyad oppressors and "imams of tyranny." For in the end, the Umayyads' posing as divinely appointed protectors of the community and its armies did them little good. They had the misfortune, as we have already seen, of holding power during an age when the categories of just rule in Islam were being discovered and worked out.

Opposition to the Umayyads took many forms, but most of it crystallized into two groupings which came to constitute the classical opposition parties of Islam.[13] One of these, the Shiʿa, began as the faction or "party" of the Prophet's son-in-law and cousin, the fourth caliph ʿAli (d. 661). It was, however, the death of ʿAli's son al-Husayn, at the hands of an army sent by the Umayyad caliph Yazid in 680, at Karbalaʾ in Iraq, that galvanized the Shiʿa: we have seen (chapter 5) that Shiʿis have always considered al-Husayn the "martyr of martyrs." In the chaotic conditions of the Second Fitna or civil war (683–692), branches of the nascent Shiʿa made ample use of the vocabulary of jihad and martyrdom. They directed their violence both against others and against themselves. So for instance, one of the first groups to take up the cause of the slain al-Husayn was that of the tawwabun (penitents). These began as a group of men in Kufa who felt remorse at not having helped al-Husayn at Karbalaʾ and vowed to avenge his death or else to die in the attempt. They attracted followers to their cause, but

---

[13] The classic treatment is once again by Wellhausen, *The Religio-political Factions in Early Islam*.

when they moved from penance to overt rebellion, they were out-numbered and destroyed on the battlefield.[14] This pattern, with variations, was repeated many times afterward.

Over time, the Shiʿa developed a full system of Islamic law. This included a doctrine of jihad that differed from the Sunni doctrine especially in two ways. First of all, everyone—Sunnis, Shiʿis, Kha-rijites—agreed that jihad requires the consent and direction of the imam. However, the Imami, or Twelver Shiʿis, who became the sect's largest branch, recognized only twelve divinely appointed imams, in a sequence that ended in 873 CE. As a practical matter, performance of jihad thus became impossible for Shiʿis in most times and places.[15] Second, while everyone agreed that jihad in-cludes an aspect of fighting Muslim rebels (*ahl al-baghy*), the Shiʿi jurists defined these rebels as the opponents of the Twelve Imams; which meant, basically, all Muslims other than the Shiʿis them-selves.[16] As with the doctrine of martyrdom, the Shiʿis thus used the broader doctrine of jihad to define themselves as an oppressed group within a world that was Muslim in appearance only and where power could only be wielded iniquitously.

The second great opposition group to emerge from the fitnas, or civil wars of the seventh century, was the Kharijites. The name by which they are most often known (*khawarij*, "those who go out") shows that most other Muslims considered them to have gone over and beyond the bounds of the community. The Khari-jites were indeed radical, even though, like the Shiʿa, they have always been divided into several groups, some of these more ex-treme than others. Broadly speaking, their characteristics included (and still include) a fundamentalist approach in deriving principles and norms solely from the text of the Quran;[17] a radically egalitar-ian view of the qualifications for Islamic leadership, or the Imam-ate; an insistence on fair and equal apportionment of the revenue accruing to the Muslim community as a result of its conquests

[14] F. M. Denny's article, "Tawwabun" in *EI²*; Jafri, *Origins and Early Development of Shiʿa Islam*, 222–234.
[15] Ismaʿili or "Sevener" Shiʿism did not have this problem: see later in this chapter.
[16] Kohlberg, "The Development of the Imami Shiʿi Doctrine of Jihad."
[17] Important parts of the narrative about the Kharijites during the First Fitna may have originated in exegetical and juridical argument over this point: see Hawt-ing, "The Significance of the Slogan *La hukma illa liʾllah*."

(*fay*'); and a thoroughgoing rejection of other Muslims who did not share their views on these points. Indeed they declared such Muslims to be not Muslims at all, but infidels (*kuffar*), and in this activity of *takfir* (declaring infidel), they were eager for violence and war.

The Kharijites showed special attachment to the jihad in their preaching, their doctrine,[18] and their poetry.[19] They called themselves *shurat* (sellers), meaning that they had sold their lives in return for the divine reward promised by God in the Quran (see chapter 2). They were intensely pious, as well as warlike: indeed, we might think that "gentle ones worn out by fasting"[20] would not be well suited to vanquishing enemies with sword and spear. However, the Kharijites paid special attention to those verses of the Quran that militate against "sitting" at home (*quʿud*) while battles and campaigns are taking place (see chapters 2 and 3).[21] They did not share the view of jihad as "sufficient obligation" (*fard ʿala l-kifaya*; see chapter 7) but adhered to the ancient view that jihad is an obligation on each and every individual. And, unlike the Sunnis, they declared jihad to be one of the Pillars of the Faith.[22] The Kharijites were a major presence during the Umayyad and early ʿAbbasid periods, when they often posed a serious threat to the caliphate and its local representatives. Afterward, though they remained a force to be reckoned with in many areas, they receded from view in the central regions of the Islamic world. Even then, however, they carried on the militant piety of the early days.

It is often said that these "opposition parties"—Shiʿites and Kharijites—began as political movements and only later acquired their religious character as sectarian movements.[23] However, we

---

[18] Crone and Zimmermann, *The Epistle of Sâlim ibn Dhakwân*, esp. 52–57, 140–141, 181–182.

[19] Donner, "Piety and Eschatology in Early Kharijite Poetry," 13–19; ʿAbbas, *Shiʿr al-Khawarij*.

[20] Donner, "Piety and Eschatology," 14, citing a verse of Farwa b. Nawfal al-Ashjaʿi, in ʿAbbas, *Shiʿr*, no. 18, p. 43.

[21] Crone and Zimmermann, *Epistle*, 51f.

[22] This was the view preached by Makhul the Syrian in the early eighth century, see previous chapter. On the Kharijites, see also Morabia, *Le Ǧihâd*, 196, 215f., 250–51.

[23] This view owes much to Wellhausen's *Religio-political Factions* and to Hodgson, "How did the Early Shiʿa Become Sectarian?"

must be careful not to apply rationalizing, historicizing interpreta-
tions to this framework of analysis. For what we have before us is
the idealized sectarian structure of Islam, where books of "orthodox" heresiography neatly list, for each single movement, both its
political aspirations in history, and its doctrinal errors in theology.
The result is compelling but utterly schematic. What we can affirm is that as soon as we find opposition movements expressing
themselves, in Islamic terms, against the Islamic leadership of their
day, they do this in the language of jihad, with martyrdom above
all. They do this so much that we might even define the earliest
jihad as warfare against the enemies of God, in a situation where
the identity of those enemies is still far from clear.

When the Umayyad caliphate fell in 750, it was neither to
Kharijites nor to Shiʿites, but rather to a conspiracy which turned
out to be operating on behalf of the ʿAbbasid family, descendants
of an uncle of the Prophet Muhammad named al-ʿAbbas. In fact,
the rhetoric and program of what we now call the ʿAbbasid Revolution were overwhelmingly Shiʿi in flavor and style. The movement's partisans demanded revenge for the crimes of the usurping
Umayyads, especially their crimes against the Prophet's family.
They demanded that the imamate be restored to "the one who is
pleasing [to God] from among Muhammad's family" (al-rida min
âl Muhammad). And they demanded (here more like the Kharijites)
a reformed and just sharing of the revenues deriving from conquest. In all this they employed the language of martyrdom, but
in Shiʿi fashion, which is to say, with focus on the suffering of the
family and the denial of its rights and claims. If ʿAbbasid partisans
made use of other parts of the doctrine of jihad, this does not
figure prominently in the sources as we have them. It was afterward, when the ʿAbbasids were securely in power, that jihad in a
broad sense became a prime concern.

The ʿAbbasid Caliphate and Its Military Crisis

The victorious ʿAbbasids established the center of their caliphate
in Iraq, which already surpassed Syria as a center of economic and
cultural production. In this way, they renounced the old Umayyad
ambition of capturing the seat of the Byzantine emperor—an ambition that had already proved unrealizable in any case. However,

they soon found that they could not ignore Syria altogether. The formidable threat of Byzantium required the massing of troops on the Muslim side, troops that only Syria could supply. Four years after the ʿAbbasid Revolution, these Syrian frontier troops took part in a rebellion against the ʿAbbasid caliph al-Mansur (r. 754– 775). Al-Mansur put this rebellion down and then looked for ways to reconcile the Syrian fighters and their leadership. Settling the Arab-Byzantine frontier district with fighters and maintaining their loyalty and strength thus became a major political concern.

The problem went beyond any one frontier district. It appears, as we have seen, that the later Umayyad caliphs had tried to promote an imperial ideology of jihad. We have also seen that at that same time and afterward, many of those people who were beginning to articulate the idea of jihad in rhetoric, theology, and law had different ideas on this matter. Some of them, in particular, advocated the idea of jihad as a universal obligation on each and every (i.e., able-bodied male Muslim) individual. At stake here, of course, was the religious merit and reward in store for the individual, which he might seek through fighting in the armies (or whatever else he understood the jihad to involve); probably not for the first time and certainly not for the last, these individual quests for religious merit came into conflict with the needs and interests of the Islamic state. In this way, as the doctrine and practice of jihad took shape under the early ʿAbbasids, it became an area of endeavor for jurists and other people who very often were not under the direct control of the ʿAbbasid caliphs themselves. There certainly were exceptions to this pattern, as we see in a handful of writings, addressed to or from caliphs, that aimed to keep warfare and its ideology, together with the armies themselves, firmly under the control of the caliphs.[24] Already in the early ʿAbbasid period, however, the more typical and enduring "face of jihad" is someone like Abu Ishaq al-Fazari, striking a somewhat defiant pose vis-à-vis the ʿAbbasid authorities along the frontier; or else ʿAbdallah ibn al-Mubarak, showing general indifference to those authorities.

---

[24] For the reign of al-Mansur, see Ibn al-Muqaffaʿ's *Risala fi l-sahaba* (epistle on the Companions), edited and translated by Charles Pellat in *Ibn al-Muqaffaʿ, 'conseilleur du Calife.'* For the reign of al-Maʾmun, see Arazi and Elʿad, "L'Epître à l'armée."

All this helps to explain why it was that before long, the ʿAbbasid caliphs showed a personal involvement in the Byzantine wars that surpassed that of their Umayyad predecessors. The caliphs al-Mahdi (775–785) and his son Harun al-Rashid (786–809) led expeditions in person. Indeed, Harun made so much of his participation in the wars that we may characterize him as the first ghazi-caliph,[25] or in other words, as the first caliph who devoted himself ostentatiously to the performance of jihad. Poets at Harun's court wove this theme into their panegyrics, with emphasis on the caliph's participation in campaigning (ghazw), neatly paired with his frequent performance of the pilgrimage to Mecca. They praised Harun for his many travels, exertion, and self-sacrifice:

You have feared God according to His due,
    while exerting yourself beyond the exertion of one who
        fears God. . . .

You visit [the infidels] in person every year,
    like one who restores ties with those have severed them.

But you could, if you liked, resort to some pleasant place,
    while others endured hardship instead of you.[26]

This emphasis on the caliph's participation in warfare, on his person (nafs) and exertion (jahd), on the supererogatory nature of his efforts, and on his travels and ubiquitousness together constitutes the ghazi-caliph of panegyric. The object of praise in these poems is the imam, the divinely appointed ruler, charged with the defense of Islam and supervision of its wars. At the same time, he is a volunteer, a kind of everyman, distinguished through his personal effort and through his free choice of roles not strictly required of him. The poets recognized that this was something new: "None but you, of those who have succeeded to the caliphate / Has ever held the frontiers."[27] The combination appeared afterward, most famously in Harun's son al-Muʿtasim (r. 833–842), to whom some of the most famous panegyric verses ever written in the Arabic

---

[25] Bonner, *Aristocratic Violence and Holy War*, 99–106. The phrase "ghazi-caliph" was first used by C. E. Bosworth in the introduction to vol. 30 of the English translation of Tabari's *History* (Albany, 1989), xvii.

[26] Abu Nuwas, *Diwan*, 452, 641.

[27] Abu l-Maʿali al-Kilabi, at Tabari, *Taʾrikh*, 3:710.

language were dedicated. But why did this figure of the ghazi-caliph emerge at this time, and what purpose did it serve?

Despite the famous prosperity of the reign of Harun, the ʿAbbasid caliphate had already entered into a broad crisis, much of it military in character. The old *levée en masse* of the early Islamic conquests had long since been supplanted by units that were basically professional. The commanders of these units wanted a generous share of the revenues, and some of them demanded a leading role in the administration of the provinces. Under these circumstances, where were new soldiers to be found? How was the state to bear the growing cost of their recruitment, training, and maintenance? And how could the caliph make sure that they would be loyal to him first of all, and then to their commanders? These problems became fully apparent in the generations after Harun,[28] but they could already be seen in his day. In these circumstances, Harun's adoption of the role of ghazi-caliph meant an anachronistic harkening back to the old *levée en masse*, when being an able-bodied Muslim meant being a fighter in God's wars and a recipient of God's stipend or gift (*ʿata*). Harun sought a civilian constituency that would respond to the message of a jihad mediated through the person of the imam/caliph, and not through the commanders who were increasingly dominating the military and political scene.

Several of the later ʿAbbasid caliphs also made much of their personal involvement in the wars against Byzantium, but this did not stave off the crisis. While the office of caliph itself survived, the Islamic world experienced a redrawing of its political map and a transformation of its fiscal structures. In the armies, the trend toward professionalization only increased. Often this meant a reliance on slave soldiers, men who had first entered the armies as slaves imported from outside the Islamic world. Other types of military units coexisted with these, including volunteers for the jihad (*muttawwiʿa*), civilians driven by religious fervor but having only marginal military skills. It seems that the professionals often considered these volunteers to be an unreliable nuisance.

Nonetheless, the ghazi-caliph remains part of the story. What made it possible in the first place was the emergence of the jihad, in the later eighth century CE, as a recognizable and definable set

---

[28] A. Arazi and A. Elʿad, "L'Epître à l'armée."

of doctrines and ideas. We have seen in chapter 7 that the early ʿAbbasid epoch saw the composition and dissemination, in the Arab-Byzantine frontier area, of two of the earliest books on the jihad (by Abu Ishaq al-Fazari and ʿAbdallah ibn al-Mubarak). It also saw the arrival in the same area of numerous scholars and ascetics, most of whom were not closely tied to the ʿAbbasid state, and some of whom were even inclined to confrontation with it. For a ghazi-caliph like Harun al-Rashid, these fighter-scholars could figure as rivals. However, the caliph could also, and in fact did, try to win them over to his side. So whereas the Umayyads had, through imperial legislation, laid the foundations for some of what later became the Islamic law of war, the ʿAbbasids found themselves making war according to principles and norms established for them by the doctors of the law.

Frontier Societies: Against Byzantium

The gradual breakup of the ʿAbbasid caliphate led to the emergence of many independent dynastic states within the Islamic world, most of them founded by men who had begun their careers as military professionals. Most, though not all, of these new states and rulers remained loyal, at least in theory, to the ʿAbbasid caliph in Baghdad. However, by the middle of the tenth century CE, this caliph had become a powerless figurehead. The societies and states that emerged out of all this were varied and complex.[29] Here, we resume the previous chapter's discussion of regions and states that constituted border societies, and of the role of the jihad within them.

We have seen that the Byzantine frontier long held pride of place among the Islamic frontier districts. The Umayyad caliphs failed in their efforts to conquer Constantinople; Muslim apocalyptic writings, which can plausibly be dated to the Umayyad period, describe the conquest of the city as a transcendent religious goal.[30] They include the prophecy that Constantinople would fall

---

[29] For a thorough introduction, see Garcin et al., *Etats, sociétés et cultures du monde musulman médiéval, X^e–XVe siècle.*

[30] Canard, "Les expéditions des Arabes contre Constantinople dans l'histoire et dans la légende."

132   CHAPTER EIGHT

to a ruler who bore the name of a prophet, a prophecy that turned
out to be accurate, even though the event took place much later
than originally expected (in 1453, when an Ottoman sultan named
Mehmed or Muhammad conquered the city). These writings also
betray anxiety among the Muslims over the possibility of a Byzantine invasion along the Syrian seacoast, followed by a sequence of
events culminating in the conquest of Constantinople and the end
of the world as they knew it.[31]

With the arrival in power of the ʿAbbasids in 750, no more
attempts were made to capture Constantinople, which meant that
no strategic efforts were undertaken to eliminate the Byzantine
adversary. For many years, victories and defeats were fairly equally
distributed between the two sides. Well-publicized expeditions,
such as that of the caliph al-Muʿtasim against Amorion in north-
central Antolia in 838, did not alter this balance. Over time, however, Byzantine power consolidated, while the caliphate in Iraq
became fragmented and weak. In the tenth century, the Muslims
found themselves on the defensive, forced to improvise in the face
of looming disaster. Ambitious local commanders came forward,
especially the Hamdanid amir Sayf al-Dawla, who brilliantly reinterpreted the role of ghazi-caliph as that of ghazi-amir, engaging
the best Arabic poets of the time to sing his praises.[32] However,
Sayf al-Dawla proved unable to match his success in public relations with success on the battlefield. Indeed, no one could stop
the Byzantine Empire as it conquered Malatya (Melitene) in 936,
Massisa (Mopsuestia) and Tarsus in 965, and Antakya (Antioch) in
969. Then the Byzantine juggernaut ground to a halt, as the empire sought to consolidate its gains and to contain its new antagonist, the Fatimid caliphate in Egypt. In 1071, the Saljuq Turks
defeated the Byzantines at Manzikert, and drove them out of most

[31] Early Islamic apocalyptic literature has received considerable attention in the
last few years. In relation to these themes of warfare and the fear of a Byzantine
invasion of Syria, see Bashear, "Apocalyptic and Other Materials on Early Muslim-
Byzantine Wars"; David B. Cook, "Muslim Apocalyptic and Jihad"; idem, "The
Apocalyptic Year 200/815–16"; idem, "An Early Muslim Daniel Apocalypse";
Michael Cook, "The Heraclian Dynasty in Muslim Eschatology"; idem, "Eschatology and the Dating of Traditions"; and idem, "An Early Islamic Apocalyptic
Chronicle." Especially important has been the publication in 1991 of the Arabic
text of the eschatological *Kitab al-fitan* by the third/ninth-century writer Nuʿaym
ibn Hammad.
[32] Canard, *Histoire de la dynastie des H'amdânides.*

of Anatolia. The Crusaders arrived in the region in the following generation, another story to be taken up shortly.

The history of the Arab-Byzantine frontier is closely tied to the institution and office of the caliphate. For long periods of time the caliphs did not actually control the frontier zone directly. However, caliphs who had distinguished themselves in the jihad were remembered there long afterward. We see this in an episode that took place in the frontier city of Tarsus, in southern Anatolia, on the eve of its being handed over to the Byzantines under Nicephoras Phocas in 965. During the last Friday prayer, the time arrived for the *khutba*, the sermon in which it was customary to include a prayer for the ruling caliph. The dignitary to whom this task had been assigned refused to act as the last preacher on the *minbar* (pulpit) of Tarsus. Thereupon a man named Abu Dharr, a native of the city, stood up and began to preach, reciting the prayer in the name of the ʿAbbasid caliph al-Muʿtadid (r. 892–902), one of the great ghazi-caliphs, who by this time had been dead for more than six decades: as if Muʿtadid were still alive, or as if there had been no caliph worthy of the name since his death.[33]

The Byzantine onslaught came at a time when the ʿAbbasid caliphate in Baghdad was hopelessly weakened and when the real holders of power in Baghdad showed little interest in these wars. However, the Byzantine-Arab frontier zone had always had a flow of volunteers for military service, arriving above all from the Persian-speaking East. In this crisis of the mid-tenth century, eloquent preachers urged people to make their way through mountains and deserts to volunteer for the fight.[34] At a time when there was no imam able to fulfill the religious obligation of leading the community in its wars against external enemies; and moreover, at a time when the real armies were professional and reduced in size, and recruited largely from alien nations such as the Turks and Daylamis, volunteering for military service became more important than ever, even if it failed utterly in its formal objective of rolling back the Byzantine armies. Tarsus and al-Massisa, the two most important towns of the frontier district, were remembered later on, after their fall, as places where volunteers had gone to

---

[33] Canard, "Quelques observations sur l'introduction géographique de la Bughyat at'-t'alab," esp. 52; Bosworth, "Abu ʿAmr ʿUthman al-Tarsusi's *Siyar al-thughur*, 183–95; Bonner, *Aristocratic Violence*, 155, 176.

[34] Ibn Nubata, *Diwan*, esp. 202–207; M. Canard, *Sayf al Daula*, 167–173.

live in great numbers, supported by pious endowments in their countries of origin.[35]

Frontier Societies: Spain and North Africa

When the ʿAbbasid caliphate in Iraq reached its nadir in the mid-tenth century, Spain and North Africa both had powerful caliphal regimes of their own. We have already seen that in al-Andalus, the powerful regent Ibn Abi ʿAmir (Almanzor; d. 1002), took great pains to appear as a kind of ghazi-caliph, even as he usurped the position of his charge, the weak and hapless caliph Hisham II.[36] This performance, which included a spectacular raid against Compostela and its shrine of Santiago (St. James) in the Christian North in 997, marked the end of the Umayyad caliphate in Spain, which subsequently fragmented into statelets known as *tawaʾif* (factional kingdoms).

Meanwhile the dynasty of the Fatimid caliphs ruled in North Africa from 909, adding Egypt to their dominions in 969. They were Shiʿis of the Sevener or Ismaʿili persuasion, and owed their first rise to power to large tribal armies, Kutama Berbers from the Aurès (in present-day Algeria), inspired by the Ismaʿili religious message and prepared to die for it. Before long, however, the Fatimids found it convenient to counterbalance their Kutama fighters with other, more predictable, and dependable elements. They created militiary units of various kinds, including slave soldier units such as were now to be found nearly everywhere in the Islamic world. Within the military hierarchy, the Kutama found themselves increasingly marginalized.

Nonetheless, the Fatimids—now a settled dynastic power, organized very much along the lines of their predecessors, especially the ʿAbbasid caliphs—made considerable use of the jihad (primarily against Byzantium) in their propaganda as they tried to expand beyond their base of operations in Egypt into Palestine, Syria, and beyond. Their Ismaʿili Shiʿi doctrine favored the jihad, declaring it one of the Seven Foundations of the Faith. (Sunnis recognize only five Pillars of the Faith, and do not include jihad among

[35] Ibn Hawqal, *Surat al-ard*, 184.
[36] See above, p. 112.

them.) However, this call to jihad did not resonate much at the time: after all, the Isma'ilis constituted only an elite minority, and even though the Sunni majority managed to tolerate the rule of the Fatimids—who in their eyes were Isma'ili heretics—it was still not about to volunteer en masse for combat under the leadership of the Isma'ili Fatimid Imam. It is thus not surprising that the Fatimid caliphs presented themselves as utterly civilian figures, rather than as ghazi-caliphs. The sole exception was the charismatic al-Mansur bi-Nasr Allah (r. 946–953), who devoted his brief reign to combat against Abu Yazid, the "man on the donkey," and other Kharijite foes.[37]

The Fatimids first rose to power in central and western North Africa (in 909),[38] but once they conquered Egypt (in 969) their fortunes and interests became tied to Egypt and the eastern Mediterranean. Nonetheless, in western North Africa and the western Mediterranean world, the formation of new Islamic states at the hands of the Berbers had only begun. In the second half of the eleventh century, among the Sanhaja of the Western Sahara, a movement arose that eventually became known as al-Murabitun, the Almoravids. This was a movement of severe Sunni, specifically Maliki reform, even though some aspects of the Almoravids' Islam struck some of their contemporaries as odd. Their first ambitious leader was 'Abdallah Ibn Yasin, who had been educated as a jurist, and who brought his followers together in settlements and led them in battle. Ibn Yasin died in combat in 1058 against the Barghawata of the Far West, a people who still practiced a syncretic religion of their own—which meant that his death could properly be called a martyrdom. Afterward, the leadership passed to Yusuf ibn Tashufin, who led the Almoravids to expansion throughout what later became known as Morocco, and beyond. In 1085 he sent troops to Islamic Spain, where the Christian King Alfonso VI of León and Castile had just captured the ancient capital of Toledo and seemed unstoppable. Here, although the refined Andalusians were reluctant to accept these rustics as their overlords, they had little choice: as one of their kinglets is reported to have said, better to herd camels for Yusuf than swine for Alfonso. The Almoravids soon became masters of Islamic Spain. In all this rapid and remarkable expansion, the

---

[37] Halm, *The Empire of the Mahdi*, 310–337.
[38] See above, p. 110.

Almoravids received impetus from the jihad, both as a motivating force among the tribesmen who fought in their armies, and as a legitimizing element among the civilian populations that found themselves under Almoravid rule, in Spain and elsewhere.[39]

Ribat

One point of controversy regarding the Almoravids has regarded their name, al-Murabitun (those who perform *ribat*). It used to be thought that *ribat* signified primarily a type of building associated with a particular social practice, that is, a Muslim military monastery. In this way, it was thought that Ibn Yasin originally gathered his followers into monastic establishments for an intensive spiritual preparation. In this view, their military activity would have been, to some degree, secondary. Now, however, we know that the meaning of *ribat* is complex and varies according to region and epoch.[40] The word has a complex history, beginning with the Quran, where it means "binding" or "linking together." In general usage, *ribat* comes to denote an activity that is often nearly the same as the activity of jihad itself. And in some cases this ribat does in fact become associated with a certain type of building. Where this happens, the activity of ribat often becomes remote from the conduct of war, and more and more associated with ascetic and mystical practices. To return to the Almoravids, however, their original *ribat* probably did not denote a building or institution, but most likely referred simply to the "bond," the "link" that held them all together: the *Murabitun* were a group of men bound together by a common religious link, which clearly involved both asceticism and warfare.

This question of ribat also comes up with regard to the eastern frontier in Central Asia. There the adversary was nothing like the hard-edged, inflexible Byzantium,[41] nor the strangely violent

[39] Messier, "The Almoravids and Holy War"; H. T. Norris and P. Chalmeta, "al-Murabitun," in *EI²*.

[40] See the *EI²* article "Ribat," by Jacqueline Chabbi. See also the recent work by Christophe Picard and Antoine Borrut described in the "Readings" for this chapter, below, p. 156.

[41] Summed up in the image of a gold coin by Louis Massignon, "Le mirage byzantin dans le miroir bagdadien d'il y a mille ans," esp. 438–440.

Western European Crusaders, but rather the Turks, brilliant warriors and nonmonotheists about whom the Prophet, in a famous hadith, had once supposedly said, "Leave the Turks alone so long as they leave you alone" (*utruku l-atrak ma tarakukum*). As we have seen, the Islamic governments of the Tahirids and Samanids created strings of defensive fortresses against the Turks. We are told of burgeoning ribats along the eastern frontier, garrisoned by a constant influx of volunteers. However, these establishments gradually lost their military purpose as the Turks converted peacefully to Islam. In the early eleventh century, many Turks entered the Islamic world, largely unopposed, and caused some havoc before a new order arose from among the Turks themselves, in the form of the Saljuq sultanate(s), which ruled over much of Iran, Iraq, and Anatolia. Meanwhile, the buildings and establishments along the eastern frontier became devoted to the arts of peace. It was here, in a flowering of Sufism, that the internal, spiritual aspect of jihad was developed and deployed. The study of ribat is thus about more than the derivation or evolution of a word: it is about transformations in social practice.

The Crusades

By now we have seen jihad and ribat involved in the formation of several new Islamic states, always associated with some kind of renewal of religion. One of the most dramatic of all these episodes comes in the confrontation with the Crusades.

By the late eleventh century, western Europeans were known in the Near East and the eastern Mediterranean as seamen and merchants, as mercenaries in the Byzantine imperial service, and as the Norman conquerors of formerly Muslim Sicily. However, the First Crusade caught the Muslims of Anatolia and the Levant by surprise, just as it surprised those Europeans and Byzantines whose territory the Crusaders had already crossed during their long, violent overland trek. As the European Crusaders, or as the Muslims called them, "Franks" (*Ifranj*) proceeded from Anatolia southward into Syria and Palestine, they sowed terror wherever they went. Their siege of Jerusalem culminated, famously, in an orgy of killing in 1099.

The reasons for this extreme violence are beyond us here. However, it is not difficult to see why the populations of Syria and Palestine—Christian and Jewish, as well as Muslim—were unprepared for it. By this time, the Arab-Byzantine wars had receded from memory. After Byzantium's onslaught of the mid-tenth century, northern Syria had become a buffer between the empire and the Fatimid caliphate of Cairo. The Fatimids maintained frequent diplomatic relations with Constantinople and mostly avoided military entanglement.[42] But even an accurate memory of the Arab-Byzantine wars would not have prepared the Syrians and Palestinians for what was coming. Those wars had lasted well over three centuries and involved enormous resources, human, and monetary. They had brought the major regional powers of the time into direct conflict—unlike the Crusades, which had a peripheral character, at least at their beginning. And of course the Arab-Byzantine wars had not been polite, bloodless affairs: many thousands perished in them, and many thousands more were deported or enslaved. Nonetheless, the Arab-Byzantine wars had been conducted within certain limits, at least in retrospect. The Crusaders, with their crazed longing for Jerusalem and their enthusiasm for violence and bloodshed, must have seemed an entirely different type.

This misunderstanding has led some modern specialists to claim that the Muslims during the age of the Crusades never learned to distinguish between Byzantines and Latins (western Europeans).[43] With regard to the modern Western understanding of Islam, this point is not trivial. Some of its implications appear in Bernard Lewis's recent and influential *What Went Wrong*.[44] In this view, the Muslims enjoyed cultural, intellectual, and material superiority over the western Europeans for many centuries. And while Muslim historians and geographers gathered knowledge about what they recognized as the other true civilizations, especially China and India, few of them showed any interest in those

[42] Stern, "An Embassy of the Byzantine Emperor to the Fatimid Caliph al-Muʿizz,"; Marius Canard, "Le cérémonial fatimite et le cérémonial byzantin"; Hamdani, "Byzantine-Fatimid Relations before the Battle of Manzikert."

[43] Gabrieli, "The Arabic Historiography of the Crusades," 98; and Lewis, "The Use by Muslim Historians of Non-Muslim Sources," 181, in Lewis and Holt, eds., *Historians of the Middle East*.

[44] Lewis, *What Went Wrong?*

boggy, frozen, barbaric lands that made up western Europe. Muslim attitudes toward non-Muslims were formed at home, in the Muslim lands, and included both tolerance and a sense of superiority. Thus the Muslims were unprepared, especially from the fifteenth century onward, when the Europeans grew prosperous and powerful and eventually outflanked the principal Muslim power of the time, the Ottoman Empire. Now for years these same Ottomans had adapted European technology and often made better use of it than the Europeans themselves. But in the modern age, the Ottomans failed to keep up. Their vocabulary for understanding the West did not advance far beyond what it had been in the early Middle Ages. Efforts at reform came too late. In this view, the Crusades represent both a first moment of European expansion into the Islamic heartland and, at the same time, a first failure on the part of Islam to recognize its adversary for who he truly was.

Yet many Muslims in the age of the Crusades did come to understand a great deal about Byzantines and Latins and the differences between them.[45] Already at the beginning, the Syrian jurist al-Sulami (d. 1106) tied the catastrophic events of the First Crusade to recent Frankish and Norman successes in Sicily and Spain. Al-Sulami did this in a *Book of Jihad*, one of the most remarkable works ever composed on this subject. God has visited this punishment on the Muslims, al-Sulami wrote, because of their neglect of religious duties, especially the jihad. The problem was political: while the conduct of jihad was the duty of the caliph in Baghdad, the political reality in Syria at the time amounted to a quarreling group of princelings—that is, in those parts of Syria not already occupied by the Crusaders. The Fatimid rulers in Cairo, and the ʿAbbasid caliph and Saljuq sultan in Baghdad, were all unable or unwilling to do their duty. The key, said al-Sulami, was in the "greater jihad" (*al-jihad al-akbar*): through repentance and through fighting their own baser impulses, the Muslims might reconstitute their own strength and, with it, their political leadership.[46] Al-Sulami pointed to the need for two developments, which

[45] Dajani-Shakeel, "A Reassessment of Some Medieval and Modern Perceptions of the Counter-Crusade."

[46] Sivan, "Genèse de la contre-croisade"; idem, *L'Islam et la croisade*; Hillenbrand, *The Crusades*, esp. 104–112.

we have already identified in other contexts. These are, first, the mobilization of what we have called (in chapter 7) fighting or embattled scholars and, second, the rise to power of ghazi-caliphs, or rather, in these circumstances, ghazi-sultans. Remarkably, al-Sulami's treatise on jihad traces the broad outline of what actually happened subsequently, in the long process we often call the Counter-Crusade.

Al-Sulami's first requirement, the mobilization of fighting scholars, emerged in the political chaos just after the First Crusade. They included al-Sulami himself, a fiery preacher, while quite a few other scholars actually took up arms. From a strictly military point of view, their contribution may have been negligible, but from a broader political point of view, it mattered considerably. In particular, legal and religious scholars had a visible role in the first major Muslim victory over the Crusaders, at Balat in 1119. The death in combat of the likes of al-Findalawi and al-Halhuli provided inspiration. They proved to all that now, in the face of enemy invasion, jihad had become *fard 'ayn*, a duty incumbent on each and every individual, in defense of the heartlands of Islam. Meanwhile, new works on the jihad, such as al-Sulami's, were recited on public occasions, together with older ones such as the *Book of Jihad* by 'Abdallah ibn al-Mubarak.[47] New books also appeared on the cities of Palestine and Syria, Jerusalem above all, which now securely occupied its place as the third holy site of Islam, after Mecca and Medina. This emphasis on Jerusalem came partly in response to the Crusaders' searing passion for that city; and here the Muslim writers could recall their own apocalyptic literature, which centuries before had already shown an obsession with an enemy invasion of Syria from outside.[48]

It took longer for a ghazi-sultan to step forward, but eventually this figure dominated the political scene. The stages are familiar. Zangi, the Atabeg of Mosul in Upper Mesopotamia (northern Iraq), reconquered the Crusader stronghold of Edessa in 1144. He died soon afterward, just as the Europeans were responding with the Second Crusade. Zangi's son Nur al-Din emerged as the hero of this encounter and seized control of Damascus, becoming ruler of all Muslim Syria by 1154. Nur al-Din projected an austere image as an ascetic and *mujahid* (participant in the jihad), an image

[47] Above, p. 100.
[48] Above, pp. 131–132.

still visible in inscriptions on monuments throughout the cities of Syria.[49] He cultivated the urban religious classes through patronage, establishing pious foundations for good works. Meanwhile, as strategic stalemate set in between the Crusaders and Nur al-Din, attention shifted to Egypt, where the Fatimid caliphate was in its death throes. A three-way struggle broke out among Egyptians, Syrians, and Crusaders. The victors were the men whom Nur al-Din sent from Syria, and among these it was Salah al-Din, known to the Europeans as Saladin, who won fame by bringing an official end to the rule of the Fatimids in Cairo in 1171. Three years later, when Nur al-Din died, a struggle began over domination of Muslim Syria. Egypt and its vast resources were now also in play. The eventual winner was, of course, Saladin. Only after many years of hard effort was Saladin able to devote himself fully to fighting the Frankish enemy, but when he did this the results came quickly, in the destruction of the Crusader army in July 1187 at Hittin, soon followed by the reconquest of Jerusalem and the greater part of Palestine. The Third Crusade, which arrived from Europe in response, reestablished a foothold for the Crusaders on the coast. However, never again would they control Jerusalem, except for a brief episode following negotiations in 1229 between the Ayyubid Sultan al-Kamil and the Emperor Frederick II. In 1291, the Crusaders finally evacuated Acre, their last major stronghold on the Levantine coast.

Saladin cut a dashing figure, commanding troops in battle and making a highly visible personal effort. Like Nur al-Din before him, he employed a network of religious scholars, poets, and historians who portrayed him as an austere ruler motivated by religion and by the desire to chase away not only the infidel, the Frankish intruder, but the internal enemy, the misguided Muslim, as well. Saladin's positive image went beyond the Islamic world, as is well known. His European adversaries came to consider him the very model of chivalry, and Dante portrayed him "standing off by himself" among the virtuous heathen in Limbo, a placement granted to only two other Muslim figures, the philosophers Ibn Sina (Avicenna) and Ibn Rushd (Averroes).[50]

[49] Tabbaa, "Monuments with a Message"; idem, *Constructions of Power and Piety in Medieval Aleppo.*

[50] *Inferno* 4:129: *E solo in parte vidi il Saladino.*

Saladin's positive image, and the concerted propaganda effort associated with it, have aroused some modern controversy. Andrew Ehrenkreutz has portrayed Saladin as a manipulative, self-seeking politician who spent more time fighting Muslim than Christian adversaries.[51] (Regarding Spain in the previous century, much the same might be said for Rodrígo Díaz, the *Cid* or *Campeador*, a Christian nobleman who spent much of his career in the military service of Muslim patrons).[52] Ehrenkreutz points to Saladin's mismanagement of the economy, especially in Egypt, which had to bear the weight of these endless wars. However, other treatments of Saladin—who has received far more scholarly attention than most figures in medieval Islam—have evaluated him as both politican and commander, and the general consensus has been positive. Despite the disappointment that Saladin himself expressed at the end of his life, his project was an overall success, the culmination of three generations' effort in the Counter-Crusade.

At the heart of this effort was the alliance between the ghazi-sultans and the fighting scholars. The armies themselves did not change much in their composition.[53] Saladin continued to rely on Turkish cavalry of slave origin and on other types of units, while civilian volunteers for the jihad remained marginal, in strictly military terms. The importance of the alliance lay in the cities, where for centuries there had been a loose distribution of power among military elites who were newcomers and outsiders in these urban societies, and civilian elites for whom participation in religious learning had special significance. Zangi, Nur al-Din, and Saladin managed to unite all these in a common purpose. And while they did not substantially alter the urban structures, they did create the basis for a new stability in the military elite, so much so that the combined reign of the Ayyubid dynasty, which began with Saladin in Egypt and Syria, and its continuator and inheritor, the Mamluk sultanate, lasted until 1517. Such political longevity had not been seen since the 'Abbasid caliphate, and presaged even greater political formations such as the Ottoman, Safavid, and Mogul empires.

---

[51] Ehrenkreutz, *Saladin*.
[52] Fletcher, *The Quest for El Cid*.
[53] Gibb, "The Armies of Saladin."

Although the Crusades are sometimes presented as local affairs, of little concern to Muslims in other regions—this is yet another point of controversy—they marked the emergence of Egypt and Syria as a unified center of power and cultural production in the Islamic world. Above all, the Counter-Crusade came together with what is often called the "Sunni revival," combining the ideology of the jihad with a rigorous attitude toward dissident Muslims, which meant mainly Shi'ites; a decrease in tolerance for "unorthodox" expressions of belief and thought, as with the mystic philosopher al-Suhrawardi, whom Saladin executed in 1191; and a narrow application of the principles of dhimma toward the local Christian and Jewish populations.

Muslim Syria and Egypt, which bore the brunt of the fight against the Crusaders, had to face a far more dangerous enemy in the Mongols, who after sacking Baghdad in 1258 and killing the last 'Abbasid caliph, turned their attention to the west. The Syro-Egyptian Mamluk armies defeated the Mongols at 'Ayn Jalut, in Palestine, in 1260, and then fought off repeated incursions over the next decades. In these difficult conditions we see the beginnings of a new interpretation of the jihad, of enormous consequence in later centuries. This comes especially in Ibn Taymiyya (d. 1328), a Syrian scholar of the Hanbali madhhab.

Ibn Taymiyya took part personally in several military campaigns, and was indeed an "embattled scholar" in every sense. He preached the jihad in a variety of writings, including a treatise of public law in which he described jihad as the summation of all virtues and religious duties.[54] For Ibn Taymiyya, however, jihad was largely about the suppression of heretics (which meant Shi'ites of various persuasions); curtailing unorthodox customs, such as the visiting of tombs (which was often done by women); and keeping dhimmis firmly in their place. All this was not simply fanaticism or madness, as some observers, including some of Ibn Taymiyya's own contemporaries, have maintained.[55] In the context of the time—the massive destruction wrought by the Mongols, the loss of huge amounts of territory to them, and the violent death of the last caliph in Baghdad—Ibn Taymiyya was describing a new Islamic polity constructed not so much on Is-

[54] Ibn Taymiyya, *al-Siyasa al-shar'iyya*, 130f.; Heck, "*Jihad* Revisited," 116f.
[55] Little, "Did Ibn Taymiyya Have a Screw Loose?"

lamic governance, but more on "Islamic identity, which [Ibn Taymiyya located] in ritual and communal practice"; a polity defined more ritually than politically.[56]

One point that has made Ibn Taymiyya especially attractive to many modern Muslim radical reformers is his negative attitude toward the rulers of the Ilkhanid Mongol empire of his own day, when these converted to Islam. Like many Sunni jurists, Ibn Taymiyya maintained that it is necessary to support and to tolerate Muslim rulers, even if they commit unjust acts on occasion, since their rule is preferable to anarchy or the rule of unbelievers. However, if a Muslim ruler is proved guilty of a serious crime, or if he hinders the practice of religion, then the situation changes completely: in this case, according to Ibn Taymiyya, the Muslims are obligated to fight him and his tyrannical regime. Consequently, when the Mongol elite of Iran and Iraq converted to Islam, toward the end of the thirteenth century, in Ibn Taymiyya's eyes they were still the same heathens as before, who had just recently come close to destroying all of Islam, still following their reprehensible customs and their non-Islamic, dynastic law (*yasa*). Their rule was Muslim in appearance only; worse, according to Ibn Taymiyya and his disciples, this rule amounted to a new *jahiliyya*, which is to say, the primitive condition of uncouth ignorance that had prevailed in Arabia before Islam. Ibn Taymiyya never condemned the Mamluk amirs and sultans of Egypt and Syria—that is, in his home country—in these terms. He directed his calls to the jihad against outside enemies, Mongols, Crusaders, or others. All the same, Ibn Taymiyya was quite controversial in his day, and spent a good deal of time in prison. In the twentieth century, he became a major authority for those who wished to turn the doctrine of jihad against the state, in the midst of the Islamic world itself, and for whom "Crusader," often paired with "Zionist," has become a current, everyday term of political abuse.

Ottoman Origins

The Ottoman sultanate and empire became the dominant Muslim power in the world, especially after it conquered Constantinople

---

[56] Heck, 117, 120.

in 1453. By many measures, including that of longevity (more than six hundred years) it was a remarkable success. Quite understandably, the question of how it came into existence has received much attention. And here again we find the jihad, or something like it, at the center of controversy.

In Europe and America, much of the argument was spurred by a short monograph, *The Rise of the Ottoman Empire* by the Austrian historian Paul Wittek, that appeared in 1938. Wittek argued against the old Ottoman imperial historiography, which had situated the founding figure Osman (d. ca. 1324) within a tribal genealogy and had linked Osman and his followers directly and organically to the earlier history of the Turks in Central Asia and Anatolia. Instead, Wittek argued that the early Ottomans were utterly devoted to frontier warfare—here known as *ghaza*—for the sake of plunder, territorial expansion, glory, and religion all at once. At that time (around 1300), the other small Anatolian Turkish principalities (*beyliks*) were no different in this way. However, Osman had the advantage of operating in northwest Anatolia, directly facing what remained of the Byzantine empire, a position that enabled him to attract more followers than his rivals. These followers were a motley crew searching for plunder and lands, and in some cases merely seeking a way to make a living; they included many who had crossed over from the Byzantine side. Wittek made much of an inscription in the early Ottoman capital of Bursa, dated to 1339 CE and describing Osman's son, the second Ottoman ruler Orkhan, as "ghazi son of the ghazi" and "marchlord of the horizons" (*marzuban al-afaq*). It was thus, Wittek claimed, an ideology of warfare, and specifically of holy warfare against Christians, that provided the raison d'être of the Ottoman state from its beginning and formed the basis of its identity and cohesion. Afterward, although the Ottomans fought on many other frontiers, they always looked first to their northwest, against the Byzantines and other nations of eastern and central Europe. Thus in 1914, when the empire went to war in alliance with Austria, its traditional enemy, it signed its own political death warrant.[57]

This "ghaza thesis," forever associated with Wittek, implies that the Ottomans were motivated mainly by a single ideological force, and that their empire could be reduced to a single historical

---

[57] Wittek, *The Rise of the Ottoman Empire*.

force or essence. The argument is not far distant from others that have been made regarding Islam itself. At any rate, regarding Ottoman origins, a rich debate has gone on in the last two and a half decades.[58] Halil Inalcik modified the ghaza thesis but maintained it within a broader interpretation of Ottoman history as a whole.[59] Rudi Paul Lindner has argued that Wittek misunderstood the way in which tribes are formed, which is actually a process of political inclusion. Lindner rejected Wittek's view of the early Ottomans as motivated by religious warfare: after all, they often fought side by side with Christian warriors and engaged in activity that might, from a religious point of view, best be described as unorthodox.[60] Colin Imber has pointed out that contemporary Byzantine sources provide no corroboration for the ghaza thesis.[61] Cemal Kafadar has argued that ghaza was an inclusive ideology, different from the formal norms of jihad as expressed by Muslim jurists.[62] Other contributions have appeared and are still appearing. Here we may mention a few themes in the light of what we have already seen in other times and places.

By the time Osman and his followers emerged, there was already a long history of frontier life in Islam, as we have seen. How do we know about this early Ottoman frontier environment in the first place? One type of source that receives attention nowadays is the popular literature of epic poems and tales about Sayyid Battal, Abu Muslim, and other Muslim heroes, poems that have much in common with medieval Christian epics about the Cid, Digenes Akritas, and so on. These epics portray a dashing life of raiding and small-scale conquest, where "religious loyalties are more important than religious beliefs, and ethical, honorable, courageous behavior is more important still."[63] However, despite the popular-

---

[58] Of great importance also has been M. Fuad Köprülü's *Les origines de l'Empire ottoman* (Paris, 1935), now translated by Gary Leiser as *The Origins of the Ottoman Empire*. I do not discuss Köprülü here, because he did not concentrate on the norms and practices of warfare.

[59] Inalcik, "The Question of the Emergence of the Ottoman State."

[60] Lindner, *Nomads and Ottomans in Medieval Anatolia*. Similar arguments regarding religious norms may be found in Jennings, "Some Thoughts on the Gazi-Thesis."

[61] Imber, *The Ottoman Empire*.

[62] Kafadar, *Between Two Worlds*.

[63] Darling, "Contested Territory," esp. 139–140; Kafadar, *Between Two Worlds*, 62–77.

ity of these poems, their value for historical reconstruction remains difficult to pin down. And this turns out to be only the beginning of the difficulties presented by the sources. In fact, the study of Ottoman origins relies mainly on chronicles that were not written down until the fifteenth century, long after the events themselves, and colored heavily by the ideological requirements of the Ottoman court and elite of their own time. All the evidence has thus been open to debate, including the famous inscription at Bursa in honor of Orkhan, the "marchlord of the horizons."

Wittek and some others have thought that this frontier life took place beyond the controls and limits of the settled Islamic states. Turks had been arriving in Anatolia in large numbers at least since the battle of Manzikert in 1071, and they brought with them the practices and beliefs of the old Central Asian frontier. This meant an Islam imbued with mysticism, or Sufism, sometimes involving antinomian practices and retaining some of the shamanistic customs of the Turks before their conversion to Islam. Among such groups as these, the figure of the holy man, the Sufi leader, held enormous authority. For these people along the wide Turco-Byzantine frontier, did the principle of ghaza have to do with this sort of mystical belief and practice, and with veneration for this figure of authority, combined together (perhaps) with actual, physical fighting? Furthermore, if ghaza was indeed a central value for the Turks of Anatolia, to what extent did it constitute a tribal or an urban value? After all, Anatolia around 1300 was not all lawless Wild West: it had cities with elites steeped in the venerable traditions of Islamic law.[64] These cities also harbored groups bound together in ascetic brotherhood (akhis, futuwwa), and perhaps others bound together through petty crime and hooliganism. The practice and ideal of ghaza may have been attractive for precisely such groups as these. Here we find another challenge to Wittek, the idea that the ideals and practices of ghaza may be sought in the crowded cities as much as in the free, open spaces of the frontier.

In all this we see a tension between religious and heroic individualism, on the one hand, and the desire to control this individualism in the name of some greater good, on the other. (The tension is as old as the jihad itself, as we have seen in Albrecht Noth's

[64] Claude Cahen, *La Turquie pré-ottomane*, esp. 148–161, 208–226, 315–320, 329–338.

distinction between "holy struggle" and "holy war.")[65] This greater good may, in turn, correspond to the interests of an "orthodox" settled elite immersed in old Islamic learning and tradition, or else it may correspond to the interests of an Islamic state and its representatives and rulers.[66] And so, when, in the modern debate over Ottoman origins, the ghaza of the early Ottomans and their allies is contrasted with the jihad of the traditional, conservative jurists, we should not take this to mean that jihad must always refer to this more conservative (and defensive) element, because, in larger historical perspective, jihad often does not. (This does not rule out the possibility, however, that people along the early Ottoman frontier did think of jihad that way.) Even more important, we should avoid the essentializing aspect of the "ghaza thesis," which makes the Ottoman empire, and even Islam itself, the historical consequence or expression of a single ideology.

All the same, there is no denying that the Ottoman empire, in its maturity, devoted enormous care and considerable resources to the prosecution of its wars against Christian European adversaries. Some of the Ottoman sultans made much of their personal role as ghazi, most famously Süleyman the Magnificent (r. 1520–1566), who began his reign with campaigns of conquest and then, at the end of his life, chose to die as a martyr, once again on campaign against the European infidels. The Ottomans, more than most Islamic rulers, maintained considerable control over their own jurists and learned classes; their ritualistic annual military campaigns may have had something to do with this. And when, in the fall of 1914, the empire entered the First World War on the side of Germany and Austria, it made a public declaration of jihad against the French, British, and Russian empires, which then ruled over many millions of Muslims in Africa and Asia. Much of the propaganda for this jihad was performed by German diplomats and orientalists, so that it became known as "the jihad made in Germany." In the end, this last Ottoman jihad had little effect on the war and its tragic outcome, but it remains a fascinating topic for study.[67]

[65] See above, p. 14.
[66] Darling, "Contested Territory," 141–145.
[67] See Hagen, "The Prophet Muhammad as an Exemplar in War": idem, *Die Türkei im Ersten Weltkrieg.*

Corsairs in the Mediterranean

Now we turn away from the steppes and the mountains to consider the sea and its place in the jihad. It was Muʿawiya, the founding figure of the Umayyad dynasty, who in the mid-seventh century first created a powerful Arab navy in the Mediterranean, a remarkable achievement for a people who then still had an aversion to ships and the sea. (This may be related to the promise, made in the hadith, that the fighter who dies fighting at sea will receive twice the reward of one who dies fighting on land.) Soon, large Muslim fleets took part in the failed sieges of Constantinople, as well as in more successful campaigns against such countries as Spain and Sicily. However, those who chose to combine a seafaring life with warfare against the enemies of Islam usually devoted themselves to depredation, rather than conquest. For centuries, Muslim raiding vessels set out to strike, unpredictably, against the northern shore of the Mediterranean. They seized all manner of booty, including treasure from churches and above all, human beings destined for the burgeoning slave markets of the Islamic world. However, the enemy could, and often did return the compliment, striking the coasts of the Islamic world, especially the western part, with similar energy and determination. Those Islamic coastlines therefore bristled with ribats, defensive strongholds where volunteers congregated. The tenth-century geographical writer Ibn Hawqal found these places (at least in Sicily) festering with immoral activity.[68] We have no way of knowing if he was right; our point here is simply that these were not sites of naval warfare. The volunteers stood watch on the land, waiting for the enemy to come to them. This does not mean that Islamic lawyers ignored the question of how to conduct warfare at sea.[69] But as the doctrine of jihad developed, it remained resolutely territorial. Sea raiding brought less prestige, on the whole, than did ribat, residing and fighting along the terrestrial frontiers.

In the western Mediterranean, this situation changed after 1492 when the Spanish, having put an end to the political presence of Islam in the peninsula, went on to conquer much of the North

---

[68] Ibn Hawqal, *Surat al-ard*, 121.
[69] V. Christides, "Raid and Trade in the Eastern Mediterranean."

African littoral. In the absence of any organized military defense against the Spanish, Muslim sea raiders took the lead. Two of these, the brothers Uruj and Khayr al-Din Barbarossa, requested the intervention of the Ottoman empire in 1519. The sultan sent troops and named Barbarossa as high commander (*Beylerbey*) in the emerging new state of Algiers. Afterward, at century's end, when peace was signed between the Habsburgs and Ottomans, the Porte sought to bring Algiers under its control by sending governors for three-year terms. These, however, could not rule the country, which remained largely under the control of two local groups: the janissaries, imperial troops sent on a regular basis from Constantinople, and known collectively as the *ojak*; and the captains of the raiding vessels, who had a corporate body of their own known as the *ta'ifat al-ra'is*. Relations between *ojak* and *ta'ifa*, the janissaries and the corsairs, were violent at times, but eventually a kind of alliance emerged between them. For, in the relatively impoverished conditions of Algiers, only the wealthy corsair captains could guarantee at least some of the ojak's needs. The corsair captains, for their part, since they commanded rather motley crews and had to be at sea much of the year, could never displace the more cohesive and better-trained troops of the ojak. Beginning in the 1640s, the ojak stripped the triennial pashas of their power, and by the end of the seventeenth century, they created the new supreme office of the *dey*, who was often one of the corsair captains. In the 1720s, the Algerines went so far as to prevent the Ottoman government from sending or even naming a pasha.[70]

In this way Algiers became a kind of ghazi state, where maritime ghazis—that is, corsairs—had a place within the ruling elite, and where the sea finally achieved the full dignity of an Islamic frontier. The residents of this frontier, who included renegades from Christian Europe, stood apart from the rest of the North African population. However, corsair captains took part in works of urban charity,[71] while much pomp and ceremony marked the comings and goings of the corsair ships. It was such considerations as these that led Fernand Braudel to think of corsair activity (*la course*) as

---

[70] Boyer, "Introduction à une histoire intérieure de la Régence d'Alger"; M. Hoexter, *Endowments, Rulers and Community*, 18–23.

[71] Hoexter, *Endowments, Rulers and Community*.

an urban phenomenon.[72] In the case of Algiers, Braudel saw *la course* as the key to the city's unity and success in commerce as well as in war, the main stimulus to its economy, and even as the element that united the city with its hinterland.[73] Now it certainly makes sense to view *la course* as part of a greater system of exchange: it depended on markets in Livorno as well as in Algiers, and there were plenty of Christian corsairs preying on Muslim coasts and ships, at the same time as the attacks of the Muslim corsairs against the Christians. But there are also reasons for taking a more negative view of the corsairs' economic, and perhaps even ideological importance.[74] In any case, corsair activity in Algiers and its neighbors peaked around the turn of the seventeenth century and then declined steeply. Just before it ended in the early nineteenth century, the young American republic had an episode of conflict with the "Barbary states," which were holding American merchant sailors captive. Here the Americans had the perplexing—and ironic—experience of seeing their (white) countrymen held in slavery, and of being unable for many years to do anything about it.[75]

The Western Sudan

In this chapter we have only been able to consider a limited number of examples of the jihad in the history of Islam before the modern age. We have left out some of the most famous episodes, such as the two sieges of Vienna by the Ottomans in 1529 and 1683. As a final example, however, we may briefly cite an interesting case that carries over into the age of modernity and colonialism, and that brings together several of this chapter's themes.

In question here is a series of movements that took place in the Western Sudan (in today's terms, northern Nigeria and surrounding areas) at the beginning of the nineteenth century, led at first by ʿUthman ibn Fudi (Usuman dan Fodio, 1754–1817) and his son Muhammad Bello (1781–1837). These were men of reli-

---

[72] Braudel, *La Méditerranée et le monde méditerranéen à l'époque de Philippe II*, 2:194.
[73] Ibid., 2:206–207.
[74] Lucette Valensi, *On the Eve of Colonialism*, esp. 47–55.
[75] Allison, *The Crescent Obscured.*

gious learning, originating among the ethnic group of the Fulani (or Fulbe), preachers and authors of works, in Arabic and in the local languages, on jihad, Sufism, and other themes. Their militant activity culminated, in 1804, in an emigration (*hijra*), followed by the defeat of a series of states (the Hausa sultanates) that were already under Muslim rule. They established their capital in the newly founded city of Sokoto, with ʿUthman, and afterward his son Bello, in the role of imam, or "Commander of the Faithful." Many of the fighters under their command were "students," eager to sacrifice themselves for the cause. Similarly, the governors of the amirates under their control were often ʿulamaʾ, men of religious learning. This militant activity went together with a movement of conversion to Islam among non-Muslims, and a movement of reform among those who already professed Islam. Meanwhile, other movements of jihad appeared, allied with or rivals of the Sokoto movement; all of them aimed to purify the local Islam from the syncretic practices that were typical of it.

Later on, the Sokoto caliphate, as it is called today, provided the basis for yet another movement of conquest and jihad, even more ambitious in scope, with the activity of another charismatic man of religious learning, Hajj ʿUmar Tal (1797–1864). Hajj ʿUmar sought to establish a new state along the entire extent of the Western Sudan, beyond any particular ethnic identification, while imposing the doctrine and practice of his mystical confraternity of the Tijaniyya *tariqa*. The result was the multiethnic state known as the Torodbe empire, which included, at its apogee, all the territory from Gidimaka to Timbuktu, and from Dinguiraye as far as the Sahara.[76] This state, which exerted only loose control over its own territory, did not survive long after the death of its founder. For now the Europeans were encroaching, especially the French from the coast of Senegambia. The main result of the Torodbe empire, like that of its predecessor, the Sokoto caliphate, was that Islam became rooted more deeply and widely in West Africa than it had been previously.[77]

[76] M. Ly-Tall, in Ade Ajayi (ed.), *Africa in the Nineteenth Century until the 1880s*, 620.

[77] Ade Ajayi (ed.), *Africa in the Nineteenth Century until the 1880s*, esp. A. Batran, "The Nineteenth-Century Islamic Revolutions in West Africa," 537–554; M. Last, "The Sokoto Caliphate and Borno," 555–599; "Massina and the Torodbe (Tukuloor) Empire until 1878," 600–635. See also *EI²* s.v. "ʿUthman b. Fudi" (D. M.

Empires, Armies, and Frontiers: Conclusions

Now we may remind ourselves once again of the beginning of Islam, which saw a transformation of individual consciousness, an awareness of moral responsibility within a tightly bound community, and then a duty and desire to fight in the path of the God who had made all these things happen. This chapter has presented a sample of the contexts in which this creative combination has been reexperienced within the political and military history of Islam. The variety of these contexts is considerable: so, for instance, the ghaza of the Turks in Anatolia at the turn of the fourteenth century had a certain amount in common with the ribat of the Almoravids some two centuries previously in North Africa and less in common, on the whole, with the jihad of the Counter-Crusade in Syria, which had formed the basis of an alliance among urban elites, civilian jurists, and military commanders. Thus, while these different historical episodes have all been processes of state formation, they have not been mere reenactments or replayings of a single, original scenario. They differ from the first experience—the rise of Islam—in several ways, which include the ever-increasing weight, as a historical factor, of the doctrine of jihad itself.

The elements of this doctrine of jihad are already present in the Quran, as well as in the early texts of sira, maghazi, and hadith (chapters 2 and 3). Jihad was also fundamentally important in the early wars of conquest, starting in the 630s (chapter 4) and during the Umayyad dynasty (661–750; see beginning of this chapter). Nonetheless, the doctrine and practice of jihad took more time to emerge than is usually imagined. It was not until the end of the eighth century that it emerged in plain view as an ideological tool of first importance and, at the same time as, in Linda Darling's phrase, a piece of "contested territory." Various groups then sought to associate themselves with the jihad, and to use it to advance their own positions. These included the governing elites, beginning with the ʿAbbasid caliphs who invented the role of the ghazi-caliph, which is to say, the ruler devoted to the performance, in his own person, of jihad. Meanwhile, other groups laid claim

---

Last), "Muhammad Bello" (J. O. Hunwick), "ʿUmar b. Saʿid b. ʿUthman Tal" (J. C. Froelich).

to this contested territory, including the many men of religious learning who moved physically to the frontiers.

The jihad in all its vicissitudes, and in all the practices associated with it (ribat, ghazw, ghaza, and so on), has always featured a certain number of protagonists. Naturally, it has often been possible for a single actor to play two or even more of these roles at the same time.

The first of these is the tribal warrior, who for us is usually rather faceless as an individual. Here, in what we might call tribal jihad, the original scenario of Islam in Arabia comes closest to reenactment. This is what Ibn Khaldun had in mind when he discussed the unifying power of religious teaching among the people of the desert. A message of Islamic reform, or even of conversion to Islam itself, galvanizes nomadic or semi-nomadic peoples and turns them into an irresistible fighting force; they conquer towns, upend states, and establish a new political formation, or as Ibn Khaldun would have said, a dynasty. However, their zeal does not last long; within the armies they are soon set aside in favor of more reliable, though more cumbersome units of regular soldiers.

The second protagonist is the ruler: first the imam/caliph, and then various independent governors (amirs), sultans, and others. It was the Umayyad caliphs who, at the beginning, went the farthest with an imperial ideal of jihad, no doubt because in their day the doctrine of jihad was still unformed and being worked out, and also because, in a very general way, basic questions regarding who held authority in matters of law and religious doctrine remained unresolved. After the Umayyads, the ʿAbbasids reinterpreted this imperial ideal of jihad through the character of ghazi-caliph, which then reappeared in many forms and guises throughout the history of Islam. The usual tendency of this kind of "ruler's jihad" is to provide legitimation for the holders of power and for the existing structures of government.

The third protagonist is the scholar, in the widest sense. Ever since the full emergence of the jihad in the later eighth century, this protagonist has been the essential, unavoidable element in every conceivable environment of jihad and in every possible state-building enterprise that seeks to use jihad as an ideology. The jihad of the scholars provides a wide range of options, as we have seen in the previous chapter. These include the actual performance of warfare; the study of the norms of warfare and the doctrine of jihad; the reenactment of various idealized versions of the earliest Islamic community and its wars; the performance of the internalized "greater jihad," involving ascetic and mystical practices; and all sorts of preaching and advising. Though it may seem rigid to outsiders, this scholarly jihad is actually quite flexible and creative. More than the tribal and imperial jihad—which can never exist without it— this jihad of the scholars and jurists has long provided models of conduct and inspiration to entire communities and nations.

The fourth and most important protagonist of the jihad is the volunteer, known as *mujahid, murabit, ghazi, mutatawwiʿ*, and several other titles. Of course, this role constantly overlaps with the other three (tribesman, ruler, scholar). But it also applies to countless obscure people who devoted themselves to these practices, undergoing suffering and, in many cases, death. The purity of their effort, their doing what they were not strictly required to do, their abandonment of their usual roles in life, their long travels, their desire to please God and, in some cases, to achieve mystical encounter with Him: all these things made them marginal, even outcasts within their own societies. Many of them were literally outsiders, like the ghazi volunteers who flocked to the frontiers, and the sailors and fighters on the corsair ships. And many performers of jihad were involved just as much in ascetic and mystical practice, in juridical studies, and in other peaceful pursuits, as they were in actual fighting; meanwhile other, more stable groups bore the brunt of the actual work of warfare. Though it may seem a paradoxical way to achieve state formation, this is the way that things often went. These performers of jihad, these outsiders and volunteers, are at the heart of this ever-recurring, state-forming enterprise of the jihad. They are the reason why this chapter has presented the jihad and its origins as a connected series of frontier societies.

Readings

The footnotes to this chapter and the general bibliography indicate some of the basic readings for the many areas and episodes mentioned in this chapter. Regarding Islamic frontier societies, much of the best work so far has been on the two extremes of the medieval Islamic world, India and Spain. However, it is important to mention the book by Andrew C. Hess, *The Forgotten Frontier: A History of the Sixteenth-century Ibero-African Frontier* (Chicago:

University of Chicago Press, 1978), which presents the shared historical space of the western Mediterranean as irrevocably split along ideological and religious lines between Muslims and Christian Europeans. Hess argues against the "Mediterranean" approach, forever associated with Fernand Braudel and more recently taken up by other historians,[78] which emphasizes the historical processes and geographical constraints which the Muslims of North Africa and the Near East, together with their western European neighbors, all had in common.

For more recent comparative perspectives, see the collections of essays in Robert Bartlett and Angus MacKay (eds.), *Medieval Frontier Societies* (Oxford and New York: Oxford University Press, 1989); Daniel Power and Naomi Standen (eds.), *Frontiers in Question* (New York: St. Martin's Press, 1999); and David Abulafia and Nora Berend (eds.), *Medieval Frontiers: Concepts and Practices* (Aldershot: Ashgate, 2002). The article by Linda Darling, "Contested Territory: Ottoman Holy War in Comparative Context" (*Studia Islamica* 91 [2000]: 133–163), evaluates modern studies of various Islamic societies and historical contexts, in addition to the much-contested problem of Ottoman origins. The "volunteers" for the jihad are dealt with in work appearing now by Deborah Tor on the eastern frontiers of the early Islamic world. For the all-important Byzantine frontier district, see my recent *Arab-Byzantine Relations in Early Islamic Times* (Aldeshot: Ashgate, 2004) and the bibliography there.

Furthermore, see Christophe Picard and Antoine Borrut, "*Râbata, Ribât, Râbita*: une institution à reconsidérer," in N. Proureau and Ph. Sénac, eds., *Chrétiens et musulmans en Méditerranée médiévale (VIIIe–XIIIe siècle). Échanges et contacts* (Poitiers: Université de Poitiers, Centre d'Etudes Supérieures de Civilisations Médiévales, 2003), 33–65; and Christophe Picard, "Regards croisés sur l'élaboration du jihad entre Occident et Orient musulman (VIIIe–XIIe siècle)," in D. Baloup and Ph. Josserand, eds., *Regards croisés sur la guerre sainte. Guerre, religion et idéologie dans l'espace méditerranéen latin (XIe–XIIIe siècle)* (Toulouse: CNRS–Université de Toulouse-Le Mirail, Collection Méridiennes, Série Études Médiévales Ibériques, 2006), 33–65.

---

[78] Braudel, *La Méditerranée*; Purcell and Horden, *The Corrupting Sea*; Wansbrough, *Lingua Franca in the Mediterranean*.

CHAPTER NINE

Colonial Empire, Modern State, New Jihad

This chapter does not offer a comprehensive outline or summary of jihad in the modern and contemporary world. This topic is vast and has been discussed in several recent books, some of which are mentioned in the notes to this chapter and the readings section at the end of this chapter. Here I wish to present a few themes for special emphasis, especially regarding continuity—or lack of it—with what has gone before.

Resistance and Reform

The encounter between the Islamic world and western Europe came to a turning point in 1798, when Napoleon arrived with his army in Egypt. Soon afterward, much of the Islamic world experienced multiple shocks from Europe's military, political, industrial, and financial strength. Most traumatical of all, the Europeans themselves arrived in force in several Muslim countries and seized direct or indirect control. Enormous changes followed in demography, politics, economic and cultural life, and just about everything else.

Jihad had a role in the first responses to this colonial domination. These were often attempts to build new structures within societies that were still relatively free of the invaders' influence, conforming to patterns that we have seen, in the previous chapter, in the premodern history of Islam. An example is the resistance to the French after their arrival in Algeria in 1830. At first the French only held the coastal cities, while an alliance of forces in the hinterland came together under the young amir ʿAbd al-Qadir (1808–1883). This alliance was built largely out of the networks of mystical brotherhoods (turuq; sing. tariqa), especially the Qadiriyya to which ʿAbd al-Qadir himself belonged. In his attempt to build a political and military organization capable of standing up to the French, ʿAbd al-Qadir sought an unaccustomed degree of central control. This brought him into conflict with the turuq as well as with other interests and groups who preferred to have a mediating figure between themselves and the central state. ʿAbd al-Qadir sought to overcome these obstacles through a rigorous, shariʿa-based Islam. He requested fatwas from respected religious authorities, especially around two questions: When Muslims fall under the rule of unbelievers—as had happened long before in Sicily and Spain—must they emigrate to the Abode of Islam? And are those who collaborate with the enemy to be considered wayward Muslims, or else apostates whose lives and property are forfeit? Meanwhile, the French abandoned their policy of occupation restreinte in 1839 and drove ʿAbd al-Qadir into exile in Morocco. He surrendered definitively in 1847.

In the same years, Russian advances in the Caucasus also provoked resistance involving the jihad. Here the charismatic Shamil (1796–1871) became recognized as Imam of Daghestan in 1834. As in Algeria, mystical brotherhoods, this time deriving from the Naqshbandiyya, provided basic networks of organization. Shamil established a rudimentary state structure in Daghestan, with support and participation from neighboring Chechnya. He mounted fierce resistance to the Russians, helped of course by the mountainous terrain, but also by the self-sacrificing determination of his mystic disciples (murids). Shamil, who had studied Arabic and the Islamic sciences in his youth, sought—like ʿAbd al-Qadir in Algeria—to impose a shariʿa-based Islam on his countrymen. The Russian empire devoted considerable resources to fighting him. Eventually Shamil surrendered and went into captivity in Russia.[1]

---

[1] For discussion of Shamil and the murids or "myuridi," see A.L. Knysh, *Islamic Mysticism*, 289–300; idem, *EI²* s.v. "Shamil."

Otherwise, perhaps the most successful example of resistance built on networks of religious brotherhoods was that of the Sanusiyya in Libya. For the most part, however, such efforts were doomed. The encounter with the Europeans proved devastating to the older structures of these Islamic societies, including their land-holding patterns and their elites.

Egypt remained free of direct foreign control until 1882, when the British bombarded Alexandria and invaded the country. For a brief time, resistance centered on Ahmad ʿUrabi (1841–1911), a leader of army officers and, at the time, minister of war in the government of the Khedive. During that moment, jihad was pro-claimed in journals and pamphlets and preached in mosques. ʿUrabi was described as "the leader of the *mujahidun*" who "has sold himself and his army to the jihad in the path of God, not caring about hardship and fatigue." Believers were called on to fight or to give financial support. However, the effort soon came to naught. In the following generations in Egypt, religious resistance remained local where it existed at all. And when, beginning in 1919, the Egyptians mounted effective resistance against the Brit-ish, it was through a secular, nationalist ideology.[2] A similar pattern prevailed in several other Islamic countries under Western domi-nation in these years.

Meanwhile, thinkers in several countries began to take a new look at the jihad, as they contemplated the place of Islam, and especially of Islamic law, within their societies. In India under Brit-ish rule, where Muslims constituted a large minority, several re-formers, of whom the most famous was Sayyid Ahmad Khan, re-vised the classic doctrine. Jihad, they said, could only be allowed in cases of outright oppression, or of obstruction of the practice of the faith. Since the British guaranteed religious liberty, Indian Muslims were under no obligation to rebel against them. For Say-yid Ahmad, the goal was a modern or modernizing Islam. Why had the Muslims fallen behind? The basis for progress and moder-nity had already been present in the earliest Islam: indeed, Euro-peans in the Middle Ages had borrowed heavily from the Muslims as they developed their own science and technology. However, centuries of decline had caused the Muslims to neglect their own

---

[2] Peters, *Islam and Colonialism*, 75–84; on ʿUrabi, see Juan Cole, *Colonialism and Revolution in the Middle East*.

heritage, which they now needed to borrow back again.³ If jihad had any role in all this, it was a liberal version of the old "internal" jihad: the Muslims must strive to achieve, or to recover, their own authentic modernity.

Meanwhile the jihad presented another problem. Europeans often said that it provided proof for the "violence" and "fanaticism" of Islam. The orientalists were especially fond of this kind of argument, since they often tended to see the doctrines and norms which they located in classical texts as the determinants of day-to-day behavior in Muslim societies. The reformers made a spirited defense against these charges. At the same time, the movement of modernist reform was greater than this: jihad was only one of its concerns, and far from the most important.

Beginning in the later nineteenth century, a body of juridical (and in some cases, apologetical) work emerged which defined the jihad as defensive warfare. This had good precedents in the classical juridical literature. For instance, when al-Shafi'i (d. 820; see chapter 7) dealt with the obligation of fighting, he saw this as a question of defending the Islamic lands against invasion and "keeping the frontiers of the Muslims blocked with men" (sadd atraf al-muslimin bil-rijal). On the other hand, there is no denying that the classical legal literature as a whole recognized offensive as well as defensive warfare. There is also no denying that Islamic states, such as the caliphate of the Umayyads and 'Abbasids (from the seventh to the tenth centuries) and the Ottoman empire (from the fourteenth century onward), regularly sent raiding expeditions into non-Muslim territory, in addition to the large-scale expeditions of conquest that they undertook from time to time. In other words, the historical experience of premodern Islamic states, together with the pronouncements of many classical Islamic jurists, would all tend to undermine this modern view of jihad as being preeminently defensive in character.

The modern jurists who made jihad into a defensive doctrine used considerable skill in handling the verses of the Quran relating to warfare and jihad (see chapter 2). They placed emphasis on the verses that call for peacemaking,⁴ and carefully contextualized the

³ Devji, Muslim Nationalism.

⁴ For instance, 8:61 (Anfal): "But if they incline to make peace, then incline to it also, and trust in God." See Peters, Islam and Colonialism, 128–129, and Fire-

more warlike verses, such as the famous "sword verse."[5] They paid less attention to the distinctions among the madhhabs (schools of law), and to the doctrine of abrogation (chapter 2), and looked more for the general ethical implications of the rules.[6] After all, what was at stake was not only the status of Islamic states as interlocutors in international relations, but also the place of the shariʿa itself within modern Islamic societies—something the domination of the European colonial powers had called deeply into question.

One achievement in this trend of thought was the elaboration of a doctrine of international law, an "Islamic law of nations," where the eighth-century jurist Muhammad al-Shaybani, author of a famous book on *siyar*, was presented as a figure similar to the seventeenth-century European jurist Hugo Grotius.[7] Even if this new doctrine had a problematic relationship to the earlier, classical Islamic doctrine, it had the important result of placing the relations of Islamic states with non-Islamic states firmly on a basis of peace. No longer is war the normal condition, interrupted—at the discretion of the Muslim authorities—only by truce or conquest. Instead the prevailing condition is peace, interrupted only by invasion or some other violation of sovereignty. In this way, the state acquired an importance that it had never held in classical Islamic law.

Fundamentalism and Islamism

This recognition of the secular state angered certain other Muslim thinkers, whom we often call fundamentalists but whom it might be better to refer to as "Islamists"[8] or, following some observers, the "Islamic radicals." These thinkers, who included the Egyptians Hasan al-Banna' (1906–1949) and Sayyid Qutb (1906–1966) and

---

stone, *Jihad: The Origin of Holy War in Islam*, throughout, for detailed discussion of the verses in question.

[5] 9:5 (*Tawba*): "But when the Sacred Months have passed, then kill and capture the infidels wherever you find them. Lie in wait for them with every strategem. But if they repent, and establish the prayers and pay the alms-tax, then let them go; for God is forgiving and merciful."

[6] Peters, *Islam and Colonialism*, 112f.

[7] Ibid.; Khadduri, *The Islamic Law of Nations*.

[8] See the discussion in Roy, *L'Islam mondialisé*, translated as *Globalized Islam*.

the Indian-Pakistani Abu ʿAlaʾ Mawlana Mawdudi (1903–1979), had preeminently political projects. They also wrote a fair amount about the jihad, within a compelling and original analysis of the dilemma of Islam in the modern world.

This analysis began with a picture of gloom. The true Islamic society, which existed in Medina at the time of the Prophet, has vanished. Most people who call themselves Muslims actually worship false values and ideals. Instead of the rule of God, they have instituted the rule of man. In this analysis, some of the radicals began to look—as they still do today—to the medieval jurist Ibn Taymiyya,[9] who had come to similarly dark conclusions about his own time. In Ibn Taymiyya's day, the Mongol rulers of Iran and Iraq had converted to Islam, but (he said) they still followed their old customs and dynastic law. Worse, they had infected their neighbors, the Mamluk rulers of Syria and Egypt, with their habits. Muslims must reject such un-Islamic rulers, whether they be Mongols in the late thirteenth century, or Gamal Abdel Nasser in the mid-twentieth. It was Sayyid Qutb who insisted forcefully and eloquently on the idea that a society that accepts such rulers and such customs is living in uncouth ignorance, or *jahiliyya*: this is the Quranic term for Arabia before Islam, the society that rejected the divine Revelation when it arrived through the prophethood of Muhammad. Thus for Sayyid Qutb and those who think like him, the so-called Islamic society actually lives in a condition of *jahiliyya*. Most of its so-called Muslims are in reality infidels who must be opposed. Qutb and his followers accordingly summoned to the jihad, which some of them described as an obligation pressing on each individual (*fard ʿala l-ʿayn*), rather than a general obligation (*fard ʿala l-kifaya*; see chapter 7), because of the gravity of the situation. Unlike the modernist reformers, they had few qualms about "offensive" jihad, even though the organizations to which they belonged, notably the Muslim Brethren in Egypt, were actually far less violent than some of the groups that have emerged in recent years.

After several years in Abdel Nasser's jails, Sayyid Qutb was hanged in 1966. Not long afterward, clandestine groups formed in Egypt, with such names as *Takfir wa-hijra* (identifying [adversaries] as infidels and emigrating) and Islamic Jihad. The new radicals

[9] See above, pp. 143–144.

produced books and pamphlets, including Muhammad ʿAbd al-Salam Faraj's *The Neglected Duty* (referring to the obligation of jihad).[10] They went farther than Ibn Taymiyya or Sayyid Qutb had done in preaching violence against Muslim political adversaries. In October 1981, one of them gunned down President Anwar Sadat, shouting "I have killed Pharaoh"—Pharaoh being the Quranic archetype of the tyrant. The following years saw an internal war between these Islamist radicals and the Egyptian state under President Hosni Mubarak. Eventually Mubarak won out, driving the radicals abroad or else deep underground.

Radical, political Islam also emerged in other countries, and has been discussed in a number of good books. Here I can only make a few observations. To begin with, many Islamist groups have devoted considerable efforts toward feeding and clothing the poor, providing medical care, and building networks of support in urban environments where the state has failed. Even though these efforts have received less attention than the many acts of violence that have taken place, they have much to do with the enduring success of some of these radical Islamist movements. Hamas in cramped, needy Gaza, is a good case in point.

Meanwhile, Mubarak's success against the radicals in Egypt has parallels in other countries. However, this triumph may have a certain pyrrhic quality. What is certain, in any case, is that the Islamist fighters have gone international and global. We see this in Usama bin Laden's fatwas of 1996 and 1998. Here, the war against the corrupt regimes in Egypt, Saudi Arabia, and other countries must be set aside and resumed later on. What matters now is for all to come together and to fight against the common enemy. This enemy is identified, as before, as a "Crusader-Zionist" alliance, but its leader, the United States of America, has now been singled out for special attention. As the jihad, in this new version, goes global, it seems bereft of its familiar contexts and objectives. Its organizers proclaim grand political projects involving the restoration of the universal caliphate. However, these projects are vague and postponed until some remote time in the future. This lack of concern with concrete political goals does not actually seem to matter greatly. Instead it is the acts of violent terrorism, described in the classical language of martyrdom but

---

[10] Full discussion in Jansen, *The Neglected Duty.*

translated into the idiom of mass culture and conveyed through the international media, that attract attention and arouse passions throughout the world.

The warriors of the new jihad are often young people who, like many of their Christian fundamentalist counterparts, begin with little knowledge of their religion's holy texts. On the level of individual psychology, some of them appear trapped, not only by their poor prospects in life, and by the enemy whom they fight, but also by existence itself. "I accept the name of terrorist if it is used to mean that I terrorize a one-sided system of iniquitous power and a perversity that comes in many forms. . . . My fight will only end in my death or in my madness."[11]

The violent radicals are a small minority, widely condemned within the Islamic world. Nonetheless, the spectacle of their violence has considerable resonance. The difficulties of minority Muslim populations, the oppression in Palestine, Chechnya, and elsewhere—all these sufferings become revealed and magnified in the murder of noncombatant civilians and in the destruction of buildings, monuments, and transportation networks. The violent drama conveys the message that all is not well, that merely reestablishing a balance will not suffice, that prosperity and civilization may have no endpoint other than destruction and ruins. "The great Blast overtook the Oppressors, and then morning found them lying prostrate in their homes, as if they had never lived and flourished there."[12]

The violence of these groups has included the introduction of violence against the self, especially in the suicide bombings that are now taking place throughout the world. We have seen (chapter 5) that these have little basis in older Islamic practice and doctrine, especially in the Sunni world. But now, under the label of "martyrdom operations," they have become a central fact, presenting a deep quandary not only to non-Muslim societies and governments but also to governments and to "establishment" religious authorities within the Islamic world itself.[13]

---

[11] Autobiographical statement by Kamel Daoudi, arrested on suspicion of plotting to blow up the U.S. embassy in Paris. *New York Times*, September 21, 2002.

[12] Quran 11:67–68 (*Hud*).

[13] See David Cook, "Suicide Attacks or 'Martyrdom Operations' in Contemporary *Jihad* Literature"; idem, "The Implications of Martyrdom Operations for

In the West, it has long been a commonplace that the way to address the "causes of terrorism" is to offer opportunities to young people for employment and advancement, by integrating their countries into the world economy. These are certainly worthy goals that must be pursued at all levels. However, even if these goals could be met, it is doubtful whether they would lead to a quick resolution of the problem of the new jihad. Intercultural and interfaith dialogue with liberal reformers in the Islamic world, though productive and praiseworthy, is also an activity for the long term. Yet now we also know that the aggressive approach—declaring open war on terrorism and occupying the territory of states that one accuses of involvement in it—simply does not work. We need to find a new political and cultural basis for rapprochement. The jihad is now the terrorists' main ideological weapon. Yet there is nothing in its long history that dooms us to repeated violence and failure. The history of the jihad has constantly involved the revival of older idioms and forms, but at the same time, it has always been a history of new political structures and of creative, new solutions.

Readings

In addition to the books mentioned at the beginning of the introduction to this book and in the notes to this chapter, Emmanuel Sivan, *Radical Islam: Medieval Theology and Modern Politics*, 2nd ed. (New Haven: Yale University Press, 1990), provides insight into the modern radicals' thought. Discussions of the Egyptian radicals of the 1980s include Gilles Kepel, *Muslim Extremism in Egypt: The Prophet and Pharaoh* (London, Berkeley, and Los Angeles: University of California Press, 1985); and Johannes J. G. Jansen, *The Neglected Duty: The Creed of Sadat's Assassins and Islamic Resurgence in the Middle East* (New York: Macmillan, 1986). For Algeria, one may begin with Séverine Labat, *Les islamistes algériens* (Paris: Le Seuil, 1995); and Luis Martinez, *La guerre civile en Algérie* (Paris: Karthala, 1998), translated as *The Algerian Civil War, 1990–1998* (London: Hurst, 2000). See also Ahmed Rashid, *Taliban: Militant*

Contemporary Islam"; idem, *Understanding Jihad*, 142–47; Bernard Freamon, "Martyrdom, Suicide and the Islamic Law of War."

Islam, Oil and Fundamentalism in Central Asia (New Haven: Yale University Press, 2000); Olivier Roy, *The Failure of Political Islam* (Cambridge: Harvard University Press, 1994); and Oliver Roy, *Globalized Islam: The Search for a New Ummah* (New York: Columbia University Press, 2004). On bin Laden and al-Qaʿida, see Peter L. Bergen, *Holy War, Inc.: Inside the Secret World of Osama bin Laden* (New York: Free Press, 2002).

Among more recent publications, of special interest is Fawaz Gerges, *The Far Enemy: Why Jihad Went Global* (Cambridge: Cambridge University Press, 2005). Raymond Ibrahim, *The Al Qaeda Reader* (New York: Doubleday Broadway, 2007), is a sourcebook of translated texts. Some recent books explore the apparent paradox—which I maintain is not a paradox at all—of the connection between charitable activity and jihad in contemporary settings. These include J. Millard Burr and Robert O. Collins, *Alms for Jihad: Charity and Terrorism in the Islamic World* (Cambridge: Cambridge University Press, 2006); and Matthew Levitt, *Hamas: Politics, Charity and Terrorism in the Service of Jihad* (Washington, DC: Washington Institute for Near East Policy, 2006).

CHAPTER TEN

Conclusions

The origins of jihad extend over the entire span of Islamic history, beginning with the nomads and semi-nomads of Arabia before Islam. Warfare and depredation loomed large in their life. They also had a style of leadership based on violence, on the waste of already-scarce resources, and on egotistical boasting: in short, on what the Quran and early Islam condemned as *jahiliyya*, "uncouthness" and "coarse ignorance."

The Quran brought about a transformation of Arabian society, in part by prohibiting this sort of violence and waste. It did not condemn wealth or social inequality: "We have raised some of [mankind] over others by degrees [ranks], so that some of them command service from others."[1] However, while the Quran allowed competition, it made sure that this competition would be channeled through the practices of generosity and almsgiving (chapter 2). Reciprocity and solidarity are thus the governing principles of Quranic economics: the individual believer imitates God by giving freely without expecting that he will get back whatever he gives; in this way, the community works as a structure of exchange.

In other parts of the Quran, as well as in that part of Muhammad's biography that is associated with Medina and the maghazi (military campaigns), we find that depredation and warfare, those activities of which the men of the *jahiliyya* used to be so fond, are

[1] Quran 43:32 (*Zukhruf*).

now allowed to reenter the community. From now on, however, these activities are directed outward, against the enemies of the community and of God. Most importantly, even if the nomadic mode of life here receives a reprieve, through the reinstatement of raiding and fighting, it is now deprived of its characteristic style of leadership. The leader of the group is no longer the one who manages to distribute the most booty among his followers, nor is it a man who destroys his own wealth in such a way as to overawe and humiliate his competitors.[2] Instead, the leader (*imam*) must be chosen on the basis of a principle of religion and piety. Meanwhile, the Quran and the Tradition promise a divine reward to the fighter: this provides him with incentive and motivation to struggle valiantly, on his own as an individual.

The brilliant early military successes of Islam led to the founding of a conquest society, which in turn provided a basis for the classical fiscal regime, as well as for the treatment of non-Muslims under the rule of Islam (chapter 6). Before long, however, the expansionist empire broke down and with it, the conquest society that would henceforth exist only as a fantasy or an ideal. It was in the period of adjustment to these new circumstances, in the later eighth century, that the jihad emerged as a recognizable doctrine and set of practices. This happened first along the Arab-Byzantine frontier, and probably also along the frontiers of Central Asia. Jihad then took root within a long, interlocking series of Islamic frontier societies, of which we have seen a representative sample in chapters 7 and 8.

Throughout this time and afterward, the jihad remained closely connected to that part of the original Islamic message that we usually, and somewhat misleadingly, refer to as "charity." In the Quran, and also in the early narrative texts of sira and maghazi, fighting in the wars is a matter of identity and belonging. It is not something for which one receives payment (here, as in pre-Islamic Arabia, the notions of payment for service and wage often cannot be distinguished from the notions of corruption and bribe.) Meanwhile, however, soon after the death of the Prophet Muhammad, the victorious early Islamic state suddenly found itself inundated with all sorts of wealth. At the same time, it had to confront the

---

[2] On this practice, see Bonner, "Poverty and Charity in the Rise of Islam," 19–21.

large-scale problems that confront all great empires, including the recruiting, paying, and supplying of its armies. As the Umayyad and then the ʿAbbasid caliphal regimes tried various solutions to their fiscal and military problems, the juridical and theological doctrines of nascent Islam slowly emerged. The "school" (or perhaps merely the local trend) of Medina, in its relative isolation, continued, somewhat longer than the others, to construct solutions to these problems in more Quranic terms, that is to say, by thinking in terms of gifts to fighters rather than payments to soldiers. Elsewhere, however, other scholars began to think differently. Is military service a religious obligation incumbent on each individual? How can the central authority (in the jurists' terms, the imam and his representatives) recruit large numbers of fighters and keep them supplied and equipped? Eventually these questions, and their answers, took the characteristic forms of classical Islam and its doctrine of jihad, including the distinction between individual and collective obligation; the insistence on religiously correct intention on the part of the person performing jihad; the insistence on the supervision of the imam or his representative, especially in offensive warfare; but also, at the same time, the emphasis on the spiritual reward in store for individuals who volunteer for combat. Again, all this was the result of a long process, and many of the underlying tensions were never completely resolved.

In this book, we have not devoted a chapter to the "internal jihad"—the "greater jihad" or "jihad against the self." Modern Western scholarship has often described this as a later, secondary or derivative phenomenon, as something that developed after the early jihad, which was supposedly all about fighting and motivating people to fight. Within the history of the doctrine, it is indeed true that the quarrel over a "greater" and a "lesser" jihad was a relatively late development. Nonetheless, the jihad from its earliest beginnings always included both a struggle against external adversaries and an internal struggle. This dual character began in the shared monotheist heritage, evident in the notions of martyrdom and of maghazi in the sense of "spiritual struggle" (chapter 5). Of course, the earliest Islam put a different emphasis on these notions of martyrdom and struggle, by associating them with combat and war. Nonetheless, the connection with the earlier monotheist traditions is there, though we may never understand it completely.

Afterward, beginning in the Arab-Byzantine frontier in the later eighth century, residence along the frontiers of Islam became a popular activity among men of learning, who are often known to us by name, as well as among throngs of nameless "volunteers." Here, we are dealing with the beginnings of jihad as a fully articulated social practice as well as a body of doctrine. And here, in the majority of cases about which we have information, we simply cannot tell precisely and to what extent individuals were engaged in devotional practices, in the transmission of learning, or in actual combat or garrison duty facing the enemy. For many, perhaps most of these people, jihad consisted precisely in the combination of these activities. Some of them satisfied the requirement for combat through formalistic gesture or symbolic performance; others undertook concrete acts of war in real time. Internal and external jihad were thus always present, to varying degrees and in different ratios.

One thing that the internal jihad did not involve, except in some fringe cases, was deliberate, physical violence against oneself. This is one reason why the "jihad against the self" of classical Islam does not help us to understand the inner torment of those Muslim youth in our own day who turn to radical Islam and the new jihad. Some of these young people seem to experience a violently split self, in which one of the halves connects to a European or American identity. Again, this is not a holdover from the classical *jihad al-nafs*, the jihad against the self: the practitioners of that jihad combated a self that was largely exterior to them and, furthermore, they almost always emerged victorious from the struggle. The struggle and split in today's youth is of a different kind. At the same time, for many of them, the classical jihad provides a frame of reference, and perhaps also a measure of relief from individual pain.

Over and again, we have seen the tension between what Albrecht Noth called "holy war" and "holy struggle": between large-scale activities of warfare, usually undertaken by a state of some kind, on the one hand, and an individualistic search for merit and blessing, with little regard for the actual outcome of battles and campaigns, on the other. We find a similar tension within the military operations conducted by many Islamic states and empires throughout history. From time to time, these states mounted large-scale operations of conquest, aiming to subdue new territories. The net results were often positive for them: expansion of the Abode of Islam, affirmation of dynastic power and legitimacy, and creation of lasting political, fiscal, and other structures. At other times, however, and in fact much more often, these premodern Islamic states and empires dispatched raiding expeditions without any territorial goals, aiming merely to inflict damage and to seize booty. The raiders in these enterprises showed stubborn tenacity, even though their yield of plunder was often not great. To a bureaucratic observer, such as the tenth-century Iraqi Qudama ibn Jaʿfar, these annual raiding operations resulted in a net loss for the caliphal treasury.[3] Yet no one, least of all Qudama, thought to challenge their purpose or importance. The raids are a constant element, always considered praiseworthy and even necessary. This is a feature of premodern Islamic states that we cannot ignore. In addition to conquest, we have depredation; in addition to political projects and state-building, we have destruction and waste.

None of this is unique to Islam: each civilization has its own modes of destruction and waste, and none on a grander scale than the United States in our own time. But here we may jump ahead once again to the new jihad that has emerged in the Islamic world in the past few years, where we see an ability and a desire to inflict destruction and waste on a monumental scale. Seen in this way, are these jihadists of today the direct heirs of the raiders and ghazis of the ʿAbbasid, Ottoman, and other premodern Islamic empires and states? For a number of reasons, the answer seems to be "no." To begin with, they do not follow the classical rules (*ahkam*) that prohibit, for instance, the deliberate killing of noncombatants, especially women and children—rules that the ghazis of old actually followed more often than not—and also outlaw suicide. Furthermore, in premodern Islam, while many military campaigns and expeditions were conducted solely for the purpose of depredation and destruction, the possibility of conquest was always present, even if only as an ideal. Today's jihadists, by contrast, seem to have no program of conquest, or to put it in more acceptable terms for today, no viable, practical project of building a new state and a new society. Finally, the contemporary jihadists, like all fundamentalists, express little interest in what went on in the Islamic world

---

[3] Qudama, *Kitab al-Kharaj*, 185–186.

under the 'Abbasids or the Ottomans. Instead, they concentrate mainly on Muhammad's Medina and on the period immediately afterward. For all these reasons, the link between the classical gha-zis and the contemporary jihadists is problematic at best.

This is not surprising, especially in light of the profound trans-formations that have taken place in Islamic societies and states in recent centuries. In fairness, however, it needs to be said that sev-eral thinkers among the contemporary radicals have confronted these problems. They often present themselves as a minority within the Islamic world, a vanguard obliged to take extreme ac-tions in order to achieve necessary goals, but in any case acting within the broad confines of Islamic law. In this view, the contem-porary violent jihadists are not, as they are often portrayed, merely nihilists who revel in inflicting damage and death on innocent ci-vilians. This field of debate is opening up only now, and is fraught with difficulty and tension.

Yet the most urgent question for the radical jihadists and, be-yond them, for fundamentalists and Islamists of all kinds (whether violent or nonviolent) is how to create a link with an authentic Islamic past and recover an authentic Islamic practice. What are the options available for doing this? Looking back at chapter 7, we may think of Abu Ishaq al-Fazari, who imitated the Messenger of God through physical participation in warfare and, at the same time, through transmission of narratives about the Prophet's cam-paigns, and also through study of the norms of *siyar*, the law of war. Or we may look to al-Fazari's colleague 'Abdallah ibn al-Mubarak, who in his *Book of Jihad* and in his personal example stressed the idea that believers must, in their jihad, internalize the norm, and must strive to live in companionship with one another. Or we may look to other scholarly heroes of the jihad who chose self-denial and asceticism, putting the search for individual purity at the heart of their participation in war. These personal examples, combined with literary activity regarding jihad and warfare, articu-late the ways in which the members of a society may relate to one another, through imitation, companionship, abstinence, or any combination of these. Participation in violence and war is only part of the story, though we must not undervalue it. Modern Is-lamist movements have, of course, long been aware of these vari-ous options: we see this especially in their charitable and social welfare networks. But from this point of view, the contemporary jihadists—the violent wing among the fundamentalists—seem different. It is hard to avoid the impression that for them the point is simply violence and killing, while care for the unfortunate, generosity, and socially and politically constructive activities, in general, are all matters of indifference.

All the same, since they are also fundamentalists, they must look back to the earliest Islam and to the Quran. And there, as we have seen, they may find a text that adamantly opposes waste and indeed, violence, within the community of believers. Sayyid Qutb, in his commentary on the Quran, was aware of the ways in which the Book calls for goods to circulate within society through the constant practice of generosity, and of the preeminent place of solidarity (ta*awun*) within Quranic and Islamic economics.[4] Qutb's followers may have neglected this Quranic message, or reduced it to pious verbiage about the requirement to give alms. But in a society that seeks seriously to live according to Quranic principles, this "economy of alms" (in Décobert's words) is not an *alternative* to the externally directed violence that must always, unavoidably, be present in the doctrine and social practice of the jihad. It is rather a *constant and necessary counterweight* to that violence. In fact, neither of the two, generosity and fighting, or (as I have expressed it) reciprocity and reward, can exist—again, in a truly Quranic universe—without the other.

In the debates over Islam that have taken place, especially since September 11, 2001, some have insisted that the jihad, and Islam itself, are all "about" peace. Others have proclaimed the opposite, that they are all "about" war. The accusation that the terrorists have "hijacked" Islam fits into this pattern of argument. But, of course, the jihad and Islam cannot be all "about" any one thing. Still others, looking at the matter from relativist and comparative perspectives, have argued that in any religious tradition there are conflicting elements that gain the upper hand at different moments in its history. If the warlike tendency in Islam has gained ground at the present moment, this has happened in other religious traditions before—most notably in European Christianity—and no doubt will change for Islam as well. But this sort of argument also does not help us to understand precisely what we have before us here.

[4] Carré, *Mysticism and Politics*, 203–227.

We may arrive at a more honest appraisal of the situation if we acknowledge that the jihad is a complex doctrine and set of practices that focus—sometimes literally, sometimes not at all literally—on violence and warfare. Through the jihad, countless Muslims have participated in a foundational myth. In doing this, they have undertaken actions with both symbolic and practical value. They have partaken in raids and campaigns recalling the nomadic lifestyle of ancient Arabia or medieval Central Asia: in this way, many city dwellers have experienced both the freedom and the hardship of that lifestyle. They have contributed to the building of Islamic states throughout the world. They have become devoted followers of pious saints, and some have become pious saints themselves. In doing all these things, they have achieved consummation of their desire for continuity with the most authentic Islamic past, which for them is always the Prophet's Medina.

At the same time, the Prophet's Medina and the Quran also teach the lesson of peace, or more accurately, of social peace achieved through the practice of generosity. If these two elements of generosity and violence, of peace and war, are in tension against each other in Islam, then that tension is permanent. However, a balance between them has often been achieved in the past and may well be achieved again, a balance between reciprocity within the community, and the reward made to individuals for their heroic achievement and striving.

Bibliography

ʿAbbas, Ihsan. *ʿAbd al-Hamid ibn Yahya al-katib*. Amman: Dar al-Shuruq, 1988.

———. *Shiʿr al-Khawarij*, 3rd ed. Beirut: Dar al-Thaqafa, 1974.

ʿAbd al-Razzaq al-Sanʿani. *al-Musannaf*. Beirut: al-Maktab al-Islami, 1983–87.

ʿAbdallah ibn al-Mubarak. *Kitab al-jihad*. Cairo: al-Azhar, Majmaʿ al-Buhuth al-Islamiyya, 1978.

Abou El Fadl, Khaled. "*Ahkâm al-Bughât*: Irregular Warfare and the Law of Rebellion in Islam." In *Cross, Crescent and Sword: The Justification and Limitation of War in Western and Islamic Tradition*, edited by James Turner Johnson and John Kelsay, 149–76. Westport: Greenwood Press, 1991.

———. *Rebellion and Violence in Islamic Law*. Cambridge: Cambridge University Press, 2002.

Abu Bakr al-Maliki. *Riyad al-nufus*. 3 vols. Beirut: Dar al-Gharb al-Islami, 1981.

Abu Daʾud Sulayman ibn al-Ashʿath. *Sunan*. Hims: Muhammad ʿAli al-Sayyid, 1969–74.

Abu Ishaq Ibrahim al-Fazari. *Kitab al-siyar*. Beirut: Muʾassasat al-Risala, 1987.

Abu Nuwas, Maʿn. *Diwan*. Beirut: Dar Sadr, 1962.

Abu Yusuf Yaʿqub. *Kitab al-radd ʿala siyar al-Awzaʿi*. Hyderabad: Lajnat Ihyaʾ al-Maʿarif al-Nuʿmaniyya, 1938.

Abulafia, David, and Nora Berend, eds. *Medieval Frontiers: Concepts and Practices*. Aldershot: Ashgate, 2002.

Ade Ajayi, J. F., ed. *Africa in the Nineteenth Century until the 1880s*. General History of Africa, vol. 6. Berkeley: UNESCO, 1989.

Allison, Robert J. *The Crescent Obscured: The United States and the Muslim World, 1776–1815*. Chicago: University of Chicago Press, 1995.

Alphandéry, Paul, and Alphonse Duprout. *La Chrétienté et l'idée de croisade.* Paris: Albin Michel, 1995.

Arazi, A. and A. El'ad. "L'Epître à l'armée." *Studia Islamica* 66 (1987): 27–70; 67 (1988): 29–73.

Arberry, Arthur J. *The Koran Interpreted.* New York: Macmillan, 1955.

Ayoub, Mahmoud. *Redemptive Suffering in Islam: A Study of the Devotional Aspects of 'Ashura' in Twelver Shiʿism.* The Hague: Mouton, 1978.

al-Baladhuri, Ahmad ibn Yahya. *Futuh al-buldan.* Leiden: Brill, 1866.

Bamyeh, Muhammad. *The Social Origins of Islam.* Minneapolis: University of Minnesota Press, 1999.

Barber, Benjamin. *Jihad versus McWorld.* New York: Times Books, 1995.

Bartlett, Robert, and Angus MacKay, eds. *Medieval Frontier Societies.* Oxford and New York: Oxford University Press, 1989.

Bashear, Suliman. "Apocalyptic and Other Materials on Early Muslim-Byzantine Wars: A Review." *Journal of the Royal Asiatic Society* series 6, vol. 3, no. 1 (1991): 173–207. Reprinted in Bonner, *Arab-Byzantine Relations,* 181–216.

Bat Ye'or. *The Dhimmi: Jews and Christians under Islam.* East Rutherford: Fairleigh Dickinson University Press, 1985.

Bataille, Georges. *La part maudite.* Paris: Editions de Minuit, 1967.

al-Bayhaqi, Abu Bakr Ahmad. *al-Sunan al-kubra.* Beirut: Dar Sadr, 1968.

Becker, Carl Heinrich. "Die Ausbreitung der Araber." In *Islamstudien,* 66–145. Leipzig:, n.p., 1924, Repr. Hildesheim: G. Olms, 1967. Appeared in English as chapters 11 and 12 of *The Cambridge Medieval History,* edited by H. M. Gwatkin and others (Cambridge: Cambridge University Press, [1913] 1967).

Bergen, Peter L. *Holy War, Inc.: Inside the Secret World of Osama bin Laden.* New York: Free Press, 2002.

Blachère, Régis. *Introduction au Coran.* Paris: Besson et Chantemerle, 1949.

Blankinship, Khalid Yahya. *The End of the Jihâd State: The Reign of Hisham ibn ʿAbd al-Malik and the Collapse of the Umayyads.* Albany: SUNY Press, 1994.

Bonner, Michael. *Arab-Byzantine Relations in Early Islamic Times.* The Formation of the Classical Islamic World, vol. 8, Lawrence I. Conrad, general editor. Aldershot: Ashgate, 2004.

———. *Aristocratic Violence and Holy War: Studies on the Jihad and the Arab-Byzantine Frontier.* American Oriental Series, vol. 81. New Haven: American Oriental Society, 1996.

———. "Definitions of Poverty and the Rise of the Muslim Urban Poor." *Journal of the Royal Asiatic Society* series 6, vol. 6, no. 3 (1996): 335–344.

———. "Jaʿaʾil and Holy War in Early Islam." *Der Islam* 68 (1991): 45–64.

———. "Poverty and Charity in the Rise of Islam." In *Poverty and Charity in Middle Eastern Contexts*, edited by Michael Bonner, Mine Ener, and Amy Singer, 13–30. Albany: SUNY Press, 2003.

———. "Poverty and Economics in the Qur'an." *Journal of Interdisciplinary History* 35 (2005): 391–406.

———. Review of Christian Décobert, *Le mendiant et le combattant*. *Bibliotheca Orientalis* 50 (1993): 500–504.

———. "Some Observations Concerning the Early Development of Jihad on the Arab-Byzantine Frontier." *Studia Islamica* 75 (1992): 5–31.

Bosworth, Clifford Edmund, trans. and ed. *The ʿAbbasid Caliphate in Equilibrium: The History of al-Tabari*, vol. 30. Albany: SUNY Press, 1989.

———. "Abu ʿAmr ʿUthman al-Tarsusi's *Siyar al-thughur*." *Graeco-Arabica* 5 (1993): 183–195.

Bowersock, G. W. *Martyrdom and Rome*. Cambridge: Cambridge University Press, 1995.

Boyer, P. "Introduction à une histoire intérieure de la Régence d'Alger." *Revue Historique* 235 (1966): 297–316.

Braude, Benjamin, and Bernard Lewis, eds. *Christians and Jews in the Ottoman Empire: The Functioning of a Plural Society*. New York: Holmes and Meier, 1982.

Braudel, Fernand. *La Méditerranée et le monde méditerranéen à l'époque de Philippe II*. Paris: Colin, 1966.

Bravmann, M. M. "The Surplus of Property: An Early Arab Social Concept." In *The Spiritual Background of Early Islam*, 229–253. Leiden: Brill, 1972.

Brett, Michael. *The Rise of the Fatimids*. Leiden: Brill, 2001.

Brunschvig, Robert. "Ibn ʿAbdalhakam et la conquête de l'Afrique du Nord par les Arabes: étude critique." *Annales de l'Institut d'Études Orientales* 6 (1942–1947): 110–155. Reprinted in *al-Andalus* 40 (1975): 129–79.

———. "Polémiques médiévales autour du rite de Malik." *al-Andalus* 15 (1950): 377–435. Reprinted in *Etudes d'Islamologie*, 2: 65–101. Paris: Maisonneuve et Larose, 1976.

al-Bukhari, Muhammad ibn Ismaʿil. *Kitab al-jamiʿ al-sahih*. Leiden: Brill, 1862–1908.

Bulliett, Richard. *Conversion to Islam in the Medieval Period*. Cambridge, MA: Harvard University Press, 1979.

Burton, John. *Introduction to the Hadith*. Edinburgh: Edinburgh University Press, 1994.

Butterworth, Charles E. "Al-Fârâbî's Statecraft: War and the Well-Ordered Regime." In *Cross, Crescent and Sword: The Justification and Limitation of War in Western and Islamic Traditions*, edited by John Kelsay and James Turner Johnson, 79–199. Westport: Greenwood Press, 1990.

Caetani, Leone. *Annali dell'Islam*. Milan: U. Hoepli, 1905–1926.

Cahen, Claude. *La Turquie pré-ottomane.* Istanbul: Institut Français d'Etudes Anatoliennes d'Istanbul, 1988.

Calder, Norman. *Studies in Early Muslim Jurisprudence.* Oxford: Clarendon, 1993.

Canard, Marius. "Le cérémonial fatimite et le cérémonial byzantin: essai de comparaison." *Byzantion* 21 (1951): 355–420.

———. "Les expéditions des Arabes contre Constantinople dans l'histoire et dans la légende." *Journal Asiatique* 208 (1926): 61–121.

———. "La guerre sainte dans le monde islamique et dans le monde chrétien." *Revue africaine* (1936): 605–623.

———. *Histoire de la dynastie des H'amdânides.* Paris: Presses Universitaires de France, 1953.

———. "Quelques observations sur l'introduction géographique de la Bughyat at'-t'alab." *Annales de l'Institut d'Études Orientales* 15 (1957): 41–53.

———. *Sayf al Dawla. Recueil de textes relatifs à l'émir Sayf al Daula le Hamdânide.* Algiers: J. Carbonel, 1934.

Carré, Olivier. *Mysticism and Politics: A Critical Reading of Fi Zilal al-Qur'an by Sayyid Qutb (1906–1966),* translated by Carol Artigues. Leiden: Brill, 2003.

Caskel, Werner. "Aijām al-'Arab. Studien zur altarabischen Epik." *Islamica* 3, no. 5 (1930): 1–99.

Chabbi, Jacqueline. "Histoire et tradition sacrée: La biographie impossible de Mahomet." *Arabica* 43 (1996): 189–205.

———. "Remarques sur le développement historique des mouvements ascétiques et mystiques au Khurasan." *Studia Islamica* 46 (1977): 5–72.

———. "Ribat." *Encyclopaedia of Islam* 8 (1994): 493–506.

———. *Le Seigneur des tribus: L'islam de Mahomet.* Paris: Noêsis, 1997.

Cheikh-Moussa, Abdallah, and Didier Gazaguadou. "Comment on écrit l'histoire . . . de l'Islam!" *Arabica* 40 (1993): 199–247.

Christides, V. "Raid and Trade in the Eastern Mediterranean: A Treatise by Muhammad b. 'Umar, the *Faqih* from Occupied Moslem Crete." *Graeco-Arabica* 5 (1993): 63–102.

Cohen, Mark R. *Under Crescent and Cross: The Jews in the Middle Ages.* Princeton: Princeton University Press, 1994.

———. "What Was the Pact of 'Umar? A Literary and Literary-Historical Study." *Jerusalem Studies in Arabic and Islam* 23 (1999): 100–151.

Cole, Juan R. I. *Colonialism and Revolution in the Middle East: Social and Cultural Origins of Egypt's 'Urabi Movement.* Princeton: Princeton University Press, 1993.

Cook, David B. "The Apocalyptic Year 200/815–16." In *Apocalyptic Time,* edited by A. Baumgarten, 41–68. Leiden: Brill, 2000.

———. "An Early Muslim Daniel Apocalypse." *Arabica* 49 (2002): 55–96.

———. "The Implications of Martyrdom Operations for Contemporary Islam." *Journal of Religious Ethics* 23 (2004): 129–151.

———. "Muslim Apocalyptic and Jihad." *Jerusalem Studies in Arabic and Islam* 20 (1996): 66–104.

———. *Studies in Muslim Apocalyptic.* Princeton: Princeton University Press, 2002.

———. "Suicide Attacks or 'Martyrdom Operations' in Contemporary Jihad Literature." *Nova Religio* 6 (2002): 7–44.

———. *Understanding Jihad.* Berkeley and Los Angeles: University of California Press, 2005.

Cook, Michael. "An Early Islamic Apocalyptic Chronicle." *Journal of Near Eastern Studies* 52 (1993): 25–29.

———. "Eschatology and the Dating of Traditions." *Princeton Papers in Near Eastern Studies* 1 (1992): 23–47.

———. "The Heraclian Dynasty in Muslim Eschatology." *al-Qantara* 13 (1992): 3–23.

———. *The Koran: A Very Short Introduction.* Oxford: Oxford University Press, 2000.

———. *Muhammad.* Oxford: Oxford University Press, 1983.

———. *Muslim Dogma.* Cambridge: Cambridge University Press, 1981.

Cook, Michael, and Patricia Crone. *Hagarism: The Making of the Islamic World.* Cambridge: Cambridge University Press, 1977.

Crone, Patricia. *Slaves on Horses: The Evolution of the Islamic Polity.* Cambridge: Cambridge University Press, 1980.

Crone, Patricia, and Fritz Zimmermann. *The Epistle of Sālim ibn Dhakwān.* Oxford: Oxford University Press, 2001.

Crone, Patricia, and Martin Hinds. *God's Caliph.* Cambridge: Cambridge University Press, 1986.

Dajani-Shakeel, Hadia. "A Reassessment of Some Medieval and Modern Perceptions of the Counter-Crusade." In *The Jihad and Its Times*, edited by H. Dajani-Shakeel and R. A. Messier, 41–70. Ann Arbor: Center for Near Eastern and North African Studies, 1991.

Darling, Linda. "Contested Territory: Ottoman Holy War in Comparative Context." *Studia Islamica* 91 (2000): 133–163.

de la Puente, Cristina. "Vivre et mourir pour Dieu, œuvre et héritage d'Abu ʿAli al-Sadafi." *Studia Islamica* 87 (1998): 77–102.

———. "El Ŷihād en el califato omeya de al-Andalus y su culminación bajo Hišām II." In *Almanzor y los terrores del Milenio*, edited by Fernando Valdés Fernández, 25–38. Aguilar de Campoo (Palencia): Fundación Santa María la Real, Centro de Estudios del Románico, 1999.

de Prémare, Alfred-Louis. *Aux origines du Coran.* Paris: Editions du Téraèdre, 2004.

———. *Les fondations de l'islam: Entre écriture et histoire.* Paris: Le Seuil, 2002.

Décobert, Christian. "Les méchanismes de la conquête arabe." *L'Histoire* 105 (1987): 10–16.

———. *Le mendiant et le combattant: L'institution de l'islam*. Paris: Le Seuil, 1991.

Dennett, Daniel C. *Conversion and the Poll Tax in Early Islam*. Cambridge, MA: Harvard University Press, 1950.

Devji, Faisal. *Muslim Nationalism: Founding Identity in Colonial India*. New York: Columbia University Press, forthcoming.

al-Dhahabi, Shams al-Din Muhammad ibn Ahmad. *Siyar aʿlam al-nubalaʾ*. Beirut: Muʾassasat al-Risala, 1981.

Dick, Ignac. "La passion arabe de S. Antoine Ruwah, néomartyr de Damas." *Le Muséon* 74 (1961): 108–133.

Djaït, Hichem. *La Grande Discorde. Religion et politique dans l'Islam des origines*. Paris: Gallimard, 1989.

Donner, Fred M. "Centralized Authority and Military Autonomy in the Early Islamic Conquests." In *The Byzantine and Early Islamic Near East. Vol. 3, States, Resources and Armies*, edited by Averil Cameron, 337–360. Princeton: Darwin Press, 1995.

———. *The Early Islamic Conquests*. Princeton: Princeton University Press, 1981.

———. *Narratives of Islamic Origins: The Beginnings of Islamic Historical Writing*. Princeton: Darwin Press, 1998.

———. "The Origins of the Islamic State." *Journal of the American Oriental Society* 106 (1986): 283–296.

———. "Piety and Eschatology in Early Kharijite Poetry." In *Fi mihrab al-maʿrifa: Festschrift for Ihsan ʿAbbas*, edited by Ibrahim as-Saʿafin, 13–19. Beirut: Dar Sader and Dar al-Gharb al-Islami, 1997.

———. "The Sources of Islamic Conceptions of War." In *Just War and Jihad*, edited by James Turner Johnson and John Kelsay, 31–69. Westport: Greenwood Press, 1991.

Dutton, Yasin. *The Origins of Islamic Law: The Qurʾan, the Muwattaʾ and Madinan ʿAmal*. London: Routledge Curzon, 2002.

Eddé, Anne-Marie, Françoise Micheau, and Christophe Picard, eds. *Communautés chrétiennes en pays d'Islam, du début du VIIᵉ siècle au milieu du Xᵉ siècle*. Paris: Sedes, 1997.

Ehrenkreutz, Andrew. *Saladin*. Albany: SUNY Press, 1972.

EI² = *The Encyclopaedia of Islam*, 2nd ed. 11 vols. Leiden: Brill, 1960–2002.

El-Cheikh, Nadia Maria. "Describing the Other to Get at the Self: Byzantine Women in Arabic Sources, 8th–11th Centuries." *Journal of the Economic and Social History of the Orient* 40 (1997): 239–250.

Elgood, Robert, ed. *Islamic Arms and Armour* (London: Scolar Press, 1979).

EQ = *Encyclopaedia of the Qurʾan*. See under McAuliffe, Jane.

Esposito, John. *Unholy War: Terror in the Name of Islam*, Oxford: Oxford University Press, 2002.

Fattal, Antoine. *Le statut légal des non-musulmans en pays d'Islam*. 2nd ed. Beirut: Dar El-Machreq, 1995.

Fierro, Maribel. "Spiritual Alienation and Political Activism: The *Ġuraba'* in al-Andalus during the Sixth/Twelfth Century." *Arabica* 47 (2000): 230–260.

Firestone, Reuven. *Jihad: The Origin of Holy War in Islam*. Oxford and New York: Oxford University Press, 1999.

Fletcher, Richard. *The Quest for El Cid*. Oxford: Oxford University Press, 1989.

Flori, Jean. *Guerre sainte, jihad, croisade: violence et religion dans le christianisme et l'islam*. Paris: Le Seuil, 2002.

Freamon, Bernard. "Martyrdom, Suicide and the Islamic Law of War: A Short Legal History." *Fordham International Law Journal* 27 (2003): 299–369.

Gabrieli, Francesco. "The Arabic Historiography of the Crusades." In *Historians of the Middle East*, edited by B. Lewis and P. M. Holt, 98–107.

———. *Muhammad and the Conquests of Islam*. New York: McGraw-Hill, 1968.

Garcin, Jean-Claude, Michel Balivet, Thierry Bianquis, and others. *Etats, sociétés et cultures du monde musulman médiéval, Xᵉ - XVᵉ siècle*. Paris: Presses Universitaires de France, 1995.

Gibb, H.A.R. "The Armies of Saladin." In *Studies on the Civilization of Islam*, 74–90. Princeton: Princeton University Press, [1962] 1982.

Goldziher, Ignaz. *Muslim Studies*. 2 vols. London: Allen and Unwin, 1967–1968.

Green, Molly. *A Shared World: Christians and Muslims in the Early Modern Mediterranean*. Princeton: Princeton University Press, 2000.

Griffith, S.W. "The Arabic Account of ʿAbd al-Masīḥ an-Naǧrānī." *Le Muséon* 98 (1985): 331–374.

Guillaume, Alfred. *See under* Ibn Ishaq.

Hagen, Gottfried. "The Prophet Muhammad as an Exemplar in War: Ottoman Views on the Eve of World War I." *New Perspectives on Turkey*, edited by Ç. Keydar and A. Önçu, 22. (2000): 145–172.

———. *Die Türkei im Ersten Weltkrieg. Heidelberger Orientalistische Studien*, vol. 15. Frankfurt am Main: Peter Lang, 1990.

Halm, Heinz. *The Empire of the Mahdi: The Rise of the Fatimids*, translated by Michael Bonner. Leiden: Brill, 1996.

Hamdani, Abbas. "Byzantine-Fatimid Relations before the Battle of Manzikert." *Byzantine Studies* 1 (1974): 169–179.

al-Harawi, Abu l-Hasan ʿAli. *Guide des lieux de pèlerinage*, translated by J. Sourdel-Thomime. Damascus: Institut Français de Damas, 1957.

Hasluck, F. W. *Christianity and Islam under the Sultans*, 2 vols. Oxford: Oxford University Press, 1929.

Hawting, G. R. "The Significance of the Slogan *La hukma illa li'llah*." *Bulletin of the School of Oriental and African Studies* 41 (1978): 453–463.

Heck, Paul L. "*Jihad* Revisited." *Journal of Religious Ethics* 32, no. 1 (2004): 95–128.

Hess, Andrew C. *The Forgotten Frontier: A History of the Sixteenth-century Ibero-African Frontier*. Chicago: University of Chicago Press, 1978.

Hillenbrand, Carole. *The Crusades: Islamic Perspectives*. New York: Routledge, 2000.

Hinds, Martin. "Maghazi and Sira in Early Islamic Scholarship." In *Studies in Early Islamic History*, edited by L.I. Conrad and P. Crone J. Bacharach, 188–198. Princeton: Darwin Press, 1996.

Hodgson, Marshall. "How Did the Early Shiʿa Become Sectarian?" *Journal of the American Oriental Society* 75 (1955): 1–13.

Hoexter, Miriam. *Endowments, Rulers and Community: Waqf al-Haramayn in Ottoman Algiers*. Leiden: Brill, 1998.

Hoyland, Robert G. *Seeing Islam as Others Saw It: A Survey and Evaluation of Christian, Jewish and Zoroastrian Writings on Islam*. Studies in Late Antiquity and Islam. Princeton: Darwin Press, 1997.

Husted, W. R. "Karbalaʾ Made Immediate: The Martyr as Model in Imami Shiʿism." *Muslim World* 83 (1993): 263–278.

Ibn Abi Shayba, ʿAbdallah ibn Muhammad al-Kufi. *al-Kitab al-musannaf fi l-ahadith wal-athar*. Bombay: Dar al-Taj, 1979–1983.

Ibn Abi Zamanin. *Qudwat al-ghazi*. Beirut: Dar al-Gharb al-Islami, 1989.

Ibn Hawqal. *Surat al-ard*. Leiden: Brill, 1938.

Ibn Ishaq. *The Life of Muhammad: A Translation of Ibn Ishaq's Sirat Rasul Allah*, translated by Alfred Guillaume. Oxford: Oxford University Press, 1955.

Ibn al-Jawzi, Jamal al-Din Abu l-Faraj. *Sifat al-safwa*. Hyderabad: Matbaʿat Daʾirat al-Maʿarif al-ʿUthmaniyya, 1968–72.

Ibn Khaldun, ʿAbd al-Rahman. *The Muqaddimah: An Introduction to History*, translated by Franz Rosenthal. Princeton: Princeton University Press, 1967.

Ibn al-Muqaffaʿ, ʿAbdallah. *Risala fi l-sahaba*. (See under Pellat, Charles).

Ibn Nubata. *Diwan khutab Ibn Nubata*. Beirut: Matbaʿat Jaridat Bayrut, 1893–1894.

Ibn Qudama, ʿAbdallah ibn Ahmad. *al-Mughni*. Cairo, 1968–1970.

Ibn Qutayba, ʿAbdallah ibn Muslim. *ʿUyun al-akhbar*. Cairo: Dar al-kutub, n.d. Reprint, Cairo: al-Muʾassasa al-Misriyya al-ʿAmma lil-taʾlif wal-tarjama wal-tibaʿa wal-nashr, 1986.

Ibn Taghribirdi, Abu l-Mahasin Yusuf. *al-Nujum al-zahira*. Cairo: al-Muʾassasa al-Misriyya al-ʿAmma lil-Taʾlif wal-Tarjama wal-Tibaʿa wal-Nashr, 1964.

Ibn Taymiyya, Ahmad. *Al-Siyasa al-sharʿiyya*. Beirut: Dar al-Kutub al-ʿArabiyya, 1966.

Imber, Colin. *The Ottoman Empire, 130–1481*. Istanbul: Isis Press, 1990.

Inalcik, Halil. "The Question of the Emergence of the Ottoman State." *International Journal of Turkish Studies* 2 (1980): 71–79.

Jackson, Sherman. "Domestic Terrorism in the Islamic Legal Tradition." *Muslim World* 91 (2001): 293–310.

———. "Jihad and the Modern World." *Journal of Islamic Law and Culture* 7 (2002): 1–25.

Jafri, S. Husayn M. *Origins and Early Development of Shiʿa Islam*. London and New York: Longman, 1979.

Jansen, Johannes J. G. *The Neglected Duty: The Creed of Sadat's Assassins and Islamic Resurgence in the Middle East*. New York: Macmillan, 1986.

Jarrar, M. *Die Prophetenbiographie im islamischen Spanien: Ein Beitrag zur Überlieferungs- und Redaktionsgeschichte*. Frankfurt am Main: Peter Lang, 1989.

Jennings, Ronald C. "Some Thoughts on the Gazi-Thesis." *Wiener Zeitschrift für die Kunde des Morgenlandes* 76 (1986): 151–161.

Johnson, James Turner. *The Holy War Idea in Western and Islamic Traditions*. University Park: Pennsylvania State University Press, 1997.

Juergensmeyer, Mark, ed. *Terror in the Mind of God: The Global Rise of Religious Violence*. Comparative Studies in Religion and Society vol. 13. Berkeley: University of California Press, 2000.

Kafadar, Cemal. *Between Two Worlds: The Construction of the Ottoman State*. Berkeley: University of California Press, 1995.

Kelsay, John, and James Turner Johnson, ed. *Cross, Crescent and Sword: The Justification and Limitation of War in Western and Islamic Traditions*. Westport: Greenwood Press, 1990.

———, ed. *Just War and Jihad: Historical and Theoretical Perspectives on War and Peace in Western and Islamic Traditions*. Westport: Greenwood Press, 1991.

Kennedy, Hugh. *The Armies of the Caliphs*. London: Routledge, 2001.

———. "The Financing of the Military in the Early Islamic State." In *The Byzantine and Early Islamic Near East III: States, Resources and Armies*, edited by A. Cameron, 361–78. Princeton: Darwin Press, 1995.

Kepel, Gilles. *Jihad: The Trail of Political Islam*, translated by Anthony F. Roberts. Cambridge, MA: Harvard University Press, 2002.

———. *Muslim Extremism in Egypt: The Prophet and Pharaoh*. London, Berkeley, and Los Angeles: University of California Press, 1985.

Khadduri, Majid. *The Islamic Law of Nations: Shaybani's Siyar*. Baltimore: Johns Hopkins University Press, 1966.

al-Khatib al-Baghdadi. *Taʾrikh Baghdad*. Baghdad, 1931.

Knysh, Alexander L. *Islamic Mysticism: A Short History*. Leiden: Brill, 1999.

Kohlberg, Etan. "The Development of the Imami Shiʿi Doctrine of Jihad." *Zeitschrift der Deutschen Morgenländischen Gesellschaft* 126 (1976): 64–86.

———. "Medieval Muslim Views on Martyrdom." *Mededeelingen der Koninklijke Akademie van Wetenschappen* (Amsterdam), Afdeeling Letterkunde, Nieuwe Reeks 60, no. 7 (1997): 279–307.

Köprülü, M. Fuad. *The Origins of the Ottoman Empire*, translated by Gary Leiser. Albany: SUNY Press, 1992.

Kraemer, Joel L. "Apostates, Rebels and Brigands." *Israel Oriental Studies* 10 (1980): 34–73.

———. "The Jihād of the *Falāsifa*." *Jerusalem Studies in Arabic and Islam* 10 (1987): 288–324.

Labat, Séverine. *Les islamistes algériens*. Paris: Le Seuil, 1995.

Lewis, Bernard. *The Assassins: A Radical Sect in Islam*. New York: Oxford University Press, 1987.

———. *The Jews of Islam*. Princeton: Princeton University Press, 1984.

———. "The Use by Muslim Historians of Non-Muslim Sources." In *Historians of the Middle East*, edited by B. Lewis and P. M. Holt, 180–191. Oxford: Oxford University Press, 1962.

———. *What Went Wrong? The Clash between Islam and Modernity in the Middle East*. Oxford: Oxford University Press, 2002.

Lewis, Bernard, and P. M. Holt, eds. *Historians of the Middle East*. Oxford: Oxford University Press, 1962.

Lindner, Rudi Paul. *Nomads and Ottomans in Medieval Anatolia*. Bloomington: Indiana University Research Institute for Inner Asian Studies, 1983.

Little, Donald P. "Did Ibn Taymiyya Have a Screw Loose?" *Studia Islamica* 41 (1975): 93–111.

Lyall, Charles. *The Diwans of ʿAbid ibn al-Abras, of Asad, and ʿAmir ibn al-Tufail, of ʿAmir ibn Saʿsaʿa*. London and Leiden: Brill, 1913.

Malik ibn Anas. *al-Muwattaʾ*. Edited by M. F. ʿAbd al-Baqi. Cairo: Dar Ihyaʾ al-Kutub al-ʿArabiyya, ʿIsa al-Babi al-Halabi, 1951.

———. *Muwattaʾ al-Imam Malik . . . riwayat Muhammad ibn al-Hasan al-Shaybani*. Cairo: al-Majlis al-Aʿla lil-Shuʾun al-Islamiyya, 1967.

Martinez, Luis. *The Algerian Civil War, 1990–1998*. London: Hurst & Co., 2000.

Massignon, Louis. "Le mirage byzantin dans le miroir bagdadien d'il y a mille ans." *Annuaire de l'Institut de Philologie et d'Histoire Orientales et Slaves* 10 (1950): 429–448.

———. *The Passion of al-Hallaj*, translated by Herbert Mason. 4 vols. Princeton: Princeton University Press, 1980.

McAuliffe, Jane, ed. *Encyclopaedia of the Qurʾan*. Leiden: Brill, 2001–.

Menocal, María Rosa. *The Ornament of the World: How Muslims, Jews and Christians Created a Culture of Tolerance in Medieval Spain.* Boston: Little, Brown, 2002.

Messier, Ronald A. "The Almoravids and Holy War." In *The Jihad and Its Times*, edited by H. Dajani-Shakeel and R. A. Messier, 15–29. Ann Arbor: Center for Near Eastern and North African Studies, 1991.

Miquel, André. *La géographie humaine du monde musulman*, vol. 2. Paris and The Hague: Mouton, 1975.

al-Mizzi, Jamal al-Din Abu l-Hajjaj Yusuf. *Tahdhib al-kamal fi asma' al-rijal.* Beirut: Mu'assasat al-risala, 1985–.

Morabia, Alfred. *Le Ğihâd dans l'Islam médiéval: Le "combat sacré" des origines au XIIème siècle.* Paris: Albin Michel, 1993.

———. "Ibn Taymiyya: Dernier grand théoricien du ğihâd medieval." *Bulletin d'Etudes Orientales* 30 (1978): 85–100.

Mottahedeh, Roy Parviz, and Ridwan al-Sayyid. "The Idea of *Jihad* in Islam before the Crusades." In *The Crusades from the Perspective of Byzantium and the Muslim World*, edited by Angeliki E. Laiou and Roy Parviz Mottahedeh, 23–29. Washington, D.C.: Dumbarton Oaks Research Library and Collection, 2001.

Motzki, Harald. *The Biography of Muhammad: The Issue of the Sources.* Leiden: Brill, 2000.

———. *The Origins of Islamic Jurisprudence: Meccan Fiqh before the Classical Schools*, translated by Marion H. Katz. Leiden: Brill, 2002.

al-Muttaqi al-Hindi. *Kanz al-'ummal fi sunan al-aqwal wal-a'mal.* Aleppo: Maktabat al-Turath al-Islami, 1969.

Neuwirth, Angelika. "Du texte de récitation au canon en passant par la liturgie." *Arabica* 47 (2000): 194–229.

Nöldeke, Theodor, Friedrich Schwally, Gotthelf Bergsträsser, and Otto Pretzl. *Geschichte des Qorans.* 2nd ed. Hildesheim: G. Olms, 1961.

Noth, Albrecht. "Der Charakter der ersten großen Sammlungen von Nachrichten zur frühen Kalifenzeit." *Der Islam* 47 (1971): 168–199.

———. *Heiliger Krieg und heiliger Kampf in Islam und Christentum.* Bonn: Ludwig Röhrscheid Verlag, 1966.

———. "Isfahan-Nihawand: Eine quellenkritische Studie zur frühislamischen Historographie." *Zeitschrift der Deutschen Morgenländischen Gesellschaft* 118, no. 2 (1968): 274–296.

———. "Les 'ulama' en qualité de guerriers." In *Saber religioso y poder político en el Islam*, edited by Manuela Marin, 175–195. Madrid: Agencía Española de Cooperación Internacional, 1994.

Noth, Albrecht, and Lawrence I. Conrad. *The Early Arabic Historical Tradition: A Source-critical Study.* 2nd ed., translated by Michael Bonner. Princeton: Darwin Press, 1994.

Nu'aym ibn Hammad. *Kitab al-fitan.* Beirut: Dar al-Fikr, 1991.

Paret, Rudi. *Der Koran: Kommentar und Konkordanz*. Stuttgart: Verlag W. Kohlhammer, 1977.

Partner, Peter. *God of Battles: Holy Wars of Christianity and Islam*. London: HarperCollins, 1997.

Paul, Jürgen. *Herrscher, Gemeinwesen, Vermittler: Ostiran und Transoxanien in vormongolischer Zeit*. Beirut and Stuttgart: Franz Steiner Verlag, 1996.

———. "The Histories of Samarqand." *Studia Iranica* (1993): 69–92.

———. "The State and the Military: The Samanid Case." In *Papers on Inner Asia*. Bloomington: Indiana University Research Institute for Inner Asian Studies, 1994.

Pellat, Charles. *Ibn al-Muqaffaʿ, 'conseilleur du Calife.'* Paris: Maisonneuve et Larose, 1976.

———. Peters, F. E. *Muhammad and the Origins of Islam*. Albany: SUNY Press, 1994.

Peters, Rudolph. *Islam and Colonialism: The Doctrine of Jihad in Modern History*. The Hague, Paris, and New York: Mouton, 1979.

———. *Jihad in Classical and Modern Islam: A Reader*. Princeton: Markus Wiener, 1996.

Pipes, Daniel. "What Is Jihad?" *New York Post*, December 31, 2002.

Power, Daniel, and Naomi Standen, eds. *Frontiers in Question: Eurasian Borderlands, 700–1700*. Basingstoke: Macmillan; New York: St. Martin's Press, 1999.

Purcell, Nicholas, and Peregrine Horden. *The Corrupting Sea: A Study of Mediterranean History*. Oxford: Blackwell, 2000.

al-Qadi, Wadad. "The Religious Foundation of Late Umayyad Ideology and Practice." In *Saber religioso y poder político en el Islam*, edited by Manuela Marin, 231–273. Madrid: Agencía Española de Cooperación Internacional, 1994.

Qudama ibn Jaʿfar. *Kitab al-kharaj wa-sinaʿat al-kitaba*. Baghdad: Dar al-Rashid lil-Nashr, 1981.

Rashid, Ahmed. *Jihad: The Rise of Militant Islam in Central Asia*. New Haven: Yale University Press, 2002.

———. *Taliban: Militant Islam, Oil and Fundamentalism in Central Asia*. New Haven. Yale University Press, 2000.

Regan, Geoffrey Regan. *First Crusader: Byzantium's Holy Wars*. Houndmills: Sutton, 2001.

Richard, Jean. *L'esprit de la Croisade*. Paris: Editions du Cerf, 2000.

Riley-Smith, Jonathan. *The First Crusade and the Idea of Crusading*. Philadelphia: University of Pennsylvania Press, 1986.

Rippin, Andrew. "Muhammad in the Qur'an." In *The Biography of Muhammad: The Issue of the Sources*, edited by Harald Motzki, 298–310. Leiden: Brill, 2000.

Robinson, Chase R. *Empire and Elites*. Cambridge: Cambridge University Press, 2000.

Rodinson, Maxime. *Europe and the Mystique of Islam*. Seattle: University of Washington Press, 1991.

———. *Muhammad*. Translated by Anne Carter. New York: Pantheon, 1971.

Rosenthal, Franz. "On Suicide in Islam." *Journal of the American Oriental Society* 66 (1946): 239–259.

Roy, Olivier. *The Failure of Political Islam*. Cambridge, MA: Harvard University Press, 1994.

———. *L'Islam mondialisé*. Paris: Le Seuil, 2002. Translated as *Globalized Islam: The Search for a New Ummah*. New York: Columbia University Press, 2004.

Rubin, Uri. "Muhammad and the Islamic Self-Image." In *The Biography of Muhammad: The Issue of the Source*, edited by Harald Motzki, 3–17. Leiden: Brill, 2000.

Russell, Frederick H. *The Just War in the Middle Ages*. Cambridge: Cambridge University Press, 1975.

Sachau, Eduard. "Das Berliner Fragment des Musa Ibn Ukba: Ein Beitrag zur Kenntniss der ältesten arabischen Geschichtslitteratur." *Sitzungsberichte der Königlich Preussischen Akademie der Wissenschaften*, 445–470. Berlin, 1904.

Sachedina, Abdulaziz. "The Development of Jihad in Islamic Revelation and History." In *Cross, Crescent and Sword: The Justification and Limitation of War in Western and Islamic Traditions*, edited by J. T. Johnson and J. Kelsay, 35–50. Westport: Greenwood Press, 1990.

———. "Justifications for Just War in Islam." In *War and Its Discontents: Pacifism and Quietism in the Abrahamic Tradition*, edited by J. Patout Burns, 122–169. Washington, DC: Georgetown University Press, 1996.

Said, Edward. *Orientalism*. New York: Vintage, 1978.

Salgado, Felipe Maíllo. "Consideraciones acerca de una fatwà de Al-Wanšarisi." *Studia Historica* 3, no. 2 (1985): 181–192.

———. "La guerra santa según el derecho mâliki: Su preceptiva: Su influencia en el derecho de las comunidades cristianas del medievo hispano." *Studia Historica* 1, no. 2 (1983): 29–66.

al-Sarakhsi, Shams al-Din Muhammad. *Sharh al-siyar al-kabir li-Muhammad ibn al-Hasan al-Shaybani*. Cairo, 1971.

Schacht, Joseph. *Introduction to Islamic Law*. Oxford: Oxford University Press, 1964.

———. *The Origins of Muhammadan Jurisprudence*. Oxford: Oxford University Press, 1950.

Schöller, Marco. "Sira and Tafsir: Muhammad al-Kalbi on the Jews of Medina." In *The Biography of Muhammad: The Issue of the Sources*, edited by Harald Motzki, 18–48. Leiden: Brill, 2000.

Sénac, Philippe. *La frontière et les hommes (VIIIe–XIIe siècle). Le peuplement musulman au nord de l'Ebre et les débuts de la reconquête aragonaise.* Paris: Maisonneuve et Larose, 2000.

Serjeant, R. B. "The Constitution of Medina." *Islamic Quarterly* 8 (1964): 3–16.

Sezgin, Fuat. *Geschichte des arabischen Schrifttums*, vol. 1. Leiden: Brill, 1967.

al-Shafi'i, Muhammad ibn Idris. *Kitab al-umm.* Cairo: Maktabat al-Kulliyat al-Azhariyya, 1961.

———. *al-Risala.* Cairo: Mustafa al-Babi al-Halabi, 1938.

al-Shaybani, Muhammad ibn al-Hasan. *Kitab al-siyar al-kabir.* Edited by M. Khadduri as *al-Qanun al-duwali al-islami: Kitab al-siyar lil-Shaybani.* Beirut: al-Dar al-Muttahida lil-Nashr, 1975. Translated by M. Khadduri as *The Islamic Law of Nations: Shaybani's Siyar.* Baltimore: Johns Hopkins University Press, 1966.

———. *Muwatta' al-Imam Malik.* See under Malik ibn Anas.

Shboul, Ahmad. "Byzantium and the Arabs: The Image of the Byzantines as Mirrored in Arabic Literature." In *Proceedings of the First Australian Byzantine Studies Conference.* Canberra, 1981. Reprinted in Bonner, *Arab-Byzantine Relations*, 235–262.

Siddiqi, Muhammad Zubayr. *Hadith Literature: Its Origins, Development and Special Features.* Cambridge: Islamic Texts Society, 1993.

Sijpesteijn, Petra. "The Collection and Meaning of *Sadaqa* and *Zakat.*" Unpublished paper, 2002.

Sivan, Emmanuel. "Genèse de la contre-croisade. Un traité damasquin du début du XIIe siècle." *Journal Asiatique* 254 (1966): 199–204.

———. *L'Islam et la croisade.* Paris: Librairie d'Amérique et d'Orient, 1968.

———. *Radical Islam: Medieval Theology and Modern Politics*, 2nd ed. New Haven: Yale University Press, 1990.

Stenning, J. F., ed. and trans. *The Targum of Isaiah.* Oxford: Clarendon, 1949.

Stern, Samuel. "An Embassy of the Byzantine Emperor to the Fatimid Caliph al-Mu'izz." *Byzantion* 20 (1950): 239–258.

Stillman, Norman. "The Non-Muslim Communities: The Jewish Community." In *The Cambridge History of Egypt*, edited by Carl F. Petry, 198–210. Cambridge: Cambridge University Press, 1998.

al-Tabari, Abu Jarir. *Ikhtilaf al-fuqaha'.* Leiden: Brill, 1933.

———. *Ta'rikh al-rusul wal-muluk.* Leiden: Brill, 1879–1901. Translated as *The History of al-Tabari.* Edited by Ehsan Yarshater. 39 vols. Albany: SUNY Press, 1985–98.

Tabbaa, Yasser. *Constructions of Power and Piety in Medieval Aleppo.* University Park: Pennsylvania State University Press, 1997.

————. "Monuments with a Message: Propagation of Jihad under Nur al-Din." In *The Meeting of Two Worlds*, edited by V. P. Goss, 223–240. Kalamazoo: Western Michigan University Medieval Institute Publications, 1986.

Theodoret, Bishop of Cyrrhus. *Commentaire sur Isaïe*. Paris: Cerf, 1982.

Tolan, John. *Saracens: Islam in the European Imagination*. New York: Columbia University Press, 2002.

Tor, Deborah (D. G.). *Violent Order: Religious Warfare, Chivalry, and the ʿAyyar Phenomenon in the Medieval Islamic World*. Istanbuler Texte und Studien 11. Würzburg: Ergon Verlag and Orient-Institut Istanbul, 2007.

————. "Privatized Jihad and Public Order in the Pre-Saljuq Period: The Role of the Mutatawwiʿa." *Iranian Studies* (2005).

Touati, Houari. *Islam et voyage au moyen âge*. Paris: Le Seuil, 2000.

Tritton, K.A.S. *The Caliphs and Their Non-Muslim Subjects: A Critical Study of the Covenant of ʿUmar*. 1930. Reprint, London: F. Cass, 1970.

Urvoy, Dominique. "Sur l'évolution de la notion de ǧihad dans l'Espagne musulmane." *Mélanges de la Casa de Velázquez* 9 (1973): 335–371.

Valensi, Lucette. *On the Eve of Colonialism: North Africa before the French Conquest*, translated by K. J. Perkins. New York and London: Africana, 1977.

Van Ess, Josef. *Theologie und Gesellschaft im 2. und 3. Jahrhundert Hidschra*. Berlin and New York: Walter de Gruyter, 1991–97.

von Bredow, Mathias. *Der heilige Krieg (ǧihād) aus der Sicht der malikitischen Rechtsschule*. Beirut and Stuttgart: Franz Steiner Verlag, 1994.

von Grunebaum, Gustave. *Medieval Islam*. Chicago: University of Chicago Press, 1953.

Waldman, Marilyn. "The Fulani Jihad: A Reassessment." *Journal of African History* 6 (1965): 333–355.

Wansbrough, John. *Lingua Franca in the Mediterranean*. Richmond, Surrey: Curzon Press, 1996.

————. *Quranic Studies*. Oxford and London: Oxford University Press, 1977. New ed., with notes by Andrew Rippin. Amherst, N.Y.: Prometheus, 2004.

————. Review of Cook and Crone, *Hagarism*. *Bulletin of the School of Oriental and African Studies* 41 (1978): 155–156.

————. *The Sectarian Milieu: Content and Composition of Islamic Salvation History*. Oxford: Oxford University Press, 1978.

al-Waqidi, Muhammad ibn ʿUmar. *Kitab al-maghazi*. Oxford and London: Oxford University Press, 1966.

Watt, William Montgomery. *Muhammad at Mecca*. Oxford: Clarendon, 1953.

————. *Muhammad at Medina*. Oxford: Clarendon, 1956.

Watt, William Montgomery. *Muhammad's Mecca: History in the Qur'an*. Edinburgh: Edinburgh University Press, 1988.

―――. *Richard Bell's Introduction to the Qur'an*. Edinburgh: Edinburgh University Press, 1970.

Wellhausen, Julius. *The Arab Kingdom and Its Fall*. Calcutta: University of Calcutta, 1927.

―――. "Arab Wars with the Byzantines in the Umayyad Period." Translated by M. Bonner in Bonner, *Arab-Byzantine Relations*, 31–64.

―――. "Prolegomena zur ältesten Geschichte des Islams." *Skizzen und Vorarbeiten* 6 (1899): 1–160.

―――. *The Religio-political Factions in Early Islam*, translated by R. C. Ostler and S. M. Walzer. Amsterdam: North-Holland, 1975.

Wensinck, Jan Arent. *Concordance et indices de la tradition musulmane*. Leiden: Brill, 1992.

―――. "The Oriental Doctrine of the Martyrs." *Mededeelingen der Koninklijke Akademie van Wetenschappen* (Amsterdam), Afdeeling Letterkunde 53, serie A (1922).

Wilfong, Terry G. "The Non-Muslim Communities: Christian Communities." In *The Cambridge History of Egypt*, edited by Carl F. Petry, 175–197. Cambridge: Cambridge University Press, 1998.

Wittek, Paul. *The Rise of the Ottoman Empire*. London: Royal Asiatic Society, 1938.

Wolf, K. B. *Christian Martyrs in Muslim Spain*. Cambridge: Cambridge University Press, 1988.

Woods, David. "The 60 Martyrs of Gaza and the Martyrdom of Bishop Sophronius of Jerusalem." *Aram* 15 (2003): 117–118. Reprinted in Bonner, *Arab-Byzantine Relations*, 429–50.

Index